Steps Toward Restoration

For Fr Joseph
With love and admiration,
from one who knows what
you have sacrificed for
us.

Steps Toward Restoration

*The Consequences of
Richard Weaver's Ideas*

Edited by Ted J. Smith III

ISI Books
Intercollegiate Studies Institute
Wilmington, Delaware
1998

Cataloging-in-Publication Data

Steps toward restoration : the consequences of Richard
        Weaver's ideas / edited by Ted J. Smith III.—1st ed.—
        Wilmington, DE : Intercollegiate Studies Institute,
        1998.
        p. cm.
        ISBN 1-882926-26-9
        1. Weaver, Richard M., 1910–1963. 2. Politics
and literature—United States—History—20th century.
3. Conservatism—United States—History—20th century. 4.
Criticism—United States—History—20th century.
I. Smith, Ted J.
PS29.W43 S74 1998   97-73009
814/.54-dc2l   CIP

Published in the United States by:

Intercollegiate Studies Institute
P. O. Box 4431
Wilmington, DE 19807-0431
www.isi.org

Manufactured in the United States of America

Contents

Preface

TED J. SMITH III

On Friday afternoon, March 27, 1998, more than 100 persons assembled for the beginning of a two-day symposium at Belmont Abbey College, a Catholic liberal arts college and Benedictine monastery located in Belmont, North Carolina, just across the Catawba River from Charlotte. The purpose of the symposium was to mark the 50th anniversary of the publication of Richard M. Weaver's *Ideas Have Consequences*.

For those Americans born after World War II and accustomed to a domestic political landscape dominated by principled debate between ascendant "conservatives" and increasingly defensive "liberals," it may be difficult to realize how much that landscape has changed in recent years. In the 1940s, widespread popular agreement on the desirability of government-assisted "progress" meant that serious political discussion centered on the clash between liberals and Marxists of various stripes concerning the optimal rate and extent of government expansion. Although far from insignificant as a political force, conservatism consisted largely of an *ad hoc* and self-interested defense of the *status quo* by members of the propertied classes.

Three books published over the course of a decade profoundly altered this state of affairs. Despite being written from substantially different perspectives, together they provided an intellectually coherent foundation for an effective conservative challenge to the political hegemony of the Left. The first of the three was Friedrich Hayek's *The Road to Serfdom*, an incisive analysis of the inherent deficiencies of socialism first published in England in early 1944 and reissued in America later that year by the University of Chicago Press. The second was Weaver's *Ideas Have Consequences*, a foundational critique of modern (*i.e.*, liberal) society and culture released by the same press in February 1948. The third was Russell Kirk's *The Conservative Mind*. Published in 1953 by the Henry Regnery Company, it made the constructive case for the movement by tracing the history of conservative thought from Edmund Burke to George Santayana and beyond. From these seeds more than any others, the modern conservative movement has grown.

The idea for the Richard M. Weaver Symposium originated with Dr. Robert Preston, the president of Belmont Abbey College. My involvement dates to May 1996, when I received a letter from Dr. Preston which outlined his plans and offered me the pleasant task of helping to design the program. At a meeting two months later, we decided that the conference should focus less on the content of *Ideas Have Consequences*, which had already been the subject of extensive discussion, and more on its origins and effects, including some examination of the reasons for its phenomenal success. Accordingly, nine speakers were asked to present papers at the symposium, all of which are included here in revised and edited form. The papers divide readily into four groups.

The two papers in the first group focus primarily on the author of the book. My essay argues that *Ideas Have Consequences* was the product of two major strands in Weaver's earlier thought, as shaped and refined by several key individuals at the University of Chicago. It is followed by a personal portrait of Weaver by Wilma Ebbitt, his close friend and colleague at Chicago for the last 18 years of his life.

The next two papers elucidate several of the book's central themes. Robert Preston outlines Weaver's main philosophical argument, explores its implications for individual freedom, and offers an assessment of Weaver's program for recovery. Mark Malvasi links the critique of modernity developed in *Ideas Have Consequences* to its sources in Weaver's doctoral dissertation, published five years after his death as *The Southern Tradition at Bay*.

The third group comprises two detailed studies of the effects of the book. George Nash examines its influence on the conservative intellectual movement in America over the last half-century, including recent reassessments of its worth by representatives of different factions within the movement. Lawrence Prelli portrays *Ideas Have Consequences* as a masterwork of rhetoric and argues that much of its persuasive impact derives from the underlying conceptual structure of its key arguments.

The last group of papers offers more personal assessments by three individuals who were strongly influenced by the book and its author. Marion Montgomery, who has numbered Weaver among *The Men I Have Chosen for*

Fathers (Columbia: University of Missouri Press, 1990), uses a discussion of his first encounter with *Ideas Have Consequences* to introduce a detailed critique of Weaver's early neo-Platonism from the perspective of Thomistic philosophy. Ben C. Toledano demonstrates the depth and cogency of Weaver's thought by extending his analysis to contemporary society, but finds it necessary to supplement his "means of restoration" with a more explicit emphasis on Christian belief and conduct. The group concludes with a revised and edited transcript of M. Stanton Evans's remarks at the conference banquet in which he discusses Weaver's ideas and influence from the perspective of one who knew him during the last years of his life.

The publication of this collection was made possible by the efforts of a number of individuals whose contributions merit our thanks and recognition. Foremost among them are Dr. Preston and his staff at Belmont Abbey College, especially Mr. R. Lawton Blandford, Jr., the executive director of the College's Bradley Institute for the Study of Christian Culture, who served as general coordinator of the Weaver Symposium. The success of the conference as a whole was due in large measure to their meticulous planning and flawless execution. Crucial financial support for the symposium was provided by the Earhart Foundation, The Ingersoll Foundation, and the Intercollegiate Studies Institute (ISI). Among those at ISI who worked so hard to bring this book into print, I am especially grateful to Mr. Jeffrey O. Nelson, vice president for publications, and Miss Brooke Daley, director of the ISI book program, for their encouragement, patience, and expert assistance. To all of these, and to all of the conference speakers and participants as well, I extend my warmest thanks.

Richmond, Virginia
August 1998

How Ideas Have Consequences *Came to Be Written*

TED J. SMITH III

O n February 16, 1948, the University of Chicago Press released for sale a slim new book with the deceptively bland title of *Ideas Have Consequences*. The event was preceded and followed by a massive, two-pronged marketing campaign, one of the largest ever mounted by the Press. It had begun two months earlier when major bookdealers throughout the country were sent a letter announcing the book's publication. This was followed in early January with a letter and sheets of talking points to "key publicity persons" and telegrams to "key dealers."[1] Next came a full-page advertisement in the January 17 issue of the leading trade journal, *Publishers' Weekly*, which announced: "We are starting with $7,500 to advertise one of the most important books we have ever published" and offered 100 advance reading copies to "anyone in bookselling" who requested one.[2] On January 22, Press director William Terry Couch dispatched a letter to book review editors in which he compared *Ideas Have*

Consequences to Friedrich Hayek's *The Road to Serfdom*. The American edition of Hayek's foundational critique of socialism had generated enormous controversy—and commensurate sales—when it was published by the Press in 1944, and Couch predicted a similar outcome for the new book. As he noted:

> Well, we have another author, a professor, who has written another book that violates the union rules. The title of the book is, IDEAS HAVE CONSE-QUENCES. The professor is Richard M. Weaver of the college [*sic*] of the University of Chicago. You may expect to hear him and us in the next few weeks called stupid, ignorant, reactionary and wicked, etc. You may also hear others say the opposite—we expect so—but we don't govern our publishing by the prospects for applause.[3]

By all indications, the initial phase of the campaign had its desired effect. Another full-page advertisement in the February 21 issue of *Publishers' Weekly* announced: "1st printing exhausted three weeks before publication; 2nd large printing on the way."[4] It is also clear that at least some major dealers took pains to promote the book. For example, Marshall Field and Company in downtown Chicago featured it in a spotlighted display at the main entrance to the book department. As described by the Press's sales manager, Donald Barnes, the display had a "surrealist" theme, and he called attention to "the use of polished driftwood and root-knots, the tattered copper screening and the very, very daliesque shadow frame portraying modern man in awful misery."[5]

For those familiar with the actual contents of *Ideas Have Consequences*, the use of a "surrealist" display featuring a "daliesque shadow frame" to promote the book may seem somewhat strange. But it was very much in keeping with the general tone and content of the massive advertising campaign that immediately followed its publication. The campaign was based initially on two full-page advertisements which appeared in most of the major literary periodicals of the day, including *The Atlantic Monthly, The Chicago Sunday Tribune Magazine of Books, Christian Century, The Nation, The New Republic, New York Herald Tribune Book Review, The New York Times Book Review,* and *The Saturday Review of Literature.* Both of the advertisements were illustrated with an image of the book in its dustjacket, and one emphasized elements of the dustjacket design in its main visual. The dustjacket itself was executed in shades of bright orange and light grey, peppered with a dense scattering of ragged, black and white newspaper headlines and leads such as "11th Red Veto Jolts U.N.," "Riot Torn India Free Today," "Jail 1,000 Strikers," and "Girl Delinquency Found Increasing." Stark, ugly, and modernistic, it conveys a sense of strident insistence which was faithfully echoed in the ads. One blared: "A calm, quiet, courageous book! A shocking, infuriating, revolutionary book! It may shatter your strongest convictions!" The other demanded to know: "If you believe our civilization is the most advanced in history— How do you explain these headlines?"[6]

It would be a serious understatement to say that the author was displeased with these efforts. As he noted in a letter to Robert Heilman:

> The dustjacket is an atrocity, and I still shudder every time I see it. My first impulse was to strip it off all the copies I sent my friends and write a note

of explanation. How they ever thought that such a thing was suitable for a work of this content is more than I can guess.

He was also less than pleased with the expensive full-page advertisements, as indicated by his comments about one of them to Heilman:

> I don't know whether you saw one of these, but it was a sensationalistic, atom-bombshell affair, the very thing to draw a negative reaction from an already high-pressured public. As one of my colleagues remarked all too truly, it reminded one of advertisements of prophylactics.[7]

He was equally pointed in a comment to Cleanth Brooks:

> I cannot avoid a certain feeling of frustration over my dealings with the Press. I think that I handed them a piece of philosophy, and they have done everything in their power to present it as a piece of journalism.[8]

Despite these shortcomings, the promotional campaign did achieve at least some of its goals. Advance sales were excellent and a great deal of discussion was generated, as indicated in particular by the publication of more than 100 reviews of the book. As anticipated, however, the reviews were decidedly mixed in tone: those in regional newspapers and religious periodicals were generally quite favorable, while those in organs of the liberal establishment tended to sneering vituperation. The most damaging were a review by Howard Mumford Jones in the February 22 issue of *The New York Times Book Review*, which characterized the book as "irresponsible," and an essay by Dixon Wecter in the April 10 issue of *The Saturday Review of Literature,* which began with an attack on Robert Maynard Hutchins and his efforts at Chicago and ended by holding up *Ideas Have Consequences* as an emblem of the university's deficiencies. The reaction to the latter on the University of Chicago campus was particularly strong, and for a time Weaver had serious doubts about whether he would be able to keep his job. He described the reaction to the Wecter review in a letter to Cleanth Brooks:

> It created a great sensation here, and the bookstore had to order additional copies of this issue. To say that I became a marked man after this is to use the language of understatement. Murmurs began to be heard that the book should never have been published at all because it was unfairly taken to represent the philosophy of the University of Chicago.... R. S. Crane [chairman of the English Department] was irritated by the book from the outset, and since the appearance of Wecter's piece, in which the English department here was branded "bush league," he has been infuriated with me. We no longer speak....[9]

The fact that Weaver was concerned about his job calls attention to the truly extraordinary character of these events. At the time *Ideas Have Consequences* was published, Richard Weaver was a young man of 37, just five years out of graduate school and with a total of only eight published essays and book reviews to his credit. Although a faculty member at a highly prestigious university, he held only a one-year appointment as an instructor in the undergraduate College, where his principal assignment was to teach the freshman-level course in English composition. Because they were evaluated primarily on their performance in the classroom, there was little time or incentive for members of the College faculty to engage in any extensive program of research and publication, and few in fact did. For someone in Weaver's position to produce a book offering a sweeping indictment of the entire course of Western civilization over the past 500 years and a trenchant critique of the core values of modern American society is indicative, at the least, of a very advanced level of audacity. And for a major university press to place its full resources and reputation behind such a book is exceptional almost to the point of uniqueness. It is therefore worthwhile to inquire just how the book came into being.

At the most basic level of analysis it is clear that *Ideas Have Consequences* was the product of two somewhat independent strands in Weaver's thinking. The first of these has roots so deep in Weaver's intellectual development that it will be useful to sketch the course of his career up to the time when the idea for the book was first suggested to him.

Richard Malcolm Weaver was born in Asheville, North Carolina, on March 3, 1910, the first of four children of Richard M. "Dick" Weaver and Carrye (later "Carrie") Lee Embry Weaver. Dick Weaver, a popular and outgoing local businessman, was the junior partner in Chambers & Weaver, a successful livery stable and automobile agency. Carrye Weaver was born in Fayette County, Kentucky, but spent most of her adult life in nearby Lexington. In 1902, at the age of 28, she founded Embry & Co., a successful millinery shop which her brother William eventually expanded into one of the leading department stores in the city. Dick and Carrye met in 1907 and were married in November of the following year. It was his second marriage, her first.[10]

On December 16, 1915, Dick Weaver retired to bed early complaining of dizziness. A few hours later he was dead, the victim of a stroke at the age of 45.[11] His widow and children remained in North Carolina for a year or two, but she then moved the family to Lexington, where she opened a new millinery shop in direct competition with Embry & Co. That venture soon failed, however, and Carrye was forced to seek employment in her brother's store, where she worked as buyer and manager of the millinery department until her retirement in about 1939.[12]

Little is known about Richard Weaver's early education. In North Carolina, he apparently attended classes at a tiny private school conducted in one room of the teacher's home.[13] After his family moved to Lexington, he enrolled as a third grade student in a public elementary school a few blocks from his home. But he did not return the following year and it seems likely that he attended classes through the eighth grade at some private school in the Lexington area.[14]

The record of Weaver's education becomes more detailed after September 1924, when he enrolled as a freshman in the Academy of Lincoln Memorial University in Harrogate, Tennessee. By all accounts, he was an unusually serious and highminded student who displayed a marked interest in moral and philosophical issues. In November 1925 he joined with Vadus Carmack —a fellow student in the Academy—and William Maury

Mitchell—a student in the University, four years his senior, who was to become Weaver's lifelong friend—to form the Societas Philosophiae Scientiaeque. The purpose of the society, which met each Sunday afternoon, was to "promote the exchange of ideas, investigate theories, propagate principles, know the truth, follow an argument wherever it goes and develop ourselves."[15] In addition, although he had not been raised in an especially religious family,[16] Weaver participated enthusiastically in Christian youth activities on campus, serving as an officer (most likely the president) of the Christian Endeavor Society.[17] In 1927, after only three years in residence, he graduated from the Academy as valedictorian of his class.

Weaver's intellectual development continued at the University of Kentucky, where he enrolled as a freshman in the fall of 1927. He first formed a commitment to the cause of world peace as espoused by various Christian youth organizations. In May of 1929 his oration "Our Big Business of War" won top honors in a statewide contest sponsored by the Intercollegiate Peace Association. Seven months later he published his first article, a brief report on the status of the college peace movement in Kentucky for a symposium entitled "A Panorama of Peace" in *The Intercollegian*, a monthly magazine for college students produced by the YMCA and YWCA.[18] From these beginnings, Weaver soon came to embrace the full ideology and agenda of international socialism. One impetus was the campus Liberal Club, which he helped to form in March of 1929 and served thereafter as vice president and president. Although neither large nor particularly active, the club achieved substantial notoriety for its perceived links to the League for Industrial Democracy and its stands on issues such as compulsory military training.[19] In 1932, the year he received his undergraduate degree, Weaver formalized his commitment to socialism by joining the American Socialist Party. Although he later commented that "My disillusionment with the Left began with this first practical step," he served as secretary of the Lexington "local" for about two years and helped to plan an October 1932 campaign appearance in Lexington by Socialist presidential candidate Norman Thomas.[20]

As graduation approached in the spring of 1932, Weaver applied to a number of Southern universities for financial aid to support him in graduate school. He received only one positive response, however, an offer of a small scholarship from the University of Kentucky. Accordingly, in September 1932 he enrolled there as a full-time student in the master's program in English. But the following spring he again applied to other schools for aid, and this time his efforts were rewarded with an offer of a modest scholarship from Vanderbilt. Although it meant repeating most of his graduate course work,[21] Weaver readily accepted the offer and enrolled as a master's student in English at Vanderbilt in the fall of 1933. After completing the master's degree in a single academic year, he enrolled immediately in the doctoral program in English, and by June of 1936 he had completed the course work and all other preliminary requirements for the Ph.D. degree.

The period at Vanderbilt (1933–36) was enormously important in terms of Weaver's intellectual development. As he noted later in his autobiographical essay "Up from Liberalism," he was strongly attracted by the ideals of socialism, but in the course of his work for the Socialist

Party he discovered that he did not much care for social-
ists as persons. In contrast, at Vanderbilt Weaver encountered a number of Southern Agrarians, most notably
Robert Penn Warren and John Crowe Ransom (who
directed his master's thesis), and found that "although I
disagreed with these men on matters of social and political doctrine, I liked them all as persons." As a result,
Weaver left Vanderbilt "poised between the two alterna-
tives" of socialism and agrarianism.[22]

It took Weaver four years to fully resolve this dilemma.
In the summer of 1936 he left Nashville and began searching for a full-time teaching position to provide financial
support while he worked on his dissertation, a study of
Milton almost certainly begun under the direction of John
Crowe Ransom. But the task of finding a job proved more
difficult than anticipated, and by late August Weaver was
so desperate that he seriously considered volunteering to
fight for the Republican forces in Spain.[23] Finally, at the
last possible moment, he was offered a one-year appointment as an instructor in English at the Alabama
Polytechnic Institute (now Auburn University) which he
accepted with great relief. Despite receiving a renewal of
his contract, he began searching again in the spring to
find a better job. This eventually produced a very attractive offer of a position as acting assistant professor and
director of forensics in the Department of English at Texas
A&M University. Clearly delighted, Weaver accepted the
appointment and taught there for the next three years
(1937–40).

The job at Alabama Polytechnic initiated a period of
relative affluence for Weaver which allowed him to
indulge his keen interest in travel. In June 1937 he bought

his first car, a black, 1934 Ford V-8, which he used to drive between Lexington and College Station, including a memorable 1,500-mile odyssey from Texas to Kentucky via New Orleans, Mobile, Birmingham, Nashville and Louisville at the end of the 1937–38 academic year. Over the Thanksgiving breaks of 1937 and 1938, he drove groups of friends and colleagues to Monterrey, Mexico. In July 1938 he sailed to Europe and spent a month in Paris. And the following year he spent what he described as "the pleasantest summer of my life" studying at Harvard and seeing the sights of New England.[24]

In other respects, however, this was a period of growing discontent for Weaver. Work on the dissertation was not going well, and what little enthusiasm he had for the project dissipated in the summer of 1938 when John Crowe Ransom left Vanderbilt for Kenyon College and was replaced as dissertation director by Claude Finney. It was also at about this time that Weaver finally lost faith in the Left. As he announced in a January 1939 letter to his friend John Randolph: "I am junking Marxism as not founded in experience."[25] That rejection was soon followed by what he later described as "a kind of religious conversion" to the "Church of Agrarianism."[26] Finally, Weaver was becoming increasingly dissatisfied with his job at Texas A&M, in large part because of the attitude of militant scientism and philistinism he encountered there among students and colleagues alike.

These frustrations came to a head in the late summer of 1939. While driving back to Texas after his stay at Harvard, Weaver was transfixed by an epiphanic insight. As he later described the experience in "Up from Liberalism," "it came to me like a revelation that I did not *have* to go back to this job, which had become distasteful, and that I did not *have* to go on professing the cliches of liberalism, which were becoming meaningless to me."[27] He therefore decided to quit his job at the end of the academic year, abandon the Vanderbilt doctorate and "start my education over."[28] In January 1940 he began the process of applying for admission to the doctoral program in English at Louisiana State University, where he hoped to study under Robert Penn Warren, Cleanth Brooks and others associated with *The Southern Review*. His intentions were made clear in his application for a graduate fellowship: "My travels have made me a Southern nationalist rather than an internationalist, and I now want to do an important piece of research in the history of my section."[29]

The intellectual origins of *Ideas Have Consequences* can be traced directly to Weaver's decision to begin his doctoral work anew at LSU. He enrolled for classes at the Baton Rouge campus in the fall of 1940, and within six months started writing a new dissertation under the direction of H. Arlin Turner. The project was completed in December 1942 under the direction of Cleanth Brooks, who had assumed that role two months earlier when Turner was called into military service.

The dissertation is entitled "The Confederate South, 1865–1910: A Study in the Survival of a Mind and a Culture." It is, by any measure, a very original and rather peculiar work for a graduate student in English to undertake. As indicated by its subtitle, it is a study of the mind and culture of the South as articulated in Southern letters—essays, military memoirs, fiction, diaries and reminiscences—in the postbellum period. Weaver begins the work with an analysis of the Southern "heritage," which he reduces to four principal components.[30] The first is a feudal system of society—derived from Europe but an authentic product of organic growth—which is, characteristically, stable, agrarian, harmonious (as opposed to unified) and hierarchical. One consequence of this organic hierarchy is the existence of a self-conscious aristocratic class. The second component is a code of chivalry, "a romantic idealism closely related to Christianity, which makes honor the guiding principle of conduct," at least among members of the aristocratic class.[31] Third, and closely related to the second, is a system of instruction designed for the education of gentlemen. Intended ultimately to foster the growth of virtue, that education is "moral in the sense that it would give the youth a system of values," and "humanistic" in the sense that it is "so framed as to instill the classic qualities of magnificence, magnanimity, and liberality."[32] Above all, it avoids specialized training, providing instead a "well-rounded regimen" designed to prepare the graduate "to perform all general duties, both public and private, of peace and of war."[33] Last is a distinctive approach to religion, which Weaver calls "the older religiousness," characterized by the simple, unquestioning acceptance of, and willing submission to, a body of religious doctrines. In this view, and in direct contrast to the dominant tradition in New England, religion is less a "reasoned belief" than a "satisfying dogma."[34]

From this heritage have sprung a number of enduring features of the Southern mind and culture. The first is a complex, holistic and nuanced view of reality, marked by a sense of the inscrutable, of the existence of supernatural power, where life is a profound mystery and, because absolutes exist, tragedy is possible. The second is an intellectual posture marked by an appreciation of intuitive, poetic and mythic insight and a corresponding distrust of mere rational intellect and the reductive simplifications of abstract theory and ideology. The third feature is a disdain, even a contempt, for materialism, commercialism and the empty blandishments of an unreflected "progress." Fourth is a natural attitude of piety, which Weaver defines as "the submissiveness of the will, and a general respect for order, natural and institutional."[35] From piety derive such other traits as humility, which involves the recognition and acceptance of proper restraints, and a respect for personality which, almost paradoxically, permits the exaggerated individualism so characteristic of the South.

Although clearly sympathetic to its people and culture, Weaver is no mere apologist for the South. Throughout his analysis he points repeatedly to its faults and excesses, especially a tendency to indulge in an extravagant and sentimental romanticism. And in an "Epilogue" added in 1945 he identifies two "great errors in its struggle against the modern world": a failure to study its position with enough care to discover the philosophical foundation on which its defense could be based, and a progressive loss or "surrender" of initiative.[36] But with all its faults and failures, the South is redeemed by its unique status as *the last non-materialist civilization in the Western World*."[37] And because of this status, the South can serve a unique and vital function.

Looking at the whole of the South's promise and achievement, I would be unwilling to say that it offers a foundation, or, because of some accidents of history, even an example. The most that it offers is a challenge. And the challenge is to save the human spirit by re-creating a non-materialist society. Only this can rescue us from a future of nihilism, urged on by the demoniacal force of technology and by our own moral defeatism.[38]

This quotation, like much of the discussion in the "Introduction" and "Epilogue," clearly foreshadows the analysis developed in *Ideas Have Consequences*. But that work was still several years in the future when Weaver graduated from LSU in May of 1943. After a long and frustrating search he eventually secured a position as an instructor in the Army Specialist Training Program at North Carolina State University. But that job lasted only eight months, and by the end of April 1944 he was again looking for work. This time, thanks to the active support of Cleanth Brooks, the outcome was more favorable. On September 6, 1944, Weaver received a telegram from Dean Clarence Faust of the University of Chicago offering a one-year appointment as an English instructor in the undergraduate College. He accepted the offer with evident pleasure and taught at Chicago for the rest of his life.

Despite these distractions, Weaver was able to maintain a substantial program of research and publication in the years immediately following his graduation. Beginning in 1942 while he was still a graduate student at LSU, he submitted for publication a steady stream of essays on Southern subjects derived from his dissertation research, most of them to *The Sewanee Review*. They appeared over the next few years as "The Older Religiousness in the South" (1943), "Albert Taylor Bledsoe" (1944), "The South and the Revolution of Nihilism" (1944) and "Southern Chivalry and Total War" (1945).[39] Weaver also worked steadily at revising his dissertation for publication, especially during his first year at the University of Chicago (1944–45). In July 1945 he took the manuscript to Chapel Hill and spent a week discussing it with the director of the University of North Carolina Press, William Terry Couch, and Couch's assistant, George Scheer. Couch agreed to publish the work if Weaver would add an introduction and epilogue to clarify its focus. That task was completed by the end of the summer.[40]

Although all of Weaver's writings in the period 1941–45 focus on Southern history and culture, it is possible to discern in the later of them—especially the essay "Southern Chivalry and Total War" and the materials added to the dissertation in the summer of 1945—a new and more negative tone. Directed against contemporary American (*i.e.*, Northern) culture, it reflects Weaver's growing revulsion and dismay at American (and Allied) conduct in World War II. This sickened rejection of contemporary culture constitutes the second major strand in Weaver's thinking at the time *Ideas Have Consequences* was written.

The progression of Weaver's views can be seen quite clearly in his comments to his old friends and former Nashville roommates John and Esther Randolph. In January 1942, at the very beginning of hostilities for America, he wrote:

My outlook for the future is far more pessimistic than yours. I do not want an Axis victory, but I see nothing to hope for through an Allied victory. This idea that peace can be brought about by economic equality is the most fatuous of all delusions. The world is faced with an indefinite period of chaos—years that will be filled with "prison and palace and reverberation" and "torchlight red on sweaty faces." It will not regain order and stability until it returns to the kind of poetic-religious vision of life which dominated the Middle Ages.[41]

At the end of 1942 he declared:

I am utterly pessimistic about the results of the war. The present ideological alignment is just too phony to last. Here is Churchill, the British imperialist, fighting to free Europe from German national socialism (it is amazing how few people can see that fascism is actually a form of socialism trying, by crude violence, to preserve some of the traditional values). Here we are, serving as "the arsenal of democracy," and pinning our hopes for victory on the fighting power of the most ruthless of all dictatorships, Stalin's Russia. I believe it will appear increasingly that the real war is between Anglo-American rightism and the various forms of European leftism.[42]

Two years later his views had become more thoroughly pessimistic:

My reaction to the war is even more negative than yours. I have never believed in it, and I believe in it less now than I did in the beginning. This war is not going to improve anything. We are going to get out of it poorer, more disillusioned, more bankrupt in purpose than ever before.... The war is like some giant automaton set going by an evil spirit. Nobody thinks it is creating anything, nobody wants it to go on, but nobody can stop it.[43]

When the war finally did end in August 1945, Weaver's disillusionment was complete:

Well, the last round of competitive homicide is over, and I have an immense sense of relief. I have really suffered in this war. I have not gone hungry, or gotten cold, or slept without shelter, or felt fright, but I have suffered inwardly. The official lies, the cunningly manipulated hysteria, the repudiation of moral standards by sources we had been taught to respect most—these have been nauseating....

And is anything saved? We cannot be sure. True, there are a few buildings left standing around, but what kind of animal is going to inhabit them? I have become convinced in the past few years that the essence of civilization is ethical (with perhaps some helping out from aesthetics). And never has the power of ethical discrimination been as low as it is today. The atomic bomb was a final blow to the code of humanity. I cannot help thinking that we will suffer retribution for this. For a long time to come I believe my chief interest is going to be the restoration of civilization, of the distinctions that make life intelligible.[44]

In the same letter Weaver proudly announced that it appeared his dissertation would be published by the University of North Carolina Press. But those hopes were soon disappointed. In September 1945 William Terry

Couch left North Carolina to become the director of the University of Chicago Press. Although he still felt the dissertation was worthy of publication, Couch informed Weaver that its strong Southern focus precluded him from considering it for the Chicago press.[45] T. J. Wilson, Couch's successor at North Carolina, did ask to review the manuscript and it was sent to him in the spring of 1946. But it was rejected some months later, and Weaver made no further efforts to find a publisher.[46] The reason was that he had begun work on a new manuscript, which eventually appeared as *Ideas Have Consequences*.

It is clear that in the early fall of 1945 Richard Weaver was acutely aware of the contrast between the culture of the South he had described in his dissertation and the culture of contemporary America as revealed especially in the conduct of World War II. It is less evident how that awareness led to the writing of *Ideas Have Consequences*. In "Up from Liberalism" Weaver offers this account of the origins of the book:

> I recall sitting in my office at Ingleside Hall at the University of Chicago one Fall morning in 1945 and wondering whether it would not be possible to deduce, from fundamental causes, the fallacies of modern life and thinking that had produced this holocaust and would insure others. In about twenty minutes I jotted down a series of chapter headings, and this was the inception of a book entitled *Ideas Have Consequences*.[47]

While this may very well provide an accurate account of how the structure of the book was determined, there is strong evidence that the idea for such a work was first suggested in a meeting in Couch's Chicago apartment attended by Weaver, Couch and Cleanth Brooks, who was a visiting professor at the University of Chicago during the Autumn and Winter quarters of the 1945-46 academic year. For example, in a May 1948 letter to Brooks about the reception accorded to *Ideas Have Consequences*, Weaver begins:

> I don't want to burden you with more correspondence, but since the idea we concocted at Couch's three years ago has created a mighty splash, you will probably be interested in hearing some details from this end.[48]

The content of that discussion is suggested by Weaver's comment in a July 1946 letter to Arlin Turner:

> I have seen a good bit of Couch at Chicago, and he has suggested that if I will take the conclusions of the dissertation and apply them in a general way to the modern world, I might produce a work in which the Chicago Press is interested.[49]

Regardless of the details of its inception, it is clear that Weaver began work on the new book in October or November of 1945 and produced a volume very much in line with Couch's suggestion. The finished work shows an obvious affinity with many of the main ideas of Weaver's dissertation and clear indications of the revulsion he felt toward the modern world in the aftermath of the Second World War. But the arguments in *Ideas Have Consequences* go substantially beyond his views in 1945 and show the mark of other influences as well.

The first of these is Weaver's reaction against what he called the posture of "systemic relativism" that permeated the undergraduate liberal arts curriculum at Chicago, especially as expounded by Richard McKeon in the capstone Observation, Interpretation and Integration (OII) course.[50] In this view, the pursuit of truth is limited to arraying different viewpoints nonreductively, systematizing their assumptions and methods, and proceeding within their confines. The problem with this approach is that it tends to foster a kind of brilliant but empty dialectical virtuosity. Nevertheless, Weaver did profit from his exposure to the position and its proponents, as indicated by a comment in a July 1946 letter to Arlin Turner. Regarding an early draft of the book he wrote:

> Some of the first chapters deal with metaphysics, for experience with these gifted Chicago dialecticians has taught me that there is no sense in going ahead until you have clarified your philosophical foundations.[51]

A second influence was his work in the English 3 course, which he taught for the first time in the 1945–46 academic year. In the spring of 1946 Weaver and several other young instructors argued successfully for a major revision of the course, to include, among other changes, a greater emphasis on logic and the informal fallacies.[52] His work in these areas led him to consider for the first time the implications of Occam's Razor and the nature and limits of pure dialectic.

Other influences can be traced to specific individuals, of whom three are most important. The first of these is

Pierre Albert Duhamel.[53] Duhamel arrived at Chicago in the fall of 1945 after completing his doctorate at the University of Wisconsin and was assigned to share an office with Weaver. Although Duhamel was married, his wife soon contracted pneumonia and returned to Wisconsin to recuperate with her family. Thus thrown together, Duhamel and Weaver became very close friends.

It was Weaver's habit to return home after lunch each day to write a page or two. He would then discuss his progress with Duhamel in their office that afternoon. The two also met frequently at Duhamel's home on Saturday nights to discuss great ideas over a gallon of Lowenbrau beer (an endeavor in which they were sometimes joined by Cleanth Brooks and Marshall McLuhan). So close was their friendship that when Duhamel returned to Wisconsin to visit his wife's family over spring break of 1946, he invited Weaver to come along. They stayed together at the University Club and spent their evenings drinking beer in Duhamel's old haunts on State Street in Madison.

The key factor in their intellectual relationship was that Duhamel, who received his undergraduate degree from Holy Cross, brought Weaver into contact with a Roman Catholic intellectual tradition that was largely new to him. As a result, their conversations often focused on Medieval Catholic philosophers such as Occam, but also such figures as Duns Scotus and Bonaventura (although seldom Aquinas, for whom Weaver apparently felt an aversion). Duhamel also introduced Weaver to the works of modern Catholic writers such as Eric Gill and Gerard Manley Hopkins. These contacts with Duhamel are almost certainly the source of the undertone of Roman Catholicism that many readers have noted in *Ideas Have Consequences.*

Thanks partly to Duhamel's tutelage, Weaver made steady progress on the manuscript over the course of the 1945-46 academic year. However, the bulk of the first draft was written during the summer of 1946. Weaver spent that period in residence at the University of Wisconsin, where, at Duhamel's suggestion, he enrolled in a single course in Greek to facilitate his understanding of the works of the early Greek rhetorical theorists. But most of his time was devoted to writing. By July he had completed a chapter outline that lists most of the arguments included in the finished work but lacks the discussion of Occam and nominalism now found in the "Introduction."[54] On October 26, he sent a completed first draft to Couch with a plea for criticism. The manuscript was entitled "Steps Toward a Restoration of Our World."[55]

The initial response to the manuscript was highly enthusiastic, as Weaver related in a January 1947 letter to Cleanth Brooks:

> The first reaction from this quarter astonished me completely. Couch invited me to Thanksgiving dinner, talked about little else, declared that this was "the finest piece of writing that I have received since I took over the Press here." That nearly bowled me over, but it is exactly what he said. His chief editor, Frederick Wieck, talked in similar vein, and described one of the chapters as "wonderful." Can you blame anyone for assuming, as I did then, that not much stood in the way of publication?[56]

However, as Weaver's plaintive question suggests, the book soon encountered what he described as "reader trouble." Although reviews by Cleanth Brooks and Otto von Simson recommended publication, those by E. K. Brown and Marjorie Greve were highly negative. As Weaver noted: "There are in the work certain phrases, perhaps ideas, which cause readers simply to explode."[57] But even the positive reviews pointed out many deficiencies, and in January 1947 Weaver was asked to revise the work.

A key figure in this process was Cleanth Brooks. It is ironic that Brooks is generally given credit for shaping Weaver's dissertation (published posthumously as *The Southern Tradition at Bay*). In fact, Brooks had little influence on that work, which was almost finished when he took over as dissertation director. But he did play a major role in shaping and refining *Ideas Have Consequences*. He was present at the meeting with Weaver and Couch where the idea for the book was first discussed, and he worked informally with Weaver in the earliest stages of the project to help formulate his major arguments. In the spring of 1947 he provided a set of detailed suggestions which Weaver gratefully incorporated into the text. Weaver acknowledged his influence in a letter dated May 1, 1947:

> With reference to the points of criticism, I may say that I agree with every one of them. I realized that I was on shakiest ground in my discussion of the arts, though I did do a fair amount of patient research up in Madison last summer.[58]

Three weeks later Weaver wrote:

> In re the manuscript: I have decided to overhaul completely the chapters on the arts and on language. And since my vein is flowing rather happily at the moment, I think I am effecting some solid improvements. I was appalled when after an interval of two months I looked again at the part on literature and language and saw how skimpy I had left it. Certainly the mood of creation is not the mood of criticism.[59]

Weaver completed the revisions in June of 1947. Armed with additional favorable reviews from Joseph Rotskoff and Alburey Castell, Couch submitted it to the press committee the following month. On July 11, the manuscript was formally accepted, and a week later Weaver was issued a contract for publication of the work, now entitled "The Adverse Descent."[60]

Once the contract was signed, the fate of the book was passed to the capable hands of William Terry Couch. It would be difficult to overestimate the significance of Couch's role in this endeavor. He may well have made the initial suggestion for the work, and he guided the manuscript through the long process of writing, review, and revision. Now he would add his stamp in at least three other ways.

The first was his decision to throw the full weight of the University of Chicago Press behind the book.[61] The initial press run was set in August at 3,500 copies. But as the reader reports and endorsements accumulated, Couch was impressed by the extremely intense responses—both positive and negative—the book tended to generate. This suggested that it could well be as controversial, and as profitable, as Hayek's *Road to Serfdom*. He therefore increased the initial printing to 4,000 copies in September and to 7,500 copies in December, with provisions for a second printing of equal size. He also authorized an advertising budget of $7,500, an extraordinary amount for a book with a retail price of $2.75.

Couch's second major contribution was to work tirelessly to secure prominent endorsements for the book. Some individuals, such as C. S. Lewis, declined to comment, citing the pressure of other obligations. Others responded with harsh criticism. For example, Philip Wylie commented:

> I have now read IDEAS HAVE CONSEQUENCES and I am passionately unimpressed by the book; while I still believe in the title, I think that for any valid consequences, real ideas are necessary, and I find in this volume an almost total absence of any ideas save a few odds and ends the author has borrowed and then misunderstood. I have assigned this dreary little volume a place in my bookcase behind the other books so that it will by no chance have the consequence of boring or confusing any of my guests or friends.[62]

But in the end Couch was able to assemble an impressive array of endorsements from such notable figures as Cleanth Brooks, John Abbot Clark, Donald Davidson, Norman Foerster, Charles Clayton Morrison, Reinhold Niebuhr, Melvin Rader, John Crowe Ransom, Allen Tate, and Paul Tillich. These were duly featured on the dustjackets and in the advertising campaign.

But perhaps Couch's greatest contribution was the title of the book. He first suggested *Ideas Have Consequences* in a memorandum dated October 4, 1947. Six days later Fred

Wieck reported that Weaver "had come around to the view that this title was very strong," and stressed that "I did not have to force the title down his throat, nor did I have to bludgeon him into swallowing it. His statement expresses his sincere conviction."[63] Despite these claims, it is clear that Weaver deeply disliked the title, and his resentment erupted in an angry public exchange with Couch at a party on October 25. In the heat of the moment Weaver apparently went so far as to suggest he might withdraw the book from the Press, and Couch responded with a formal offer to release him from his contract. Fortunately for all concerned, Weaver reconsidered his position, and the next day sent Couch a written apology for "my rudeness at the party." He explained:

> For some time I have been conscious of violating my own prescript—that is to say, I have been conscious of becoming egotistic about the book in question, of attaching to it an importance which it does not have. That may account for an exaggerated sensitivity about titles and other things. I ought to take more of my own advice and get a perspective on things.[64]

That matter settled, the book went smoothly into press. But the result was that a phrase Weaver later described as "hopelessly banal"[65] has now become indissolubly linked with his name.

****

The fate of the book and its author were left hanging in the balance some pages ago, and it remains to discuss how they fared. In the end, *Ideas Have Consequences* met neither the fondest expectations nor the darkest fears of those who brought it into being. Most likely as a result of both the less than inspired advertising campaign and a number of prominent negative reviews such as those by Jones and Wecter, it generated only relatively modest sales. Couch had hoped that as many as 30,000 copies would be bought. But by mid-1948 the total stood at less than 8,000,[66] and in the following year returns outnumbered sales by a ratio of almost two to one.[67] As Couch noted in a letter in July 1948:

> IDEAS HAVE CONSEQUENCES has had at least one serious consequence for me. It has lost us a fair sized chunk of money, and I am now discovering that dollars make a lot of difference to this place. Unless I am able to get rid of some of the sacred cows around here it will be a long time before I will be able to take any long chances like this again.[68]

As far as Richard Weaver is concerned, the fears for his job proved groundless. In fact, just three months after the book was published he was promoted from instructor to assistant professor and issued a three-year contract, the first multi-year contract he had received in 12 years of teaching. And despite some incidents of petty harassment and the evident disdain of certain colleagues, he went on to enjoy a conventionally successful academic career at Chicago. More important, *Ideas Have Consequences* established Weaver as a leader in the fledgling conservative movement, a status he held until his death in 1963.

Finally, it must be noted that Couch's pessimistic conclusion was perhaps a bit premature. Although not an immediate bestseller, orders for copies of the second printing continued at a respectable rate through the end of 1958, when stocks were at last exhausted and the book was declared out of print.[69] But demand for the book continued, and within a matter of months the Press decided to reissue it in paperback under its Phoenix imprint. The new edition was duly published in late 1959 or early 1960,[70] and by August 1960 more than 3,000 copies had been sold.[71] And *Ideas Have Consequences* has remained in print continuously ever since.

ENDNOTES

1. Undated and unsigned typescript sheet headed "Richard M. Weaver IDEAS HAVE CONSEQUENCES." Located in Box 483, File 6, of the University of Chicago Press Records in the Special Collections of the Regenstein Library at the University of Chicago and quoted by permission.

2. University of Chicago Press advertisement, *Publishers' Weekly* (January 17, 1948), 206-07.

3. Form letter from W. T. Couch dated January 22, 1948. Located in Box 483, File 5 of the University of Chicago Press Records and quoted by permission.

4. University of Chicago Press advertisement, *Publishers' Weekly* (February 21, 1948), 1036.

5. Letter from Donald B. Barnes to Jocelyn Kahn dated March 19, 1948. Located in Box 483, File 5, of the University of Chicago Press Records and quoted by permission.

6. See, *e.g.*, *The Saturday Review of Literature* (March 6, 1948), 7, and (March 20, 1948), 3.

7. Letter from Richard Weaver to Robert Heilman dated July 2, 1948. Located in the Robert Heilman Papers in the Manuscripts and University Archives Division of the University of Washington Libraries and quoted by permission.

8. Letter from Richard Weaver to Cleanth Brooks dated January 28, 1948. Located in Box 15, Folder 320, of the Cleanth Brooks Papers in the Beinecke Rare Book and Manuscript Library at Yale University.

9. Letter from Richard Weaver to Cleanth Brooks dated May 31, 1948. Located in Box 15, Folder 320, of the Cleanth Brooks Papers.

10. The details of Dick and Carrye's relationship are confirmed by correspondence and other documents acquired from Weaver's sister, Polly Weaver

Beaton, and now in the author's possession. See also the entry on them in Pearl M. Weaver, *The Tribe of Jacob* (Asheville: Miller Printing, 1962), 112. Additional confirmation was provided by William Embry, Jr., in a telephone interview conducted by the author on January 4, 1996.

11. From a local newspaper obituary dated December 17, 1915, acquired from Mrs. Polly Weaver Beaton and now in the author's possession.

12. Telephone interview with William Embry, Jr., January 4, 1996.

13. For a brief description of his earliest educational experiences, see Richard M. Weaver, *The Role of Education in Shaping Our Society* (Bryn Mawr: Intercollegiate Studies Institute, undated pamphlet), 10.

14. Interview with Mrs. Dee Amyx conducted in Lexington, Kentucky, on January 23, 1997.

15. From the handwritten "Charter" of the society acquired from Mrs. Polly Weaver Beaton and now in the author's possession. The fullest account of Weaver's activities at the Academy is found in his unpublished 1958 eulogy "William Maury Mitchell," which is included in a comprehensive collection of Weaver's shorter writings forthcoming from Liberty Press in 1999.

16. Interviews with Embry Lee Weaver and Polly Weaver Beaton conducted in Weaverville, North Carolina, on August 11, 1995.

17. The nature and extent of Weaver's participation in the Christian Endeavor Society are indicated by a number of entries (including two speeches and four prayers prepared for oral presentation at meetings) in a notebook of his from that period acquired from Mrs. Polly Weaver Beaton and now in the author's possession. For extensive excerpts from that notebook, see Fred Douglas Young, *Richard M. Weaver 1910–1963: A Life of the Mind* (Columbia: University of Missouri Press, 1995), 18–20.

18. See "Richard Weaver Is Winner in Contest," *Kentucky Kernel* (May 24, 1929), 8; "Richard Weaver Wins Peace Prize," *Lexington Leader* (May 24, 1929); and Richard M. Weaver, "Kentucky," in "A Panorama of Peace: A Symposium," *The Intercollegian* 47 (December 1929), 72.

19. For a detailed discussion of the Liberal Club and Weaver's early political views, see Clifford Amyx, "Weaver the Liberal," *Modern Age* 31 (Spring 1987), 101–06. See also the file of newspaper clippings on the Liberal Club in the Archives of the University of Kentucky.

20. Richard M. Weaver, "Up from Liberalism," *Modern Age* 3 (Winter 1958-59), 22.

21. An examination of Weaver's transcripts from Kentucky and Vanderbilt shows that only one course from his year of work at Kentucky was accepted as transfer credit for his master's degree at Vanderbilt.

22. Weaver, "Up from Liberalism," 23.

23. Letter from Richard Weaver to John Randolph dated August 23, 1936, from a copy in the author's possession. The discussion of Weaver's activities in the period 1936–40 is based primarily on his correspondence with his close friends John and Esther Randolph, with whom he shared an apartment during his last year at Vanderbilt.

24. Letter from Richard Weaver to John Randolph dated August 12, 1939. Quoted by permission of Mrs. Esther Randolph.

25. Letter from Richard Weaver to John Randolph dated January 26, 1939. Quoted by permission of Mrs. Esther Randolph.

26. Letter from Richard Weaver to John Randolph dated January 20, 1942. Quoted by permission of Mrs. Esther Randolph.

27. Weaver, "Up from Liberalism," 24.

28. *Ibid.*

29. Richard M. Weaver, Application for Fellowship to the Graduate School of The Louisiana State University, undated, p. 3. Located in the Richard M. Weaver file in the Department of English Records, RG# A0607, Louisiana State University Archives, LSU Libraries, Baton Rouge, Louisiana, and quoted by permission.

30. Richard M. Weaver, *The Southern Tradition at Bay,* ed. George Core and M.E. Bradford (Washington: Regnery Gateway, 1989 [1968]), 31–95.

31. *Ibid.,* 31.

32. *Ibid.,* 61–62.

33. *Ibid.,* 63.

34. *Ibid.,* 82–83.

35. *Ibid.,* 82.

36. *Ibid.,* 373–74.

37. *Ibid.,* 375, emphasis in original.

38. *Ibid.*

39. Richard M. Weaver, "The Older Religiousness in the South," *The Sewanee Review* 51 (April 1943), 237–49; "Albert Taylor Bledsoe," *The Sewanee Review* 52 (Winter 1944), 34–45; "The South and the Revolution of Nihilism," *The South Atlantic Quarterly* 43 (April 1944), 194–98; and "Southern Chivalry and Total War," *The Sewanee Review* 53 (Spring 1945), 159–70. All of these have been reprinted in *The Southern Essays of Richard M. Weaver,* ed. George M. Curtis III and James J. Thompson, Jr. (Indianapolis: Liberty Press, 1987). At least one essay, "The Anatomy of Southern Failure," was submitted to *The Sewanee Review* in 1944 but rejected. An edited version of this essay will appear in the comprehensive collection of Weaver's shorter writings forthcoming from Liberty Press in 1999.

40. For a description of Weaver's meeting with Couch, see his letter to Cleanth Brooks dated July 9, 1945, in Box 15, Folder 320, of the Cleanth Brooks Papers.

41. Weaver to Randolph, January 20, 1942, quoted by permission.

42. Letter from Richard Weaver to John Randolph dated December 27, 1942. Quoted by permission of Mrs. Esther Randolph.

43. Letter from Richard Weaver to John Randolph dated January 16, 1945. Quoted by permission of Mrs. Esther Randolph.

44. Letter from Richard Weaver to John Randolph dated August 24, 1945. Quoted by permission of Mrs. Esther Randolph.

45. See the letter from Richard Weaver to Arlin Turner dated July 3, 1946, located in the Richard Weaver file in the Arlin Turner Papers (2nd 84:A) in the Special Collections Library at Duke University.

46. According to Louis H. T. Dehmlow in an interview with the author conducted in Wilmette, Illinois, on November 1, 1992, the envelope containing the returned manuscript lay unopened in a corner of Weaver's office until after his death, when it was discovered by Dehmlow. It was eventually published in 1968 as *The Southern Tradition at Bay*.

47. Weaver, "Up from Liberalism," 30.

48. Weaver to Brooks, May 31, 1948.

49. Weaver to Turner, July 3, 1946, quoted by permission.

50. It would be more accurate (and charitable) to label McKeon's perspective "skeptical pluralism." For a detailed explication and application of this approach, see Ted J. Smith III, "Diversity and Order in Communication Theory: The Uses of Philosophical Analysis," *Communication Quarterly* 36 (1988), 28–40.

51. Weaver to Turner, July 3, 1946, quoted by permission.

52. See, *e.g.*, Weaver's letter to Cleanth Brooks dated April 25, 1946. Located in Box 15, Folder 320, of the Cleanth Brooks Papers.

53. The account that follows is based on interviews with Duhamel conducted in Boston, Massachusetts, on May 17 and November 11, 1994.

54. See the eight-page typescript headed "Weaver, Richard M." and date-stamped July 31, 1946, located in Box 483, Folder 5, of the University of Chicago Press Records.

55. See the Letter from Richard Weaver to William Couch dated October 26, 1946. Located in Box 483, Folder 5, of the University of Chicago Press Records.

56. Letter from Richard Weaver to Cleanth Brooks dated January 13, 1947. Located in Box 15, Folder 320, of the Cleanth Brooks Papers.

57. *Ibid.*

58. Letter from Richard Weaver to Cleanth Brooks dated May 1, 1947. Located in Box 15, Folder 320, of the Cleanth Brooks Papers.

59. Letter from Richard Weaver to Cleanth Brooks dated May 24, 1947. Located in Box 15, Folder 320, of the Cleanth Brooks Papers.

60. As noted by Joseph Scotchie, *Barbarians in the Saddle* (New Brunswick: Transaction, 1997), 58, the exact wording of this title has been the subject of some controversy. The wording used here is confirmed by a signed copy of the original contract acquired from Mrs. Polly Weaver Beaton and now in the author's possession. An unsigned copy of the contract can be found in Box 483, Folder 5, of the University of Chicago Press Records.

61. The discussion that follows is based on various documents located in Box 483, Folders 5 and 6, of the University of Chicago Press Records.

62. Letter from Philip Wylie to Elizabeth L. Titus dated April 16, 1948. Located in Box 483, Folder 5, of the University of Chicago Press Records and quoted by permission.

63. Memorandum from FW (Fred Wieck) to DB and EW dated October 10, 1947. Located in Box 483, Folder 6, of the University of Chicago Press Records and quoted by permission.

64. Letter from Richard Weaver to William Couch dated October 26, 1947. Located in Folder 27 of the William T. Couch Papers in the Southern Historical Collection of the Library of the University of North Carolina at Chapel Hill and quoted by permission.

65. Weaver to Heilman, July 2, 1948, quoted by permission.

66. *Ibid.*

67. Letter from Ethel Kellstrom to Richard Weaver dated August 26, 1949. Located in Box 483, Folder 5, of the University of Chicago Press Records.

68. Letter from William Couch to Selma Fuller dated July 13, 1948. Located in Folder 29 of the William T. Couch Papers and quoted by permission.

69. Although the book was technically out of print, as late as June 1959 the Press still had a number of slightly damaged copies which it was selling at a discount of 40%. See, *e.g.*, the letter from Jo Anne Schlag to Stephen Miles dated June 10, 1959, and located in Box 483, Folder 9, of the University of Chicago Press Records.

70. The uncertainty about the publication date stems from the fact that the Phoenix reprint carries no unambiguous year of publication. Weaver's "Foreword" is marked "September 1959," and that is the date which appears in standard catalogue entries, including the Library of Congress. However, a number of items of Weaver's correspondence strongly suggest that the book was not issued until February or March of 1960. See, *e.g.*, the memorandum from William Wood to Richard Weaver dated March 16, 1960, located in Box 483, Folder 9, of the University of Chicago Press Records.

71. See the letter from William Wood to Richard Weaver dated August 22, 1960, located in Box 483, Folder 9, of the University of Chicago Press Records.

Richard Weaver:
Friend and Colleague

Wilma R. Ebbitt

Until quite recently readers of Dick Weaver's books have been interested primarily in his ideas as set forth therein. If readers formed a mental picture of the author, it was likely to be a bleak pen-and-ink sketch of a solitary thinker, withdrawn and remote, even perhaps emotionally impaired.

But now Fred Douglas Young's intellectual biography is in print, and a great deal of biographical information is in circulation. Those who knew Dick grow old and swap memories of him, in and out of the classroom. From this group, ever shrinking in number, must come the scope and the color for a full-bodied portrait.

I speak as a friend and colleague of Dick's in the College of the University of Chicago from 1945 to 1963, the year of his death. I joined the composition staff in 1945 after completing my graduate work and taking my first uncertain steps as a teacher at Brown University. Dick had come to Chicago a year earlier after three years of teaching at Texas A&M University and graduate work at Vanderbilt and Louisiana State University. He was older than most of the newcomers and always maintained a kind of seniority that went beyond age and experience. He was respected, even by those who sometimes found him a little absurd. My husband, an inveterate cartoonist, captured a verbal image:

> Dick was a short, stocky man who lived in brownish three-piece suits and spoke in sentences that revealed to New England ears only a trace of a "Southern accent." He had a large, round head with a big jaw. His hair was dark and spiky, and his skin was pitted. He was pleasantly homely. Though he cleared his throat a great deal, and sometimes his sinuses, his manners were courtly, if not always graceful.
>
> He had a ready smile, and when he grinned, it was a side grin, with his big chin thrust forward and his eyes twinkling through his spectacles. But he could also be grave, severe, impressively silent. All in all, colleagues found him an agreeable, somewhat old-fashioned man and a first-rate teacher.

What amused some of the younger staff members was Dick's routine; and here, as elsewhere in this talk, I shall repeat what I have recorded in earlier memoirs, trusting that it will be new to some in my audience.[1] I don't know when Dick got up in the morning—it was unquestionably early—or how he breakfasted, but after he left his rented room on a typical weekday, he walked a mile to the campus, arriving in time to teach two early-morning classes. He preferred this early start, and his preference was honored without argument. At 11:30 he lunched alone at the Commons, settling as a rule for soup and either a sandwich or a piece of pie. Then he hiked back to his room, where he wrote two pages and had a nap. Restored, he returned to the campus to meet another class and then confer with students, attend meetings, or do library research. He dined at the Commons at 5:30, worked in his room until 9:30, drank a beer, and retired.

It was a simple routine and not an unusual one for a bachelor of Dick's generation. Today, health addicts might deplore the pie and the beer, and gourmets would certainly deplore the Commons, but many would applaud the four miles of walking each day. Those familiar with Chicago's weather can only shake their heads in wonderment.

The newcomer in 1945 who came to know Dick best was P. Albert Duhamel, from Holy Cross by way of the University of Wisconsin. During Al's four years at Chicago, he and Dick shared an office as well as many intellectual interests. Dick, Al once said, "was as methodical in [his] daily regime as he was in his thinking."

A footnote here. One interest Dick and Al shared was not intellectual. Both men were railroad buffs. They collected timetables and, I think, worked out complicated itineraries. I say "I think" because neither was forthcoming about just what they were up to. But it seemed to be an enjoyable hobby, and it may have been related to Dick's fondness for trains. He always used them to travel from and return to Weaverville, to home and family.

Dick had a pattern for his weekends as well as for his week. He worked in his office on Saturday morning and then took the Illinois Central commuters' train to Chicago's Loop, where he rummaged through the stock of secondhand bookstores and sometimes visited Berghoff's old-fashioned German restaurant and beer hall, an institution that has survived, I believe. Returning to the campus, he might indulge in relaxing talk with an acquaintance, perhaps in Jimmy's, a hangout for graduate students and faculty, before heading home with the early edition of the Chicago *Tribune*. On Sundays he wrote.

This account of Dick Weaver's weekend routine is notable for what it does not include. Then as now, Chicago had lots to offer: the splendid Art Institute, art galleries, concert halls, theaters, nightclubs, restaurants, and sports, sports, sports. For that matter, the University campus provided a crowded schedule of music, drama, and lectures of all varieties, often by notable speakers. Did Dick patronize any of these? If he did, it seems likely that he went alone; colleagues have not mentioned accompanying him to any extracurricular events. But after his books were published, he may have met with like-minded acquaintances who had no connection with the University. In any case, Dick's thriftiness would have limited his indulgence in entertainment.

The stories of Dick and his difficulties with driving in Chicago—especially with left turns—have been repeated enough, I think. On one occasion when he took my husband and me and Margaret Perry, a mutual friend, to dinner in downtown Chicago, we went by car, but it was Margaret's car, and Margaret did the driving. The restaurant Dick took us to was part of a sort of arty, upper-class club where Adlai Stevenson's former wife presided for a time.

That dinner party took place long after Dick and I became friends. As a newcomer, I didn't find it easy to get to know him. One reason was that, as a member of the staff, Dick simply did not chat. He engaged in conversation only when he had something to say pertaining to the curriculum or course development or examinations. (I never heard a word of gossip from Dick.) But in time I found myself depending on his classroom experience, his good sense, his wisdom in and out of our staff meetings.

Much has been made of the value of these priceless weekly meetings, and I subscribe to every bit of praise they received. The format was simple. One member of the staff would undertake (or be obliged) to present his pedagogical view of the unit the students would face the following week, analyzing the text or texts, advancing theory where appropriate, and offering suggestions for writing assignments. The presentation was followed by discussion and often by debate, in which objections were aired as well as affirmations.

Dick participated fully in the business of the staff, but he was not a star performer at these meetings. Again, he didn't talk for the sake of talking. And he made no attempt to push his own presentations or to inflate them. Tom Rogers, a new instructor in 1955, was struck by the imposing silence of the older man, as well as his helpfulness in time of need.

Contributing to Dick's reticence, I think, was an awareness that most of the staff members were ten or more years younger than he—Tom Rogers was about fifteen years younger—and therefore especially sensitive to his criticisms. At any rate, Dick responded to the efforts of others with great tact.

A number of staff members shared in the writing of the excellent article "Looking for an Argument,"[2] and I'm sure all of them would testify that Dick was the major figure in this cooperative enterprise. In it, he introduced the classical *topoi* to English composition in the College, a genuine contribution, as was his splendid textbook, *Composition*, in 1957.[3]

In my opinion, Dick Weaver did work of inestimable value to the composition courses while avoiding the limelight. At the time of his death, he had just begun serving as chairman of the staff. I have no doubt that he sighed when he was persuaded to take on that job. He could hardly have welcomed it. For whether or not he was a "born" teacher as some thought, he was unquestionably *not* a born administrator.

Dick was an excellent teacher. Reputations are created in the classroom, and all the comments about his teaching that have reached me over the years offer unqualified praise. Though I never studied under him or observed him in action, he and I had a number of students in common; so I gained some insight into what went on in his classroom. He was always punctual, always cordial, always maintaining order and taking pains to communicate the essential details of assignments.

I was not surprised to learn that Dick embraced the belief that a good teacher hopes and expects that his students will go beyond his own accomplishments. Nor was I surprised to find, just last August, a reference to him in the *University of Chicago Magazine* as "one of the great teachers in the College during its formative Hutchins years." The alumnus who wrote that also spoke of Dick's "devotion to teaching undergraduate writing."[4] Recognition of this unswerving commitment was widespread in the College at that time. It was an intellectual commitment of the highest order.

To achieve his reputation as a teacher in the College, Dick had to master the difficult art of guiding discussions, a technique that was fundamental to the Chicago approach. What were wanted were *active* learners, not passive listeners who simply absorbed, or failed to absorb, lectures. Almost certainly Dick had learned from lectures and taught by lecturing—and lecturing well. But in the College, word of his success with the discussion method circulated among both students and faculty.

I am left with the impression that Dick's solid reputation as a teacher was based on mutual respect in his classes. Students sensed his dedication—a dedication by no means universal in composition courses. He recognized their willingness to learn; I can recall overhearing him in conversation with some students and being struck by how closely his mode of address duplicated his speech to colleagues. What he did *not* do is seek the favor of students or offer them entertainment or attempt to proselytize them. His job was to teach; theirs, to collaborate in a joint effort.

Although I think it's clear by now that Dick was no anchorite, a few words about his social life at the College will add some color to the sketch. He liked conviviality. He liked to have a drink in his hand, and he liked to be in the company of agreeable women. He was a beer drinker to whom *whiskey* meant "party." And vice versa. He could drink considerable amounts of beer without showing much effect, but on occasion bourbon was his downfall. Indeed, "The Night that Dick Fell" is as popular a chapter in his oral biography as is "Three Rights to Make a Left Turn."

Let me emphasize that Dick's falls were very rare and never messy. If he went down, he went down smiling. He was always among friends, and friends saw to it that he reached home quickly and safely. I think he was liked all the better for displaying what some would call a weakness.

One story about Dick and bourbon strikes me as especially revealing. Periodically, the composition staff met at the home of Paul Diederich, the examiner, to deal with grading standards. Paul, a kind and gentle man, rewarded those who worked through the evening by laying on the liquor thereafter. Like most of us in those years, he had no money to spare, and he economized on the bourbon. To a fault, one might say. As a result, he was visited one morning-after by a pale but resolute Dick Weaver, who forbade him ever, ever again to serve the poison that he had dispensed the night before. Even a well-bred Southern gentleman had to be blunt in time of crisis.

It was at one of Paul Diederich's work-and-play evenings that Dick took a political stand. A group of us were trashing the Chicago *Tribune*—a popular sport among the decidedly liberal instructors—when Dick announced that he could defend logically and philosophically any of the *Trib's* editorials. This claim astounded us, and if anyone but Dick had made it, a noisy brouhaha would have almost certainly followed. But no one wanted to argue with Dick while drinks were available, and when sobriety reigned, politics was a topic to be skirted in Dick's presence.

Members of the staff and their wives entertained on many weekends. Dick was seldom invited. When he was, he accepted, attended, and always seemed to have a splendid time. Margaret Perry was especially kind to him, and he responded with warm gallantry, once offering, for example, to help her don her overshoes.

I think it needs to be said that Dick Weaver's social life was similar to that of many bachelor professors. Those who choose bachelorhood or have bachelorhood thrust upon them are unlikely to be included in all the parties that their married colleagues enjoy or endure. Bachelors are apt to be loners to some degree. But they are also likely to find good company outside the staffs to which they belong. Dick fit that pattern. He had a friend in the philosophy department and another friend who was associated with the Oriental Institute, not to mention those who had no connection with the University of Chicago. He was no isolate.

Nor was Dick unique in his permanent attachment to *home*. Again, I associate the strong homing instinct with bachelorhood. Dick seized on the spring break to rush home to Weaverville and was surprised that others passed up this opportunity to "escape" Chicago. He failed to realize that married academics, and many single ones as well, put down roots where their careers planted them. But I know another bachelor professor who "escaped" as regularly as Dick did but who made his escape from the natural beauty of Penn State's Happy Valley to the environs of, yes, Chicago.

Like most of us, Dick had numerous personas, but perhaps his were more distinct from one another. The jovial party-goer was hardly recognizable in the silent observer. at staff meetings. People who know him only through his books might be surprised to learn of the enjoyment he got from literature. His memory was loaded with aphorisms he had harvested from his wide reading. He had not one but a dozen of them appropriate for just about any occasion, and while they could be somber, many were light and sparkling. He loved a clever turn of phrase. I remember his recommending George Moore's *Hail and Farewell,* and I suspect that what caught his fancy were such flashes of wit as "There is no one in the world that amuses one as oneself" and "I write according to my soul and act according to my appearance." Dick himself was given to anecdotes, but applauded wit in any form with enthusiastic knee slappings.

And then there was the persona that produced the books. I have often been asked how Dick's colleagues on the composition staff reacted to them. I have to reply "Scarcely at all," though those who read them were certainly startled by the aggressiveness—indeed, the belligerence—they exhibited, so foreign to the voice of moderation we heard in our staff meetings. Now it strikes me as odd that then we simply took it for granted that Dick had produced *Ideas Have Consequences,* a work that contained formidable stretches of argument that could have been used in the courses we were teaching.

As I puzzle over the lack of staff response to *Ideas,* I wonder if it wasn't because of the nature of the book. *Ideas* was the kind of book produced not by an English professor but rather by a moral philosopher. And another reason was that almost everyone at that lively time was writing a book or an article, or was planning to write, or was talking about writing. So colleagues checked out Dick's book, found that it was no threat to what they had in mind, and returned to their own garden patch.

Remember, too, that the primary responsibility of every one of us was to teaching—a very demanding responsibility in the College.

Dick's second book, *The Ethics of Rhetoric*, earned more attention and more praise, and in my opinion deserved it. But today my topic is the man, not his works.

As should be clear by now, I never knew Dick Weaver the recluse, or the hermit, or the monk, or even the exile, for if Chicago meant exile to Dick, the College, where he spent most of his time, meant community. There, he was happy in his work, in his freedom, in his privacy, and, when opportunity arose, happy to let the good times roll. He was among friends who adjusted to his eccentricities as he adjusted to theirs.

Dick's life was cut short, but not before he had had his say in the books he had published. And I believe the reception of those books, including the roars and the catcalls, gave him great fun. As an author, Dick loosened up, and so did his purse strings. I remember a splurge, an indulgence: Dick bought himself a cashmere coat—and philosophical consistency be hanged!

The last time I saw Dick, he had just returned from his routine escape to Weaverville during the spring break. But this time the visit had not had its usual restorative effect. When I asked how he was, he grimaced and rubbed his upper arm. "Some pain here," he said.

A few days later he failed to meet his early class. The routine had ended.

ENDNOTES

1. Wilma R. Ebbitt, "Richard M. Weaver, Teacher of Rhetoric," *The Georgia Review* 17 (Winter 1963), 415–18; Wilma R. Ebbitt, "Richard M. Weaver: Friend

and Colleague," presented at the Conference on College Composition and Communication, St. Louis, March 19, 1988.

2. Manuel Bilsky, McCrea Hazlett, Robert E. Streeter, and Richard M. Weaver, "Looking for an Argument," *College English* 14 (January 1953), 210–16.

3. Richard M. Weaver, *Composition: A Course in Writing and Rhetoric* (New York: Henry Holt and Company, 1957).

4. Charles L. Fierz, "Weaver Teaching Writing," *The University of Chicago Magazine* 89 (August 1997), 4–5.

Ideas Have Consequences
Fifty Years Later

ROBERT A. PRESTON

I first read *Ideas Have Consequences* by Richard M. Weaver sometime in the late sixties. For me, being trained in scholastic philosophy, and always struggling to make the subject of metaphysics understandable and relevant to college students, it was an answer to prayers. For almost 30 years, *Ideas* has been a companion text to one of the traditional textbooks on Thomistic metaphysics in my course, and it has been a most happy marriage, at least for me, if not for my students. But I hope that I am not being unduly optimistic when I say that, for most of my students, Weaver became a guide to their understanding of what has gone wrong in a society they were now only beginning to examine. It is a pleasure for me to have the opportunity to discuss once again *Ideas Have Consequences*, this time from the perspective of 50 years after its publication, and to join with scholars who have a fuller knowledge of Weaver's writings than I, to review the importance of this undeservedly little-known thinker for an understanding of the present age.

To begin our discussion, I am going to argue that Weaver possesses a vision of an organized society and a unified culture from the perspective of one of the two golden ages of the Western tradition, that of the high Middle Ages from the 10th to the 14th centuries.[1] From this perspective he provides a critique of the slow decline of society beginning in the 14th century caused by what he calls "the fateful doctrine of nominalism"[2] to the present time, where that doctrine is now the dominant view. To make my case, I will deal with five points:

1. The basic metaphysics underlying Weaver's position;
2. An explanation of nominalism, *i.e.*, the movement from intellectualism to voluntarism;
3. The impact of this philosophical change as it manifests itself in the meaning of freedom;
4. Weaver's prescience in his grasp of the consequences of the move from intellectualism to voluntarism; and
5. A critique of Weaver's solution to our current societal malaise.

Weaver's vision is based upon two premises: the world is intelligible and the human person is free. The actual source of this intelligibility Weaver does not discuss because his strategy is to make his argument as non-religious as possible, but it is clear that he finds that source of intelligibility in a supreme mind, whether that mind be called the architect of the universe or the creator.

In appealing to the intelligibility of the universe, Weaver is siding with the philosophical realists against the nominalists. The difference between the two schools is that the realists admit of two realities: the universal and the individual. An example of this is that each person is an individual existent who shares in the universal of human nature. In the traditional metaphysics of realism, we are at once one and many. We are all one in our human nature and many in our individuality.

The significance of this is easy to see. It is the universal that provides the basis of intelligibility. If we can find an essential characteristic of human nature, then we know that this characteristic is possessed by every individual human.

Weaver will use such terms as *universal, essence, nature* and *form* interchangeably. It is upon the reality denoted by these terms that truth is based because the universal transcends space and time. It has its reality based in an order beyond the spatial and temporal, that is, beyond the order of change and motion.

It is also the realm of the universal that is the basis of truth. Weaver accepts the traditional definition of metaphysical truth as that which cannot be otherwise than it is, and truth in this sense is unchanging and always and everywhere the same. If, for example, we determine lying to be the willful deception of someone in authority who has the right to know, and if we further determine that justice in society cannot be achieved if lying is tolerated, then we can see that whenever this principle is violated it is a moral violation. And this is not simply true of our society today, but it is true of every society that has or will exist. Thus, the basis of Weaver's argument is the four-square acceptance of the metaphysics of realism because only a dualism of the spiritual and the physical will provide him with the order of truth and those stable social values from which he criticizes the present age.

The doctrine of nominalism, often also called empiricism, positivism, or materialism, holds that only the individual is real. The universal is seen as a mental fiction useful in organizing the disparate aspects of reality so that they may be more easily studied or categorized. Nominalism explicitly denies any such reality as human nature being grounded outside the knowing mind. In fact, it denies the knowing mind in favor of sense perception alone. Reality is not intelligible, it is sensible only.

The implications of this doctrine are fearful. There is no order of truth in the traditional sense, there are only facts; there are no universally valid moral principles, but only relative moral standards; there is no hierarchy of meaning within reality to serve as a basis for judging which human attainments are higher than others; the denial of the intelligibility of the universe entails the denial of understanding and wisdom as the basis of authority and law, and substitutes wealth and power; the purpose of each individual human life within the created order loses its meaning, and the purpose of human life is not discovered by analysis of the real, but chosen by each individual to be whatever he or she wants it to be; and finally, the arts follow this downward spiral from dealing with the grand themes of medieval and renaissance art, through the sentimentalism of the romantic era, to the prevailing desire for immediacy.

Weaver traces the rise of nominalism in the 14th century with William of Ockham, through its further development by the British Empiricists in the 18th century to its popular acceptance in the 20th century. For its rapid spread from the end of World War I until the time of his writing of *Ideas*, Weaver credits what he calls "the great stereopticon." That is, the movies, the press and the radio. Television had not achieved the status that it has today, but if Weaver had revised *Ideas* he certainly would have included television as even a greater force for cultural and social dissolution.

Weaver condemns the great stereopticon because, he says, it provides the public with "a sickly metaphysical dream."[3] It encourages the view that the purpose of life is happiness through comfort, it is antithetical to critical thinking by promoting passivity in its readers, hearers and viewers, and it undermines an adequate view of reality by espousing the doctrine of presentism and the endless round of becoming.

For Weaver, a proper metaphysical dream is based upon "an unsentimental sentiment." It is an inchoate feeling that reality is the result of planning, and if the human person is willing to study the created order, he will find therein the meaning and purpose of human life that provides a social bond that unites mankind in an ongoing pursuit of a just society and high cultural attainments.

This metaphysical dream provides a basis of agreement for the important issues of life, and without this agreement men cannot live in harmony and peace. It is the loss of the common metaphysical dream that is the root cause of our society's problems. In Weaver's words,

> ...a waning of the dream results in a confusion of counsel, such as we behold on all sides in our time. Whether we describe this as decay of religion or loss of interest in metaphysics, the result is the same; for both are centers with power to integrate,

and, if they give way, there begins a dispersion which never ends until the culture lies in fragments.[4]

What Weaver labors to make clear is that unless we agree on primary issues, we cannot argue in the sense that the philosopher means by the term "argue." The purpose of argument is to achieve clarification and understanding. It demands prior agreement on such basic issues as the nature of reality and the meaning of words. For this reason the realist and the nominalist cannot argue in the proper meaning of that term. Lacking prior agreement on basic issues, they can only carry on a semblance of argument that leads nowhere.

This is the plight of our age. We lack the ability to address the profound issues that are at the basis of a meaningful culture, and so we distract ourselves with discussion of issues of secondary importance, relegating the former to private concern while the latter occupy the public sphere.

To exemplify the dramatic change in perspective that has come about, I wish to examine the basic notion of freedom as it is viewed within a metaphysics of realism, and contrast it with the notion of freedom as espoused by nominalism. In the doctrine of realism where reason has priority over will, freedom is defined as the ability to do what one knows to be good. This is the controlling view of Aristotelian ethics. Man must discover through reason the good, which is defined as those activities that perfect him both as an individual and as a social being. From the repetition of these activities, good habits or virtues are developed. The practice of virtue, in turn, develops a person's character, so a person becomes honest, courageous, just and temperate. As one practices the virtues, one gains deeper understanding of what constitutes the good action, and thus is capable of more accurate judgment of the truly good action even in complex situations.

On the basis of his theory that the practice of virtue increases knowledge of what constitutes the virtuous action in the practical order, Aristotle is led to posit as the criterion of good actions, the good person. If you wish to know what is the just action in any particular situation, Aristotle can only answer: "Ask the just person." Thus, according to this theory, to become free is to achieve self-control, that is, to possess the ability to follow reason's guidance in making rational choices, often in spite of the contrary inclination of one's animal nature. Plato's warning "beware of pleasure and pleasant things," was heeded by Aristotle who saw true education as the process by which the student learns to judge what constitutes pleasure in the proper human sense of that term.

Central to this view is the position that reality provides the basis for both metaphysical and moral truths. The human endeavor is to study reality in search of these truths and to apply them to complex situations with as much accuracy as possible. Each generation is aided by the wisdom of the past, and is called upon to contribute further to the ongoing study and understanding of what is really real.

Contrasted with this view is the nominalistic definition of freedom as the ability to do what one wants. Here we give priority to will over intellect, and education is the process of developing within each individual the intellectual abilities to achieve a desired end. Reason becomes the servant of appetite. In denying a created order, nominalism must emphasize not the discovery of meaning in reality, but the positing of meaning by each individual. We no longer discover meaning outside of ourselves in an ordered universe, but we are free to determine for ourselves what meaning our life will have. Because of this emphasis on the individual will, we have seen freedom of speech change from its traditional role of providing protection for the pursuit of truth in open intellectual and political dialogue, to protection of any form of speech no matter its intent.

Weaver, with one of his characteristic pithy statements, writes: "The Separation of Religion From Education, one of the proudest achievements of modernism, is but an extension of the separation of knowledge from metaphysics."[5] This observation is germane to the issue of freedom. By the separation of knowledge from metaphysics, Weaver is referring to nominalism's denial of any doctrine of truth objectively realized. This leads to Bacon's view of knowledge as power, or the utilitarian view that the purpose of knowledge is to assist in the attainment of desire.

The separation of religion from education refers to the denial of moral truths, leaving each individual to search within himself for some basis of right and wrong, sometimes known in educational circles as "values clarification." Weaver's point was made recently at the University of Chicago when the faculty member selected to give the 1997 "The Aims of Education Address" told the freshmen with some degree of approbation:

> Not only is there a powerful imperative at Chicago to stay away from teaching the truth, but the university also makes little effort to provide you with moral guidance. Indeed, it is a remarkably amoral institution. I would say the same thing, by the way

about all other major colleges and universities in
this country.[6]

That Weaver saw this development fifty years ago is
wonderful testimony to his prescience, and one can only
speculate as to his reaction had he been sitting in
Rockefeller Chapel for this address to the freshmen. It
would seem that, if our "best and brightest" are being
indoctrinated with the doctrine of nominalism, in fact,
have been for quite a while now, then any sort of reversal
would be most doubtful. From the hallowed halls of our
great universities comes our leadership, and to whatever
extent Weaver's analysis is valid, to that extent there is
reason to be apprehensive about our country's future.

Weaver finds an answer to our present dilemma in
what he calls "The Last Metaphysical Right," *viz.*, private
property. One must first understand clearly what Weaver
means by private property because it cannot be identified
with the notion of private property as understood by capitalism. Private property for Weaver is that property
which can be identified with the individual: the family
farm, the privately owned home or the small business. It
is not stocks and bonds, nor is it the impersonal corpora-
tion overseen by professional managers and owned by
thousands of shareholders. Weaver writes:

> Respecters of private property are really oblig-
> ated to oppose much that is done today in the name
> of private enterprise, for corporate organizations
> and monopoly are the very means whereby prop-
> erty is casting aside its privacy.[7]

What is this "privacy" that private property provides?
For Weaver private property is the ground of personal

responsibility, and it is the source of personal growth, allowing a person to complete himself. A person needs private property in order to perfect himself because there is an inalienable bond between a person and his property.

> ...Somehow [private property] is needed to help him express his being, his true or personal being. By some mystery of imprint and assimilation man becomes identified with his things, so that a forcible separation of the two seems like a breach in nature.[8]

More importantly, private property becomes for Weaver the lever by which he can pry a crack in the monism of materialism and make room for dualism. If private property is, as he believes, a priority among middle class values, then Weaver can argue that the middle class must recognize that private property, in his sense of that term, requires also that one admit of the reality of the spiritual along with the physical.

The reason that Weaver has called private property a metaphysical right is to show that is not grounded in the material order of change and temporality, but has its basis in the unchanging order of the spiritual. For Weaver, right and obligation are correlatives. If one wishes to preserve the right of private property, then one must admit also of the obligations of stewardship which entail the preservation and development of property for one's children and grandchildren.

Behind this line of argument is the recognition of the notion of community. Membership in the community belongs to three groups: the dead, the living and the unborn. The living owe a debt to the dead which they can only pay to the unborn. This is the basis of the idea of stewardship. The living inherit the property from those who have gone before, and they must protect and enhance it for the benefit of those yet to come. This is the spiritual order that transcends the immediate.

Weaver's dedication to the principles of Southern Agrarianism, which is never explicitly mentioned in *Ideas*, becomes clear in his use of private property as the answer to the problems of the current crisis. He was prejudiced in favor of rural life over urban life, and the farmer over the city dweller.

However, he is speaking to a public which is for the most part ignorant of the principles upon which his argument is based. The right of private property and its corresponding responsibilities of stewardship resonates only with a declining percentage of the population, even in Weaver's beloved Southern culture. In fact, perhaps we should say especially in Weaver's beloved Southern culture, which has chosen to throw off the burden of agrarianism in favor of technology and commerce. It is an ancient adage that : "The corruption of the best is always the worst."

To the last metaphysical right Weaver would add the necessity of a special type of education if we are to set matters aright. He calls for the restoration of the study of language, in particular poetry, foreign languages and rhetoric. The study of poetry, he tells us, will teach the evocative power of language; foreign languages, particularly the translation of Latin and Greek, will provide discipline and an antidote to slovenliness in the use of language; and rhetoric provides us with stability in the meaning of words that is necessary for the understanding of law.

To these two—private property and the study of language—Weaver adds a third path back to social sanity: it is by way of piety, which he defines as "a discipline of the will through respect."[9] Piety must be directed at nature, our neighbors (*i.e.*, all other people), and the past. Piety is directed at nature because it represents a created order and commands our respect; piety is directed at our neighbors because we all share in a common human nature; and piety is directed towards the past because history reveals the existence of law and the hand of providence. These three objects of piety stand as guardians against *hubris*, that most seductive temptation of the contemporary age.

It is difficult to conclude a discussion of Weaver's thought on an optimistic note. There are those of us who agree with his basic insights, but we are lacking in both numbers and influence. Those whom Weaver called "the Progressives" have won the day. They control "the great stereopticon," the major universities and the giant corporations. We could add the Supreme Court, but that would be for another symposium at another time.

What might be interesting to discuss is the issue that, if Weaver is basically correct in his analysis, and if ideas do have consequences, and if our society has embraced erroneous ideas, then what will be our nation's future in 2023, *i.e.*, twenty-five years from now? I would be pleased to be part of a planning effort to discuss that issue next year at this time.

ENDNOTES

1. Cf. Albert William Levi, *Philosophy and the Modern World* (Bloomington: Indiana University Press, 1959), 5: "Western man looks back with longing to two great periods of cultural synthesis—the secular millennium of the Athenian city state and the other worldly paradise of the Middle Ages."

2. Richard M. Weaver, *Ideas Have Consequences* (Chicago: University of Chicago Press, 1948), 3. Page references in this paper will be to the 1976 Midway Reprint edition.

3. *Ibid.*, 104.

4. *Ibid.*, 21.

5. *Ibid.*, 93.

6. "The Aims of Education Address," presented by John J. Mearsheimer, R. Wendell Harrison Distinguished Service Professor in the Department of Political Science and the College, University of Chicago, September 21, 1997. Published in *The University of Chicago Record* 32 (1997). The address is a good example of what Weaver called "the separation of metaphysics from knowledge and of religion from education." Professor Mearsheimer took note of the fact that he was delivering the address in the Rockefeller Chapel, and told the freshmen that religion played a large role in education in the late 19th and early 20th centuries. However, "Today, elite universities operate on the belief that there is a clear separation between intellectual and moral purpose, and they pursue the former while largely ignoring the latter. There is no question that the University of Chicago makes hardly any effort to provide you with moral guidance. Moreover, I would bet that you will take few classes here at Chicago where you discuss ethics or morality in any detail, mainly because those kind of courses do not exist."

7. Weaver, 133.

8. *Ibid.*, 134.

9. *Ibid.*, 172.

Ideas Have Consequences
and the Crisis of Modernity

MARK G. MALVASI

"If the world continues its present drift toward tension and violence," wrote Richard M. Weaver in "Aspects of the Southern Philosophy," "it is probable that the characteristic Southern qualities will command an increasing premium."[1] Weaver's diagnosis of the modern crisis was inseparable from his apology for the South. Although Southern history did not project an image of accomplishment, prosperity, and success, Southerners, Weaver believed, had kept from extinction virtues integral to civilized life. The Southern tradition, in Weaver's analysis, offered a core of resistance to the most powerfully corrupting forces of the modern age: rationalism, positivism, materialism, egalitarianism, individualism, and science. While modern men exhausted themselves pursuing false gods, thus inviting confusion, immorality, and degradation, Southerners stayed at home and worshiped the old-fashioned God of their fathers.[2]

Bitterly reviled, the generation of Southerners who came of age after the Civil War enjoyed little success in

imposing their ideals, values, and beliefs on the nation
and the world. Maligned and forgotten, many scorned
their patrimony or managed only an inept defense of it.
Southerners failed to cultivate their foremost virtues,
neglecting to invoke their "mandate of civilization."[3]
They may have lost their struggle for independence, and
in the process relinquished any opportunity to attain
wealth, prestige, and power, but the legacy their ancestors forged, fought for, and passed on deserved preservation and allegiance.

Weaver was the first thinker to attempt a systematic re-
evaluation of the Southern intellectual tradition. In his
magisterial study, *The Southern Tradition at Bay*, which he
began during the early 1940s as a doctoral dissertation
under the direction of Arlin Turner and Cleanth Brooks at
Louisiana State University but which remained unpublished until 1968, Weaver asserted that Northerners had
looked to American history to certify their own nascent
world view. He found little rationale to justify such an
appropriation, save that Federal troops had won a bloody
victory in a great war. The dead could not speak. Defeat
forced the living into silence. On those rare occasions
when traditional Southerners did venture to articulate
their ideas, values, and beliefs, they did not expound
them with much eloquence or clarity. As a consequence,
few modern Americans felt compelled to listen. Virtually
by default, the North, the "majority section," appropriated the history and established the meaning of America.[4]

Yet, even in their mute and easily ridiculed veneration
of the past, Southerners knew better than to expect automatic, inexorable progress toward a level of civilization
presently beyond human conception. The history of their

region eradicated any utopian tendencies they might once have entertained. The mechanical, thoughtless dogmas of science eased the modern conscience by promising peace and prosperity without the usual exertion and suffering. Men now routinely deluded themselves that "a great machine appeared to have been set in motion" to liberate them from their responsibilities to order their lives and govern their world.[5] Weaver demurred. "We must admit," he objected, "that man is to be judged by the quality of his actions rather than by the extent of his dominion."[6]

The Southern tradition, alternately, enabled people to see that civilization lies not in the accumulation of wealth and power, but in the moral and aesthetic conceptions with which the imagination informs reality. It encouraged the recognition that civilization requires a sense of discipline, restraint, and piety. As fallible and finite creatures, human beings ought humbly and joyously to submit to the will of God. Within this tradition, and the civilization it helped to sustain, Southerners had also sought to invest life with meaning not as individuals but as members of a solemn community inspired by a shared reverence for the past and a common vision of the future.

Modern men, whom traditional Southerners regarded as largely impious and uncivilized, had abolished both the past and the transcendent as dimensions of meaning. They shed their reserve, wanting no constraints imposed on their desires and ambitions. Impatience, egotism, and vanity attained epidemic proportions among them. Weaver feared that modern men, enclosed in the artificial environment of the city, had not only abandoned their piety toward God but had lost their "sense of the difficulty of things," the knowledge that all human accomplishments require toil and sweat. Labor had ceased to be "functional in life," and had become instead "something ... grudgingly traded for that competence, or that superfluity, which everyone has a 'right' to."[7] Expecting science and technology to gratify their hearts' desires, typical moderns fell to cursing and blaspheming when the world resisted their manipulation and control. Selfish, pampered, and naive, the inhabitants of the modern, urban wasteland enacted frightening reprisals against nature and humanity when they did not get their way.

In *The History of the Decline and Fall of the Roman Empire,* Edward Gibbon wrote:

> We cannot determine to what height the human species may aspire in their advance towards perfection; but it may be safely presumed that no people, unless the face of nature is changed, will relapse into their original barbarism.... We may therefore safely acquiesce in the pleasing conclusion that every age of the world has increased and still increases, the real wealth, the happiness, the knowledge, and perhaps the virtue, of the human race.[8]

Weaver no longer shared Gibbon's optimistic faith in the inevitability or desirability of progress. On the contrary, he anticipated the coming of a nightmarish world in the very triumph of technology and the very dream of progress that eighteenth-century thinkers like Gibbon believed would release human beings from drudgery, poverty, and suffering, and would thus enable them to advance civilization in untold ways. Weaver offered a less sanguine vision of the future. In his observations, rather than in those of Gibbon, we may see ourselves and may judge the world we have made.

If the degeneration of culture and civilization proceeded, Weaver maintained, humanity in the future could expect to be as amply provided for as the inmates of a well-regulated asylum. Everyone, at least in the advanced industrial countries, would be comfortable, but everyone would also be restless, tormented by "the deep psychic anxiety" and "the extraordinary prevalence of neurosis" that Weaver thought already distinguished American society.[9] There would be little sustenance or consolation for the spiritual and immortal aspects of human nature, for individuals would have no respite from the perpetual tumult of existence. Since there would be no great demand for intellectual exertion, minds would grow shallow and people would become intellectually bored and emotionally unstable. Life would become a ceaseless, though disappointing, quest for more intense and excessive amusements, pleasures, and comforts, the only activity capable of fascinating those whose imaginations had atrophied.[10]

Modern society, Weaver concluded, was becoming ever more frenzied, bustling, and resplendent, but modern men remained melancholy, discontented, and cheerless. "One of the strangest disparities of history," Weaver proposed, "lies between the sense of abundance felt by older and simpler societies and the sense of scarcity felt by the ostensibly richer societies of today." He elaborated: "That there are abysses of meaning beneath his daily routine, the common man occasionally suspects; to have him realize them in some apocalyptic revelation might well threaten the foundations of materialist civilization."[11]

Beneath the riotous life on the surface of modernity, there is death at the heart.

Weaver's survey of the approaching crisis was prescient at the time he wrote *Ideas Have Consequences*. To recognize today in his thought an enduring wisdom about the contemporary predicament is only to discharge what George Orwell once identified as the first obligation of intelligent men: a restatement of the obvious. For, as Weaver pointed out, it is not dynamism, vigor, affluence, and power that make a civilization great. It is, rather, the resilience, magnanimity, and piety of its people. Weaver discerned that in a world in which the bonds of family, community, and tradition have been severed, people lose any sense of solidarity and interdependence. They instead retreat into private life, become disposed to think and act exclusively for themselves, and at last espouse a mean and selfish individualism.

Under such circumstances nothing is fixed and stable. Men constantly fear a diminution of fortune and status, and thus, Weaver understood, develop a passion for wealth, comfort, and leisure at the expense of the common good, for which they care not at all. Even should they live in democratic societies, everyone is subject to the same despotism of science, technology, and bureaucracy, which Weaver equated with the debased equality of slavery. "Democratic societies which are not free," wrote Alexis de Tocqueville in *The Old Regime and the French Revolution*:

> may well be prosperous, cultured, pleasing to the eye, and even magnificent, such is the sense of power implicit in their massive uniformity.... But...where equality and tyranny coexist, a steady

deterioration of the mental and moral standards of
a nation is inevitable.[12]

Weaver could not have agreed more completely with
Tocqueville's assessment. "The sin of egotism," he
explained:

> always takes the form of withdrawal. When per-
> sonal advantage becomes paramount, the individual
> passes out of the community. We do not mean the
> state, with its apparatus of coercion, but the spiritual
> community, where men are related on the plane of
> sentiment and sympathy and where, conscious of
> their oneness, they maintain a unity not always
> commensurable with their external unification.[13]

As the result of their painful history, Weaver hoped,
Southerners, in addition to acquiring a degree of humility and restraint, had escaped the most sinister and per-
ilous forms of this modern alienation. Dispossessed of
their homeland and their past, suffering all the indigni-
ties of a conquered people and an occupied nation,
Southerners clung fiercely to their traditions and neither
pitied themselves nor lamented their fate. They accepted
what they could not change. In defeat they approved the
contingencies of nature and the vicissitudes of the
human condition more gracefully than their sophisticated and prosperous Northern and modern counter-
parts. Trusting in God to bless and keep them and their
loved ones, Southerners acquired a penetrating wisdom
and a tragic spirituality amid the wreckage of their
world.[14]

The intellectual effort expended in defense of slavery,
Weaver conceded, vitiated Southern assertions of moral

superiority. But if antebellum Southerners had not achieved a complete reconciliation between their moral aspirations and their social reality, they nonetheless displayed greater sensitivity and conscience than the fanatics who proclaimed the equality of all men. Southerners understood that different men possess vastly diverse intellectual and moral endowments, and that to judge all alike would be an injustice to their individuality.[15]

They also knew that men attain their full stature as human beings only in relation to, not in isolation from, one another. If they wished to avoid a return to the state of nature, which Weaver regarded as a Hobbesian "war of all against all," then those fortunate enough to have been favored with exceptional aptitudes had to bear responsibility for the welfare of those less auspiciously situated. As Christian gentlemen, Southern slaveholders thus saw it as their obligation to care for the unfortunate creatures whom God had entrusted to them. Like virtually all antebellum proslavery theorists, Weaver insisted that aristocracy and patriarchy, which place some men in the service and under the protection of others, constitute the best, if not the only, means of perpetuating a Christian social order in the modern world.

Southerners considered the ability to formulate and enforce these kinds of social distinctions as the true measure of civilization, constituting the one sure way to impose order on an indeterminate and perplexing reality. They expressed little sympathy for bewildered moderns who shrugged that the world was incomprehensible or who protested that it could not be other than they imagined it. The modern quandary arose from adherence to the pernicious doctrines of radical individualism and absolute equality. That no man was ever born indepen- dent and free, and that no two men were ever born equal, save perhaps in their helplessness and their sinful- ness, was, Weaver ascertained, a more sensible evaluation of human nature than the contrary view. Hence, the emergence of egalitarianism as the generally preferred social philosophy troubled him, for it threatened to oblit- erate the sources of discrimination and the standards of judgment that demarcated civilization from savagery.[16]

Weaver echoed a host of antebellum social theorists who strove to fashion an alternate vision of order in the modern world. At the core of their thought lay a belief in social hierarchy, inequality, and interdependence. Notwithstanding the diversity and complexity of the antebellum Southern world view, countless individual Southerners were bound to a common vision of human and divine order, which, by the 1820s, had come to rest squarely on the foundation of Christianity. Enough Southerners believed in the justice of their cause and in the morality of their way of life to ensure four years of the bloodiest war in the history of the United States.

Without such a vision of order preserved and dissemi- nated by men of virtue, character, and intellect, Southern thinkers believed, civilization would collapse into a bar- barism and chaos that would inevitably engender despo- tism and tyranny. Only style distinguished the uncivilized brute who seized power by force from the cultivated demagogue who beguiled the unthinking masses. Southern thinkers since before the Civil War had pitted their Christian values and beliefs against all who would deny the essential sinfulness of human nature and all who would open the way to the ravages of personal immorality and social chaos. At stake were the God-fearing households and communities that they had built, as well as their sense of familial and social order and their personal integrity and honor.[17]

Nearly a century after the Civil War, Weaver could still regard the traditional South as God's bastion against all the ideologies that threatened to undo Christian civilization: individualism, anarchism, communism, socialism, utopianism, feminism, and an array of other abominations and heresies too numerous to mention. "People close to the soil appear to have longer memories than have the urban masses," Weaver proclaimed. "Traditions there live for generations; what their grandfathers did is real to them."[18] In the South, he contended, there had emerged a social order that circumscribed and restrained the evil inevitable in a world haunted by sin—a social order that imposed the sense of Christian discipline and moral responsibility necessary to compensate for all that was feeble, wicked, impious, and degenerate in human beings.

During the twentieth century, Weaver declared, Americans had unfortunately embraced faulty definitions of words such as "discrimination" and "segregation." In part, for Weaver, the crisis of modernity originated in the debasement and distortion of language. The words "discrimination" and "segregation" did not, in Weaver's mind, denote some unnatural pattern in human affairs that excluded some persons from the full benefit of social, political, and civil rights. Instead, they constituted an intuitive process of discretion, refinement, and taste whereby the "coarser natures, that is, those of duller mental and moral sensibility, [are] lodged at the bottom and those of more refined at the top."[19] Ideas of rank and inequality, Weaver suggested, are not inimical to liberty, for only an intelligible order makes freedom possible.

Denial of such ostensibly self-evident propositions scandalized Weaver, as it had antebellum Southern thinkers. Southern political theory, Weaver charged, provided a mechanism and a rationale to establish social order; Northern political theory reduced to a series of unattainable yearnings, or worse, to the onset of lawless competition. The "political romanticism" of the North confined life to the narrow context of practical judgment and material interest. Northerners regarded as antiquated and absurd Southerners' attachment to custom, tradition, and community, none of which immediately enhanced scientific utility, technological efficiency, commercial activity, or profits.[20]

With the spiritual character and condition of society always foremost among his concerns, Weaver applied the term "Yankee" as the ancient Greeks had used the term "barbarian." "Yankees" represented the apotheosis of the insipid but savage and dissolute bourgeois world that Weaver decried.[21] In a letter to Donald Davidson, he clarified his thinking:

> By the term "bourgeois" I really meant the American philistine, the sort of person who thinks that the greatest thing in life is to own and display a Buick automobile. It seems to me that it is this soulless, desiccated middle class which has done most to destroy the concept of non-material value. The levelling process results in everyone's being pushed into it. Its characteristic mentality is a perfect ideological befuddlement. The Common Man

of Henry Wallace's Common Century would be a member of this class.[22]

The South, on the contrary, was *the last non-materialist civilization in the Western World.*[23] Southern civilization extended refuge to the virtues of the spirit, to the sentimental affinities of the imagination that had no demonstrable connection with mere survival or profit, but which ratified the dignity of human nature.

Weaver did not use "sentimental" in the usual sense of a nostalgic longing for some object, place, or person now gone. By "sentimental" he meant instead the attachment to those ideas and beliefs through which men define themselves and through which they reaffirm their identity and their convictions. In *Ideas Have Consequences* he wrote of "the unsentimental sentiment" as the agent that restrains the minds and disciplines the souls of men in their quest to fashion a "metaphysical dream of the world." The "unsentimental sentiment," that deep and abiding fidelity to old forms, customs, and traditions, refines, cultivates, and civilizes human beings, moving them from "a welter of feeling to an illumined concept of what one ought to feel." Culture, in Weaver's estimation, is merely "sentiment refined and measured by intellect."[24]

The destruction of the sentimental and the spiritual dimensions of life, Weaver avowed, did not reduce men to animals, who had their own kind of dignity, but to debased and ruined human beings.[25] The dissolution of traditional bonds, the fragmentation of life, the confusion of values, the inability to distinguish good from evil anticipated the coming disorder. Weaver's already mounting sense that Western civilization had arrived at a crossroads only deepened as he witnessed the grave consequences attending the rise and spread of communism and fascism in Europe and the astonishing violence of the Second World War. In a world of measureless devastation and mass death, what did it profit a man to study lost causes? Weaver urged his contemporaries to ponder the question, certain that the answers they furnished would decide the fate and future of the West.

In his apologia for the South, Weaver did not merely chronicle the incidents and personalities, the ideas, policies, wars, and treaties that are the most conspicuous aspects of history. He also evaluated the revolutionary forces of modernism from the perspective of a traditional, religious, agrarian order. He removed events from the realm of temporal accident and sought to establish their meaning as universal truths. Weaver spoke for the South, but he also attempted to find in Southern history and culture permanent values that explain more than the struggles of a particular people living in a particular place under particular circumstances.

Southerners, according to Weaver, displayed two characteristic but catastrophic shortcomings in their encounter with the modern world. First, no Southern philosopher emerged to articulate the Southern world view in a systematic way, to state categorically the fundamental assumptions and principles on which that world rested, "to show why the South was right *finally*."[26] The South had no Thomas Aquinas, no *Summa Theologica*.

The second great Southern failure, more difficult for Weaver to forgive, was the surrender of initiative. Since 1865, Southerners, although proud and honorable in defeat, had no faith in their own imprimatur. Too many of them accepted Northern interpretations of history and

Northern definitions of culture and success. They read books written by Northern authors, while those of Southern writers gathered dust on the shelf. They imitated Northern ways and Northern manners, which suggested to Weaver that a deep sense of incompetence and inadequacy underlay the vaunted Southern arrogance and conceit. A consciousness of failure enveloped the South, making it impossible for Southerners to vindicate their way of life.[27]

However inadequately Southerners may have defended humanism, sentiment, tradition, and Christianity, the convictions for which they fought, though out of fashion, had not yet expired. The achievement and promise of the South, Weaver thought, posed a challenge to the modern world to abandon the demonic forces of science and technology and thereby to save the human spirit. Only the restoration of a "non-materialist society" could rescue humanity from the nihilism that resulted from spiritual timidity and moral defeat.[28] Weaver uttered a message of salvation, not a call for reform. He urged Southerners to recover the initiative they had lost, without awaiting Northern approbation.

The re-creation of a religious world view, the finest attribute of the South, would halt the decline of civilization in the West. Christianity would impress upon the modern world a splendid image of mankind ennobled by communion with God through Christ. Living under this religious dispensation, modern men could discard the random truths of science and materialism that brought a false equality in their wake, that were "democratic" and "egalitarian" only in the most treacherous sense.

Religion, morality, and art would again enable human beings to experience the drama of life and feel the transformative power that accompanies the struggle between good and evil. Scientists and positivists had devised a sanitized universe in which men at best occupied the position of sophisticated automatons. But those who were yet intellectually and spiritually vital wanted a challenge. They longed to live out the ancient wisdom that men must suffer unto truth. The failure to reinstate the religious world view, moral sentiments, and aesthetic sensibilities to their former primacy summoned harrowing possibilities for Western civilization: malaise, ennui, decadence, and collapse.

The tone of dark foreboding that from time to time enters Weaver's writing suggests not only a deepening pessimism about the likelihood of reversing the dissolution of the West but also a growing resolve to forestall decline. In *Ideas Have Consequences,* he acknowledged that among those who predict the end of the world are many who have a death wish. They hope that the end will come soon, for they have lost the ability to cope with life. But nothing is more certain, Weaver wrote:

> than that we are all in this together. Practically, no one can stand aside from a sweep as deep and broad as the decline of a civilization. If the thinkers of our time cannot catch the imagination of the world to the point of effecting some profound transformation, they must succumb with it. There will be little joy in the hour when they can say, 'I told you so.'[29]

Weaver at times feared the worst. His generation watched ancient empires fall and ancient faiths crumble. They saw cities obliterated, populations displaced or destroyed, nations decimated. For four centuries men had grown increasingly confident that they had achieved a level of intellectual and moral independence that rendered the antique restraints superfluous. Having attained the very summit of human progress, though, modern men now beheld unprecedented eruptions of hatred and violence. Moderns, Weaver declared, echoing the words of St. Matthew, live amid "great tribulation, such as was not since the beginning of the world."[30] They had squandered their rich estate, and as the crisis deepened, they grew more and more apathetic about the consequences.

The insatiable egocentrism, ruthless competition, moral degeneracy, and spiritual emptiness that today characterize modern life lend credibility to Weaver's earlier insights. Evidence of the ruin of American civilization abounds. To illustrate it fully would require an encyclopedic jeremiad. People from all walks of life have begun to recognize that American society and Western civilization have entered a period of prolonged crisis. The relentless indecency that spews forth daily from television, the movies, radio, magazines, music, and the arts combines to annihilate not only values, standards, manners, morals, taste, judgment, and language, but, more serious, the imagination as well. These cultural forms celebrate sensuality, sexuality, self-indulgence, perversion, boorishness, and, perhaps worst of all, a juvenility that the Dutch historian Johan Huizinga identified as "Puerilism," an appallingly vulgar expression of adolescent barbarity destructive of civilized life.[31]

In addition, unlike the situation in imperial Rome, the barbarians are not at the gate; they are already inside the city walls. "We are ending where the savages began," exclaimed the French thinker Bertrand de Jouvenel, writing in the immediate aftermath of the Second World War. "Barbarian invasions would be superfluous: we are our own Huns."[32] The most troubling prospect confronting Europeans and, perhaps to a greater extent, Americans at the end of the millennium may well be the approaching descent into a new age of barbarism, compounded by a pagan science and an often ghoulish technology. This development, if unchecked, raises lingering doubts about whether the widespread prosperity, comfort, and freedom, which have long been hallmarks of Western civilization, will not recede and disappear. As Weaver perceived, there are, in the second half of the twentieth century, many persons who lack the will and the fortitude to vindicate and save what remains of civilization in the West.

By "Western Civilization," Weaver did not mean the global dissemination of American popular culture or the unchallenged American dominance of the world. He emphasized instead the values, customs, beliefs, traditions, and faith that Americans share with the peoples of England, France, Spain, Italy, Germany, Greece, and Eastern Europe, including European Russia. He knew, of course, that given the unequalled wealth and power of the United States following the Second World War, the attitudes, ideas, and efforts of Americans would for a long time remain critical to the perpetuation of that common heritage.

Weaver also never advocated the kind of abstract,

bureaucratic internationalism that has governed the conduct of American foreign policy since Woodrow Wilson.
For Weaver, the defense of civilization rested on the
defense of tradition, morality, and civility. Civilization, in
his view, could not be imposed on a people; it had rather
to be organic and historic. He foresaw a time, however,
when upholding tradition, morality, and civility would
become more important to the survival of civilized life
than the perpetuation and expansion of wealth and
power. That era has now arrived.[33]

Modern men, Weaver resolved, had lost their moral
orientation, had, indeed, become "moral idiots," unable
to respond to the perversions, brutalities, and challenges
of their world.[34] Heartless and indifferent, they behaved
like "spoiled children," living not immorally but amorally,
without the capacity even to measure their descent and
degradation.[35] The unceasing belligerence against everything that stands outside the self is but a single manifestation of the modern crisis. The coarse-minded barbarian,
who denigrates and destroys all that is different and
unfamiliar, and the dangerously sensitive neurotic, who
mistrusts and manipulates others, were, for Weaver, the
representative personalities of modern times. Both impiously put men before God, usurping the power to dispose of others' lives.

According to Weaver, modern men can no longer
entirely credit the reality of other selves. They lack the
imagination and the sympathy to appreciate and respect
other human beings, or to recognize that the sanctity of
their own lives depends on the existence of a beneficent
and civil human community.[36] Mystified by their disaffec-
tion from nature, humanity, and God, modern men can-

not remedy their affliction, for they have come to rely exclusively on human means to do so. Having forgotten the many flaws and limitations of human nature and the unfathomable glory and perfection of God, modern men retain only a belief in the power of reason and the efficacy of science, instruments now wholly inadequate to ensure their happiness and survival.[37] Having divested themselves of an abiding sense of the divine and eternal, men must confront the rising impersonality and disorder of the modern world alone, without solace or hope.

Weaver nonetheless affirmed that modern men can continue to nourish the possibility of redemption as long as they do not succumb absolutely to the determinism of reason, science, and technology. Men may be arrogant and sinful, as they have always been, but they remain capable of experiencing Christian faith and love—capable, that is, of believing without confirming and of giving without taking. Endowed as they are with free will, they also potentially retain the capacity to distinguish between good and evil. For Weaver, therefore, the heirs of Western civilization in the twentieth century face a momentous and preeminently moral choice. Modern men have got to choose between barbarism and civilization. They must decide if they wish to live, and if they do, whether they wish to live as men, as human beings, in civilized communities, or, in Weaver's striking image, as "rats" huddled in the doorways of blackened buildings, scuttling through the rubble of wrecked cities. "One can detect signs of suicidal impulse," Weaver lamented; "one feels at times that the modern world is calling for madder music and for stronger wine, is craving some delirium which will take it completely away from reality."[38]

Weaver returned to the South for an antidote. "The Old South may indeed be a hall hung with splendid tapestries in which no one would care to live," he wrote in *The Southern Tradition at Bay*, "but from them we can learn something of how to live."[39] The sense of honor, obligation, humility, piety, faith, and love embodied in the Southern tradition offered the most complete image of a Christian community available in the modern world, and thus held out the best promise of rekindling the idea of civilization amid the darkening twilight of Christendom.

ENDNOTES

1. Richard M. Weaver, "Aspects of the Southern Philosophy," in *The Southern Essays of Richard Weaver*, ed. George M. Curtis III and James J. Thompson, Jr. (Indianapolis: Liberty Press, 1987), 208.

2. Richard M. Weaver, *The Southern Tradition at Bay: A History of Postbellum Thought*, ed. George Core and M. E. Bradford (New Rochelle: Arlington House, 1968), 30–31. For perceptive recent analyses of Weaver's views of the South and modernity, see M. E. Bradford, *Remembering Who We Are: Observations of a Southern Conservative* (Athens, GA: University of Georgia Press, 1985), 73–82; Donald Davidson, "The Vision of Richard Weaver: A Foreword," in *The Southern Tradition at Bay*, 13–24; Eugene D. Genovese, *The Southern Tradition: The Achievement and Limitations of an American Conservatism* (Cambridge: Harvard University Press, 1994), *passim*, but especially, 88–91; Fred Hobson, *Tell About the South: The Southern Rage to Explain* (Baton Rouge: Louisiana State University Press, 1983), 323–335; Lisa Jane Tyree, "The Conservative Mind of the South: Richard Weaver" (M. A. thesis, University of Arkansas, 1988); and Brenan R. Nierman, "The Rhetoric of History and Definition: The Political Thought of Richard M. Weaver" (Ph.D. dissertation, Georgetown University, 1993).

3. *Ibid.*, 388–91.

4. *Ibid.* For a more complete exposition of this perspective on the Civil War, see Frank Lawrence Owsley, "The Irrepressible Conflict," in *I'll Take My Stand: The South and the Agrarian Tradition* (Baton Rouge: Louisiana State University Press, 1977), 61–91.

5. *Ibid.*, 31.

6. *Ibid.*, 32.

7. The first quotation comes from *Ibid.*, 33, the second from Richard M. Weaver *Ideas Have Consequences* (Chicago: University of Chicago Press, 1948), 15. But also see *Ideas Have Consequences*, 1–17, 113–28, 182–84.

8. Edward Gibbon, *The History of the Decline and Fall of the Roman Empire* (London: Methuen, 1925), IV, 180–81.

9 Weaver, *Ideas*, 16.

10. *Ibid.*, 91, 105–06.

11. *Ibid.*, 14, 106.

12. Alexis de Tocqueville, *The Old Regime and the French Revolution*, trans. Stuart Gilbert (New York: Doubleday, 1983), xiv.

13. Weaver, *Ideas*, 70–71.

14. See Weaver, "Aspects of the Southern Philosophy," 189–208 and "The South and the American Union," 230–56 in *Southern Essays*. See also Weaver, *Southern Tradition*, 34.

15. Weaver, *Southern Tradition*, 35.

16. *Ibid.*, 35–39.

17. On the conservative, religious world view of antebellum Southern thinkers, see Genovese, *Southern Tradition*, 1–40; *The Slaveholders' Dilemma: Freedom and Progress in Southern Conservative Thought, 1820–1860* (Columbia: University of South Carolina Press, 1992); "'Slavery Ordained of God': The Southern Slaveholders' View of Biblical History and Modern Politics," 24th Annual Fortenbaugh Memorial Lecture, Gettysburg College (1985), 7–30; Eugene D. Genovese and Elizabeth Fox-Genovese, "The Religious Ideals of Southern Slave Society," *The Georgia Historical Quarterly* 70 (1986), 1–16; and "The Divine Sanction of Social Order: Religious Foundations of the Southern Slaveholders' World View," *Journal of the American Academy of Religion* 55 (1987), 211–33.

18. Weaver, *Ideas*, 68.

19. Weaver, *Southern Tradition*, 36–37.

20. *Ibid.*, 39.

21. *Ibid.*, 41.

22. Richard M. Weaver to Donald Davidson, February 28, 1948, in the Donald Davidson Papers, Special Collections, Jean and Alexander Heard Library, Vanderbilt University.

23. Weaver, *Southern Tradition*, 391, emphasis in original.

24. Weaver, *Ideas*, 18–23. See also *Southern Tradition*, 39–41.

25. Weaver, *Southern Tradition*, 41.

26. *Ibid.*, 389. Weaver did not see himself as that systematic Southern philosopher. In the brief "Foreword" to the edition of *Ideas Have Consequences* that was

issued more than a decade after its original publication, Weaver described the book as "not primarily a work of philosophy" but "rather an intuition of a situation."

27. *Ibid.*, 390.

28. *Ibid.*, 391.

29. Weaver, *Ideas*, 187.

30. *Ibid.*, 2.

31. Johan Huizinga, *Homo Ludens: A Study of the Play Element in Culture* (Boston: Beacon Press, 1955), 205. For Weaver's critique of radio, the movies, and the print media, see *Ideas*, 93–104, 110–11.

32. Bertrand de Jouvenel, *On Power: The Natural History of Its Growth* (Indianapolis: Liberty Press, 1993), 11.

33. Weaver, *Ideas*, 66. For a trenchant exposition of this development and its impact on the United States and Europe during the twentieth century, see John Lukacs, *Outgrowing Democracy: A History of the United States in the Twentieth Century* (Lanham: University Press of America, 1984), *passim*, but especially, 368–404, and *The End of the Twentieth Century and the End of the Modern Age* (New York: Ticknor & Fields, 1993), *passim*, but especially, 170–202. For a contemporary European, specifically a French, perspective on these issues, see Jean Raspail, "Defending Civilization," *Chronicles: A Magazine of American Culture* 22 (April 1998), 14–16.

34. Weaver, *Ideas*, 1.

35. See *Ibid.*, 113–28, for Weaver's discussion of "The Spoiled-Child Psychology."

36. *Ibid.*, 171–72.

37. *Ibid.*, 184–85.

38. *Ibid.*, 185–86. See also Eugene D. Genovese, "The Southern Tradition and the Black Experience," in *The Southern Front: History and Politics in the Cultural Wars* (Columbia: University of Missouri Press, 1995), 278–85.

39. Weaver, *Southern Tradition*, 396.

The Influence of
Ideas Have Consequences
on the Conservative
Intellectual Movement
in America

GEORGE H. NASH

On April 3, 1963, Richard M. Weaver was found dead in his small apartment in Chicago, precisely one month after his fifty-third birthday. The conservative intellectual community in America was stunned. Already an esteemed member of this community, Professor Weaver was immediately eulogized as a scholar and moralist of unusual power—indeed, as "one of the ablest cultural critics of our times."[1]

In the three-and-one-half decades since Weaver's death, his reputation among conservatives has remained high. In 1984, when his first published book—*Ideas Have Consequences*—appeared in a new paperback edition, the distinguished sociologist Robert Nisbet pronounced it "one of the few authentic classics in the American political tradition."[2] Four years later the preeminent conservative publisher Henry Regnery cited *Ideas Have Consequences* as one of just three books "which provided the intellectual basis for the modern conservative movement."[3] (The other two were Friedrich Hayek's *The Road to Serfdom* and Russell Kirk's *The Conservative Mind*.) In 1996, when the first biography of Weaver was published, the one-time Marxist historian Eugene Genovese asserted in the *New Republic* (no less) that Weaver "deserves to rank among the most significant intellectuals of America in this century."[4]

The continuing acclaim for Weaver on the American Right has been matched by devoted efforts to honor his memory. In 1964 the Intercollegiate Society of Individualists (now known as the Intercollegiate Studies Institute) established a Richard M. Weaver Fellowship program for graduate students.[5] Thirty-five years later, its beneficiaries include many of the best conservative scholars in American academia. In 1983 the Rockford Institute in Illinois created an annual Richard M. Weaver Award for Scholarly Letters; since then, some of the finest historians and social critics in the United States have received it.[6]

Meanwhile Weaver's writings—the basis for his reputation—have continued to be disseminated. During his lifetime Weaver published only three books, but between 1964 and 1970 four more came out posthumously, in part because of the exertion of his intellectual heirs.[7] Nor has interest in his work waned over the years. In 1987 the Liberty Press brought out a collection of Weaver's essays on Southern history and literature.[8] That same year President Edwin J. Feulner, Jr., of The Heritage Foundation—himself a former Weaver Fellow—selected

Weaver's brilliant essay "Up From Liberalism" for national distribution.[9] In 1995 the Intercollegiate Studies Institute produced a paperback edition of his *Visions of Order.*[10] Thus it has come about that more of Weaver's *oeuvre* has appeared in book form after his death than before it. And all this time, *Ideas Have Consequences* has remained almost continuously in print: a remarkable datum in itself. How many other books published in 1948, one wonders, managed to stay in print a mere five years, let alone fifty?

As conservative testimonials to Weaver's importance have multiplied, academia has begun to take notice. Since the late 1980s, Weaver has been the subject of no fewer than three doctoral dissertations, five master's theses, two biographies (with a third on the way), one monograph, an anthology of appreciative essays, and a steadily increasing number of scholarly articles.[11] In fact, there now exists more serious scholarship about Richard Weaver than about any other founding father of modern American conservatism, except for Eric Voegelin and Leo Strauss. To put it another way: in the past decade a Weaver "industry" has sprung up—not, to be sure, as large as the Strauss and Voegelin "industries," but one whose potential for growth seems assured.

At first glance the burgeoning interest in Weaver may seem puzzling. A reserved and unassuming bachelor, he was neither a campus celebrity nor a charismatic public speaker. A professor in the undergraduate College of the University of Chicago, he left behind no corps of talented graduate students to build on his intellectual edifice. In the variegated world of the intellectual Right, one frequently hears of Straussians and Voegelinians, Austrian

School economists and Chicago School economists, Burkeans and even Objectivists, but no Weaverites. Indeed, shortly after Weaver died, a friend remarked that "he was much admired, but seldom imitated."[12] Yet for all these apparent limitations, this "shy little bulldog of a man"[13] soon attained nearly iconic status in the pantheon of American conservatism.

Three factors help us to understand why. First, in the estimation of those who came to know him, Richard Weaver was a "remarkable" man.[14] "Still water runs deep," says the proverb, and many who befriended him sensed that here was no ordinary college professor but a figure of truly "great depths."[15] Time and again, in the appraisals of Weaver that his friends and colleagues composed over the years, one finds moving references not just to his mind but to his character: to his "dogged integrity," "rugged honesty," courage, "quiet heroism," and modesty.[16] For those who knew him personally, Weaver was a figure of genuinely moral stature.[17]

It was not just that he was an exceptionally disciplined scholar who worked literally seven days a week, or that his lifestyle seemed so austere and monastic that a friend compared him to a "little gnome."[18] No, there was something else that his friends discerned in him and found deeply affecting: a sense of vocation to which, with "almost consuming passion," he devoted himself.[19] Weaver's life was "a crusade to reestablish belief in the reality of transcendentals," a friend wrote in 1970.[20] Another friend said that Weaver kept his mind "fixed on the far goal of a grand reordering of a splintered society."[21] Weaver himself once remarked that he had been powerfully influenced by his mentor John Crowe

Ransom's concept of the "unorthodox defense of ortho-doxy."[22] But however one defines his calling, there is little doubt that, to a degree unusual among academics of his time, Weaver saw himself not just as a seeker of knowl-edge but as a soldier in a great spiritual and intellectual battle.[23] No wonder his fellow conservatives admired him. He "never gave an inch on the fundamentals,"[24] one of them asserted. This, too was part of the reason he fas-cinated—and continues to fascinate—the Right.

Weaver's mode of living seemed to enhance his quiet mystique. Living alone in a rented hotel room during most of his years in Chicago, he appeared to make few concessions to the modern world. Although he owned an automobile for most of his adult life, he found driving in Chicago to be nerve-wracking and soon gave up the effort. Nearly every summer, in fact, during his University of Chicago years, he escaped the uncongenial Windy City for his beloved ancestral home town of Weaverville, North Carolina, where (it is said) he culti-vated a little plot of land with a horse-drawn plow, never a tractor. He insisted on traveling from Chicago to Weaverville by train. Only rarely in his life did he consent to fly in a plane. "You have to draw the line somewhere," he said.[25]

Secondly, since 1963 this native Tarheel has increasingly been recognized as belonging to a vibrant, twentieth-cen-tury tradition of Southern conservatism, extending from the authors of *I'll Take My Stand* in 1930 to M. E. Bradford and Marion Montgomery in the 1990s. One scholar has concluded that Weaver was "the most influential Southern conservative since the Agrarians."[26] Another has labeled him "the Saint Paul of the Vanderbilt

Agrarians. He was born too late to be one of the twelve, but with the possible exception of Donald Davidson, he became the movement's most vigorous and eloquent defender."[27] No longer perceived (as he sometimes was in his lifetime) as a kind of solitary genius, Weaver can now be seen in context. In the community of scholarship there is now a thriving Southern Agrarian "industry" (if that is not an oxymoron), and Richard Weaver has become part of it. It is the second reason he has not been forgotten.

But neither Weaver's personal qualities, nor his prominence in the great Southern Agrarian chain of being, would alone sustain his reputation among American conservatives were it not for a third fact—his books—and for one book above all. In a separate article Ted J. Smith III has explained how *Ideas Have Consequences* came to be written. In this essay we shall examine how *Ideas Have Consequences* came to be *read*—read and assimilated—by the conservative intellectual movement since World War II. There is universal agreement among conservatives that this slender volume had "profound" and "seminal" importance.[28] According to Robert Nisbet, it "launched the renascence of philosophical conservatism in this country."[29] How, then, did its influence manifest itself? In what ways did this book change minds?

When *Ideas Have Consequences* appeared in 1948, its publisher (the University of Chicago Press) anticipated that the book would cause a sensation. Investing heavily in advertising, the Press ordered an initial printing of 7500 copies.[30] The publisher's judgment was quickly vindicated: within two years *Ideas Have Consequences* received more than one hundred reviews, to the amazement of its author.[31] Weaver had been warned that his opus would provoke wrathful rejoinders, and so, in some quarters, it did.[32] Readers—both pro and con—seemed to respond to it vehemently, he told his ideological soulmate Donald Davidson.[33]

But if the author of *Ideas Have Consequences* soon found himself under furious assault from the Left, he must have been heartened by the plaudits he received from a number of scholars who were to become luminaries of the postwar intellectual Right. In the *Kenyon Review* Eliseo Vivas—later to be a friend of Weaver—acclaimed him as "an inspired moralist."[34] In the *Journal of Politics* Willmoore Kendall, a conservative political scientist and teacher of William F. Buckley, Jr., unabashedly nominated Weaver for "the captaincy of the anti-Liberal team."[35] Still another conservative who discovered *Ideas Have Consequences* in its first month of existence was a young historian and bookstore proprietor in East Lansing, Michigan, named Russell Kirk. Quickly recognizing the importance of Weaver's volume, Kirk displayed it prominently in his bookshop and invited its author to address a literary society in East Lansing. Thus began a close and lifelong friendship.[36] Kirk was impressed by the "uncompromising intrepidity" of *Ideas Have Consequences* and publicly saluted its author as "one of the most courageous men in America."[37] He also extolled Weaver's "iron logicality" and bestowed upon him the epithet "the Calvin of criticism."[38] For Kirk and Kendall—and no doubt for others on the Right—one source of the book's appeal was its outspoken repudiation of what Kirk called "ritualistic liberalism."[39] As

Kendall put it in his review, Weaver's "real enemy" was "the more or less typical American liberal."[40]

In the cases of Kirk, Vivas, and Kendall, it is safe to say that Weaver to them was a kindred spirit rather than a mentor. But in at least one crucial instance, the influence of *Ideas Have Consequences* went much deeper. Among its early readers was a former Communist Party functionary named Frank S. Meyer. Already disillusioned with Communism, Meyer in 1948 was not yet a man of the Right. By his own account, *Ideas Have Consequences* exerted a huge influence on his "personal development towards conservatism." Even more importantly, Weaver's book, in Meyer's words, "adumbrated...the informing principle" of postwar American conservatism: "the unity of tradition and liberty." It was *Ideas Have Consequences*, Meyer later declared, which provided "much of the inspiration" for his own salient contribution to conservative thought: the position known as "fusionism." In 1970 a grateful Meyer called the publication of *Ideas Have Consequences* "the *fons et origo* of the contemporary American conservative movement."[41]

If *Ideas Have Consequences* had decisively affected the life of only one man, Frank S. Meyer—the key conservative theorist of the early 1960s—it would have to be accorded a significant footnote in our intellectual history. But of course the impact of Weaver's first published book was more far-reaching than that. "It will shock," Paul Tillich predicted, and shock it did.[42]

For Weaver's book was nothing less than a sustained philippic against the smugness and shibboleths of the twentieth century. "This is another book about the dissolution of the West," he announced in his very first sentence.[43] By the end of the first page he had labeled modern man a "moral idiot," seemingly incapable of distinguishing "between better and worse."[44] By page three he had propounded a sweeping thesis: that the disintegration of Western civilization was directly traceable to an "evil decision" six hundred years earlier. Enticed by the "fateful doctrine of nominalism" espoused by William of Occam, Western civilization had abandoned its belief in transcendental values or "universals" and thus the position that "there is a source of truth higher than, and independent of, man." "The defeat of logical realism by nominalism in the great medieval debate," Weaver asserted, was "the crucial event in the history of Western culture."[45]

For the next 184 pages Weaver unsparingly delineated what he held to be the "consequences" of this intellectual revolution. With ruthless candor he flayed the idols of the age: the Whig theory of history; the doctrine of progress; "the fallacy of scientism"; the hubris of technology; "the fetish of material prosperity"; "the worship of comfort"; industrialism; materialism; pragmatism; empiricism; liberalism; democracy; relativism; "the insolence of material success"; the "disorganizing heresy" of equality; "the foolish and destructive notion of the 'equality' of the sexes"; and more. At times his audacity was breathtaking. "Has the art of writing proved an unmixed blessing?" he asked.[46] After a coruscating indictment of the modern mass media (the "Great Stereopticon"), he asserted: "How...can one hesitate to conclude that we would live in greater peace and enjoy sounder moral health if the institution of the newspaper were abolished entirely?"[47] In other startling passages he condemned jazz music ("the clearest of all signs of our age's deep-seated predilection for barbarism") and dismissed impressionist art as an expression of nominalism and "egotism" in painting.[48] But Weaver was not engaged in cheap, attention-seeking pyrotechnics. The decadence, moral chaos, and rampant immersion in sensation that had engulfed the West were not happenstance, he insisted. They were products of a centuries-long intellectual retreat from first principles, from true knowledge (the knowledge of universals), and from the integrative "metaphysical dream" of the Middle Ages.

It is sometimes assumed that *Ideas Have Consequences* appeared in 1948 like a bolt from the blue, disturbing the complacency of mid-twentieth-century America. This was not really true. In the aftermath of World War II, the market for Weaver's cultural critique was in fact considerable. Just the year before, Arnold Toynbee had published a one-volume condensation of his six-volume *A Study of History*, a monumental inquiry into the rise and fall of civilizations. Toynbee's book was one of the spectacular publishing events of 1947. It even received a *Time* magazine cover story written by Whittaker Chambers, soon to be another of postwar conservatism's founding fathers.[49] In 1948 Professor Toynbee followed up with a book entitled *Civilization on Trial*; it, too, was heavily reviewed.[50] Few conservatives became as despairing as Chambers, who told William F. Buckley, Jr., in 1954 that it was "idle to talk about preventing the wreck of Western civilization. It is already a wreck from within."[51] But the fear that the West *might* be dying was widespread. As the threat of another world war invaded public consciousness, the question "Whither Western civilization?" was

very much in the air. *Ideas Have Consequences* both bene-
fited from and gave voice to this mood of cultural angst.

Nor is it correct to say that *Ideas Have Consequences* was
an exceptionally original book, although its thesis—that
Western civilization's troubles began with the nominalist
controversy of the fourteenth century—appears to have
been uniquely Weaver's. To the contrary: *Ideas Have
Consequences* was in many ways a derivative book, and in
identifying what it derived from, one can begin to understand its appeal to American conservatives.

Where in 1948 was Richard Weaver "coming from"?
Some hostile readers of *Ideas Have Consequences* quickly
associated him with a "chain of reaction" allegedly head-
quartered at the University of Chicago, where Robert
Hutchins and the philosopher Mortimer J. Adler—"the
Divine Doctors of the Great Books Movement"—had
been propagating a neo-medievalist gospel for years.[52]
The semanticist S. I. Hayakawa labeled this movement
"Neo-Scholasticism." Hutchins and Adler, he said, were
its "neon lights"; Richard Weaver, Russell Kirk, and Eric
Voegelin were among its "dim bulbs."[53] While Weaver, an
ardent Platonist, shared much of the pedagogical and
metaphysical worldview promulgated by Hutchins and
his allies, the young English professor drew most of his
inspiration from other sources. His references in his book
to "sentimental humanitarianism" reflected his exposure
to Irving Babbitt and the New Humanists, about whom
Weaver had written his master's thesis in 1934.[54] His concept of "the spoiled-child psychology" (the subject of his
fourth chapter) he took from the Spanish philosopher
José Ortega y Gasset, whom he quoted twice in his book.[55]
Indeed, *Ideas Have Consequences* forcefully reminded more

than one reader of Ortega's 1930 classic, *The Revolt of the Masses*.[56] Above all, Weaver's worldview in 1948 derived, as we now know, from the Southern Agrarians, whose earnest disciple, by the mid-1940s, he had become.[57] In his mordant criticisms of industrialism and technology, in his negative appraisal of urban man and urban living, and in his plea for a society based on "distinction and hierarchy," he resembled no one so much as the authors of the Agrarian manifesto *I'll Take My Stand*.[58] It was no coincidence. Not surprisingly, some of these very Agrarians had been his teachers in graduate school.[59]

Far, then, from being sui generis, *Ideas Have Consequences* was a luminous example of a diverse and well-established literary tradition of "cultural pessimism" whose past exponents had included Oswald Spengler. As usual, Weaver himself minced no words about it. "Cultural decline is a historical fact," he declared emphatically in his book; "...to establish the fact of decadence is the most pressing duty of our time...."[60] In deliberately hard-hitting and unequivocal prose,[61] he uttered concerns that "cultural pessimists" and "declinists" had been expressing for years. In Weaver the ideology of cultural pessimism gained an eager recruit, at a time when the ideology of progressivism was tottering.[62]

This leads us to the first great contribution that *Ideas Have Consequences* made to the conservative cause after 1945. By linking the rise of modernity to cultural disintegration, it put modernity itself on trial. By standing outside modernity and depicting it as a problem, Weaver dramatically extended the mental horizon of the postwar Right. The crisis of the West, as he diagnosed it, was not simply one of foreign policy (the battle against

Communism) or economics (the fight against the New Deal). No, said Weaver, Western man faced a *civilizational* catastrophe, born of "unintelligent choice" and philosophic error deep in our past.[63] It was to be a central tenet of "traditionalist" conservatism for years to come.

This idea of Weaver's soon had consequences of its own. Among those whom *Ideas Have Consequences* persuaded that the West's crisis was "total" was a young conservative activist named E. Victor Milione. In 1953 Milione became associated with the Intercollegiate Society of Individualists; eventually, he became ISI's president, serving in that capacity for more than twenty years. Armed with Weaver's insight, Milione contended that ISI must not focus narrowly on politics or economics. It must, instead, address "the 'total crisis,' the crisis of culture." Reflecting in part Milione's Weaverian vision, ISI initiated—and sustains to this day—a broadly interdisciplinary approach to its mission.[64] In a conservative intellectual community often preoccupied by short-term contests over public policy, ISI maintains the long view—thanks in considerable measure to Richard M. Weaver.

Coupled with Weaver's critique of modernity in *Ideas Have Consequences* was a second theme that wielded enormous influence over the postwar conservative mind: his unalloyed moral and metaphysical absolutism. Not surprisingly, relativistic liberals castigated him for it, finding in his "metaphysical certitudes" the intellectual scaffolding for authoritarianism.[65] But Weaver was not to be deflected. Truth, universals, and transcendentals were real, he insisted. Forty years before the vogue of nihilistic postmodernism, he discerned and indicted the growing "inroads" of relativism, "with its disbelief in truth."[66] With remarkable prescience he warned:

> The denial of universals carries with it the denial
> of everything transcending experience. The denial
> of everything transcending experience means
> inevitably...the denial of truth. With the denial of
> objective truth there is no escape from the rela-
> tivism of "man the measure of all things."[67]

By insisting upon the existence and knowability of
objective truth, and by looking (as he put it) "toward an
ontological realm which is timeless,"[68] Weaver exerted an
upward pull on American conservatives. Not for him (or
them) a form of conservatism mired in expediency and
mindless pragmatism. Following Weaver (and, a little
later, Russell Kirk), conservatives asserted instead their
fealty to an "objective moral order" and the "permanent
things." Thus in 1960, when the Young Americans for
Freedom was born, its founding manifesto affirmed belief
in "certain eternal truths" and "transcendent values."[69]
The unapologetic philosophical absolutism of the crusad-
ing conservatives of the early 1960s owed much to the
worldview and rhetorical tone of *Ideas Have Consequences*.

A third way in which *Ideas Have Consequences* made its
imprint on conservatives was its encouragement of what
might be called a Roman Catholic interpretation of modern history. At a time when most Americans probably
interpreted the story of Western civilization as an ascent
from the benighted Middle Ages, Weaver turned the
entire chronicle upside down. It was the Middle Ages, he
argued, which had evinced "a comparatively clear perception of reality"—in fact, "a greater awareness of realities than our leaders exhibit today."[70] It was "the unfixing

of relationships in the fourteenth century," he said, which had set the West on its course of "social disintegration."[71] Although *Ideas Have Consequences* deliberately avoided religious exhortation, its biases were noticeable. "The metaphysical right of religion went out at the time of the Reformation," he asserted.[72] "For four centuries every man has been not only his own priest but his own professor of ethics, and the consequence is an anarchy which threatens even that minimum consensus of value necessary to the political state."[73]

So palpable was Weaver's yearning for the lost metaphysical unity of the Middle Ages that one Protestant reviewer of *Ideas Have Consequences* denounced its author as "a propagandist for a return to the medieval papacy."[74] To another reviewer (a Roman Catholic) Weaver appeared to be advocating "the catholicity of Catholicism," only to stop "just short of saying it"—"dead in his tracks"—"as if he had suddenly seen something."[75] Other reviewers noted with amusement that Weaver's "pure Platonism" put him to the right of Thomas Aquinas.[76]

Weaver, of course, was not a Roman Catholic but an inactive Protestant who in later years occasionally attended Episcopal church services in Chicago.[77] While his worldview was basically Christian,[78] he was not a man to verbalize his religious faith, and its precise doctrinal content remains uncertain.[79] (One point that does seem clear is that he felt little affinity for the Fundamentalist Protestantism of the Bible Belt.)[80] But whatever Weaver's innermost religious convictions, the implicitly Catholic neo-medievalism of *Ideas Have Consequences* made its mark on American conservative intellectuals, not a few of whom eventually converted to the Roman Catholic faith.[81] Like John Hallowell's *Main Currents in Modern Political Thought* (1950) and Eric Voegelin's *The New Science of Politics* (1952), *Ideas Have Consequences* popularized a historical paradigm for conservatives in which the founding events of modernity—including the Reformation—came to be seen as critical episodes in the decline of the West. Thus did Richard Weaver, a Protestant from North Carolina, contribute to the noticeably Roman Catholic and Anglo-Catholic coloration of traditionalist American conservatism in the first two decades after World War II.

A fourth influence of Weaver's book on the postwar Right was subtler but equally profound. It lay in his firm conviction that ideas—above all, "our most basic ideas of human destiny"—were the decisive determinants of the course of civilizations.[82] Weaver was not the only conservative theorist to assert this after 1945, but he was one of the first and most compelling. In the wake of *Ideas Have Consequences*, a new genre of conservative criticism proliferated: distinctively intellectual histories and genealogies of declension, all seeking to answer the question: "When did Western civilization take its wrong turning?" Although their answers differed in details, one theme was invariant. Not machines, not the "class struggle," not impersonal social "forces," but ideas: these were the engines of history.[83]

In a way this was, for conservatives, a source of hope. For if (as Weaver argued) a "falsified picture of the world"[84] had produced pernicious consequences for Western civilization, then perhaps a correct picture of the world would yield better consequences. If the world today is as it is because of the sheer, unfathomable weight of impersonal forces, then resistance to its pressures may well be futile. But if our world is the product of ideas in our heads, maybe we can reform our world by changing our ideas.

Such was the hopeful prospect which Weaver held out in *Ideas Have Consequences*. The intellectual history he taught, and which countless conservatives absorbed, was anti-materialist, anti-determinist, anti-fatalist.[85] In a remarkable sentence that he wrote elsewhere shortly before he began *Ideas Have Consequences*, he asserted: "We can will our world."[86] For conservatives seeking the origin of present travails in intellectual error, it was a bracing message. *We can will our world.* Error can be refuted. Ideas have consequences.

But if this is so, it follows that the creators and purveyors of ideas—notably teachers, writers, rhetoricians, and college professors—have a supreme role to play in the redemption of our culture. It was a lesson Weaver explicitly taught in the penultimate chapter of his book, wherein he recommended the study of poetry, rhetoric, dialectic, and foreign languages as ways of restoring "the metaphysical community of language" and even "our lost unity of mind."[87]

And that leads to the fifth way in which *Ideas Have Consequences* molded postwar conservatism in its early years: it encouraged cultural traditionalists to think of themselves as a civilized aristocracy in revolt against the masses and their idols. It should not escape notice that *Ideas Have Consequences* was written by an English professor at a time when more than a few custodians of the humanities in America were appalled by the growing evisceration of the traditional liberal arts curriculum. For conservatives and other votaries of humane learning,

Weaver's outspoken attacks in his book on the cult of "progress," on the "fallacies" of scientism and technology, and on the "specialist" as "a man possessed of an evil spirit,"[88] had strong appeal. Here was a man unafraid to rebuke the ignoramuses (both lettered and unlettered) who were systematically subverting the life of the mind in America. When Weaver contrasted Europe in the Middle Ages (where "the possessor of highest learning was the philosophic doctor")[89] with the contemporary United States (where scientists, technicians, and specialists "at the borderline of psychosis"[90] held sway), the "philosophic doctors" of 1948 approved. His fighting words helped to instill in them a renewed sense of the worth of their cause.

In one area, though, Weaver's assault on the enemies of civilization did not appear to resonate, at least not at first: his scathing denunciations of the bourgeoisie and its value system. *Ideas Have Consequences* contained more than a dozen references to the bourgeoisie or middle class; not a single one of these allusions was favorable. The middle class, he asserted, was "besotted."

> Loving comfort, risking little, terrified by the thought of change, its aim is to establish a materialistic civilization which will banish threats to its complacency. It has conventions, not ideals; it is washed rather than clean. The plight of Europe today is the direct result of the bourgeois ascendancy and its corrupted world view.[91]

To Weaver the "bourgeois mentality" was "psychopathic in its alienation from reality."[92] The world that "the bourgeoisie finds congenial" was "inane." He accused the middle class of spreading the "infection" of "egotism" and self-seeking, leading to "a fragmentation of society which cannot stop short of complete chaos."[93] He asserted that the bourgeoisie "first betrayed society through capitalism and finance."[94] He scorned as "Philistine" the notion that happiness in life consisted of "a job, domesticity, interest in some harmless diversion such as baseball and fishing, and a strong antipathy toward abstract ideas."[95] He attacked "the worship of comfort" as a "form of debauchery" and contrasted it with his own philosophy that "life means discipline and sacrifice."[96]

Such vehemence invites the suspicion that some bitter personal experience may have underlain Weaver's aspersions on the bourgeoisie, and, that, indeed, appears to have been the case.[97] But whatever the origin of Weaver's fiercely anti-middle class sentiments, they did not catch on with most of his confreres on the Right. Nor did his similar strictures on "finance capitalism," industrialism, and commercialism. There were fundamentally two reasons for this. First, the developing conservative movement after World War II had a second component very different from the religious/literary traditionalism exemplified by Weaver. This was the classical liberal or libertarian wing of the Right, and for it individual freedom—including economic freedom—was the *summum bonum.* As these two disparate streams of resistance to modern liberalism came together in the 1950s, this very fact limited the audience on the Right for all-out critiques of middle America and the economics of private enterprise.

Secondly, in *Ideas Have Consequences* and elsewhere,

Weaver himself muted the anti-bourgeois thrust of his analysis, notably by his eloquent defense of individual, small-scale property ownership as "the last metaphysical right." To be sure, Weaver made it plain that he was defending property ownership for metaphysical reasons, not materialistic ones, and that his advocacy of "the distributive ownership of small properties" had nothing whatsoever to do with the "abstract" property arrangements wrought by "finance capitalism." "Big business and the rationalization of industry," he asserted, "abet the evils we seek to overcome."[98] Yet what was his scheme of independently owned homes, farms, and local businesses if not a version of a middle-class ideal? Although he did not label it as such, Weaver had endorsed the via media of Southern Agrarianism. If no partisan of what he called "monopoly capitalism," neither did he welcome what he disapprovingly labeled "pagan statism."[99] He wanted private property to be a "sanctuary" against the omnipotent State.[100] This fact probably helped to assuage the discomfort some of his conservative readers might otherwise have felt.

As it happened, Weaver's apologia for individually owned private property as "the last metaphysical right" turned out to be one of the most influential legacies of *Ideas Have Consequences*. Not only did it open a bridge to free market conservatives; more importantly, it enabled conservatives to vindicate private property rights in language that did not look like a rationalization of materialistic acquisitiveness. Unintentionally or not, Weaver helped to elevate the conservative "case" on this issue to a higher plane. It was an important service.

As for Weaver's castigation of the bourgeoisie, his

intention in *Ideas Have Consequences* may not have been as anti-capitalist as it might have appeared. When he had used the word "bourgeois" (he explained as the book started to circulate), he had been thinking of the kind of Americans whose highest aspiration was ownership of a Buick. Philistines, in short—people with shriveled souls.[101] These were the kind of bourgeois he had evidently met during his unhappy years of teaching at Texas A&M University, just prior to his conversion to Southern Agrarianism: the sort of people Sinclair Lewis had satirized in *Babbitt,* and whom H. L. Mencken had derided as the "booboisie." In part, then, the publication of *Ideas Have Consequences* was another skirmish in a long-running culture war between "alienated" literary intellectuals and a middle America they perceived as crass and materialistic. Weaver's passionately anti-bourgeois rhetoric was probably perceived by his fellow conservatives through that lens, and they would have been right. In 1948 Weaver was closer to Mencken than to Marx.

There is another sense in which it could be said that *Ideas Have Consequences* influenced American conservatism after 1945. If Weaver created the book, the book created him as a conspicuous public intellectual of the Right. In the late 1940s and 1950s Weaver became a friend of many leading figures in the conservative renascence. One of these, Henry Regnery, published Professor Weaver's second book, *The Ethics of Rhetoric,* in 1953.[102] In 1955 Weaver became a contributor to William F. Buckley, Jr.'s, *National Review* at its founding and remained so listed on its masthead until his death.[103] Eleven years earlier, in a letter to Cleanth Brooks, Weaver had declared modern liberalism to be exhausted and had yearned for a journalistic alternative to the cheap and dishonest liberalism being expounded (he said) in leading periodicals.[104] In Buckley's *National Review* he got his wish. During the next eight years he contributed thirty-six articles and reviews to its pages.[105] *National Review,* he told Buckley, was indispensable.[106]

Another conservative publication with which Weaver became affiliated was the academic quarterly *Modern Age,* launched by Russell Kirk in 1957. Weaver contributed the lead article to the inaugural issue, and several additional pieces in the next few years.[107] As an associate editor of *Modern Age* from late 1959 to 1963, he worked hard to assure its success.[108] He also had charge of its book review section.[109]

Still another conservative organization that Weaver embraced was the Intercollegiate Society of Individualists, founded in 1953. In the late 1950s he joined the society's board of directors.[110] In the next several years he lectured under the organization's auspices to campus audiences and prepared three essays which it circulated as pamphlets.[111] Weaver was openly proud of his association with ISI and pleased that its influence was expanding.[112] He esteemed the institute highly, he wrote to a friend in early 1963.[113] Barely two weeks later, and just four days before his death, he told an acquaintance that the work ISI was doing was admirable.[114]

The link with the Intercollegiate Society of Individualists, one suspects, was good for Weaver. It gave him an appreciative audience of conservative youth and drew him away, on occasion, from the almost monastic discipline of his daily life. It was also good for *Ideas Have Consequences.* In 1959, the year that Weaver's book first appeared in a paperback edition, E. Victor Milione distributed approximately six hundred copies through ISI.[115] In the next four decades ISI disseminated literally thousands of additional copies to college students and graduate students throughout the United States.[116] Thanks to the paperback revolution, and more especially to Milione and his associates, *Ideas Have Consequences* experienced a kind of second birth.

Meanwhile, as Weaver grew closer to the growing conservative youth movement, there were signs that he was beginning to modify some of the antimodernism of *Ideas Have Consequences*. Not in a wholesale manner: as late as 1959, in the Foreword to the paperback reprint of his book, Weaver wrote that he "saw no reason, after the lapse of more than a decade, to retreat from the general position of social criticism" he had offered.[117] Still, on at least a few telltale issues he appeared to be changing his mind. In early 1961, for instance, the board of directors of the Intercollegiate Society of Individualists had under consideration a proposal by William F. Buckley, Jr., to change the organization's name, on the grounds that "conservative" was now the movement's label and that the strange-sounding word "individualist" was an obstacle to the society's success.[118] Despite Professor Weaver's denunciation of the term "individualism" in *Ideas Have Consequences*,[119] he opposed Buckley's recommendation. The name Intercollegiate Society of Individualists had always seemed appropriate to him, he protested.[120] Nor was this a momentary lapse on Weaver's part. That same year he became one of three original editorial advisors of the *New Individualist Review*, a journal founded by graduate students of Friedrich Hayek at the University of

Chicago. The new publication had decidedly libertarian leanings, and, fittingly enough, its two other faculty sponsors were Professors Hayek and Milton Friedman. If Weaver felt any intellectual embarrassment about serving on the same masthead with two of the staunchest defenders of free market capitalism in the Western world, the record does not show it. He remained an advisor to the *New Individualist Review* until his death.[121]

By far the strongest evidence of a developing reorientation in Weaver's conservatism appeared in an address delivered in April 1959 at the University of Wisconsin and delivered again, at an ISI-sponsored gathering in Chicago, in September 1962. On the latter occasion his lecture was entitled "How to Argue the Conservative Cause."[122] Although it is possible to find continuities between the contents of this speech and *Ideas Have Consequences*, two themes were startlingly novel. First, Weaver asserted that, in the great contemporary debate over Communism and collectivism, the vast majority of the American people were soundly committed to the conservative cause: the cause of freedom. It was the intellectuals and educated people, he said, who had absorbed liberal and collectivist ideas, while it was people farther down the social scale who had remained mostly untainted. From an intellectual nonconformist who less than a dozen years before had excoriated bourgeois complacency and "the spoiled-child psychology of the urban masses," it was a remarkable reversal. The ordinary citizen, Weaver now told his listeners, was a sensible fellow. The one-time antagonist of philistinism now found virtue in middle America. Weaver was in a new frame of mind that April day, a frame of mind that anticipated the coming era in which conservatives would shuck off their minority-mindedness and proclaim themselves the vanguard of the silent majority.

Even more surprising was the second new theme in Weaver's 1959/1962 speech: his rousing defense of the American economic system. An economy rooted in freedom, incentives, and initiative, he proclaimed, had rewarded Americans with the best standard of living in the world. Capitalism—yes, capitalism—had produced an incomparable cornucopia of plenty. Weaver exhorted his listeners not to feel guilty or defensive about the material achievements of their capitalist system. A society founded upon freedom of enterprise, he averred, was a natural product of unchanging human nature. Such a society, he predicted, would survive.

It is impossible to know where Weaver might have taken these arguments in the years ahead. Less than seven months after he gave this lecture for the second time, he died. Moreover, around the time he was publicly praising capitalism for its bounteousness, he was also continuing to write sympathetically about Southern Agrarianism and contemplating a return to the South to teach. To the end of his days he remained a critic of industrialism and technological "progress."[123] Nevertheless, by the last years of his life Weaver had significantly softened the militantly anti-materialistic, anti-bourgeois, anti-capitalist biases of *Ideas Have Consequences*. Perhaps at the height of the Cold War against an atheistic and collectivist enemy, the United States of America looked better to him than it had in the late 1940s. In his 1959 (and 1962) speech on the "conservative cause," he appeared to think so. To Weaver on these occasions, the United States of America was a success to be celebrated against its leftist critics.

All this is, perhaps, a useful reminder that important thinkers do not stop thinking and that authors sometimes outlive their earliest books. But books—and, particularly, great books—can outlive their authors, and such was the fate of Weaver's *Ideas Have Consequences*. When Weaver died in 1963, his writings did not die with him. "Strong books, like high deeds, confer immortality," Russell Kirk wrote at the time, and his words proved prophetic.[124] In the first three decades (and more) after Weaver's death, *Ideas Have Consequences* continued to be read, admired, and cited on the American Right.[125] The very phrase "ideas have consequences" became a cliché, as conservatives (reflecting Weaverian thinking) engaged in what they called "the battle of ideas."

Yet even as conservatives everywhere acclaimed Weaver, a subtle change in their perception of him now occurred: a tendency to see in him a mirror for their own preoccupations. This in itself was a tribute to his importance: his intellectual legacy was deemed valuable enough to be argued over and claimed. But it meant that from now on, to some degree, the author of *Ideas Have Consequences* would be a contested figure on the Right.

One of the first to appropriate Weaver after his passing was Frank S. Meyer, the chief ideologist of the fractious conservative movement in the 1960s. In 1964 Meyer—hard at work on articulating the philosophical synthesis called fusionism—dedicated a book on the subject to the memory of Weaver, whom he labeled the "pioneer and protagonist of the American conservative consensus."[126]

In 1970 (as noted earlier), Meyer contended that *Ideas Have Consequences* was the veritable fountainhead of his fusionist philosophy. Meanwhile, in 1965, Willmoore Kendall—conservatism's great contrarian—used a review of Weaver's posthumous volume *Visions of Order* to berate the "high priests" of the conservative establishment from which Kendall was increasingly estranged. Weaver's conservatism was "unique," said Kendall; only Weaver, among his fellow conservatives, stood on the "right" side on certain pivotal issues.[127] When one of Kendall's *bêtes noires,* Russell Kirk, eulogized Weaver in the Foreword to *Visions of Order,* Kendall accused Kirk of trying to make Weaver into his "alter-ego."[128]

As various conservatives sought (as it were) to "capture" Weaver for their agendas, an event occurred which drastically altered their perception of him: the publication, in 1968, of a slightly expanded version of his 1943 doctoral dissertation under the title *The Southern Tradition at Bay.* During his lifetime Weaver had often published articles on Southern subjects, including sharp criticisms of racial integration and the emerging civil rights movement.[129] But none of the three books he published in his lifetime had been overtly Southern in content. Moreover, he had taught nearly twenty years at the University of Chicago, no Southern citadel. It was only five years after his death that the profoundly formative, Southern Agrarian dimension of his thought became fully apparent. From this point forward, the prevailing interpretation of Weaver was unequivocal: he was "the most prominent disciple of the Vanderbilt Agrarians"[130]—indeed, their "best expositor"[131]—and even "the most unreconstructed of them all."[132]

The growing recognition of the Agrarian roots of Weaver's conservatism soon had reverberations on the Right. Traditionalist Southern conservatives speedily hailed him, both as a prophet of the evils of modernity and as a dogged defender of the antimodern South. In the 1970s a group of his admirers attempted to establish a Richard M. Weaver College in South Carolina.[133] In the 1980s and early 1990s the *Southern Partisan* printed two largely unknown addresses by him at family reunions many years before, as well as a lengthy cover story lauding his achievement.[134] Whenever the Agrarians and their disciples were discussed, Weaver's name was likely to be mentioned with respect.[135]

Not surprisingly, the increasing emphasis on Weaver's Southernness evoked a fresh interpretation of *Ideas Have Consequences*. With *The Southern Tradition at Bay* belatedly in print, it now seemed to some conservatives that *Ideas Have Consequences* should be read as a companion volume to it, an indictment not just of modernity-in-general but of Northern modernity in particular. But if Weaver was now to be understood not as a conservative-in-general but as a quintessentially *Southern* conservative, a new possibility opened up: *Ideas Have Consequences* could become a weapon against Yankees—including Yankee conservatives—with whom latter-day Southern Agrarians and their allies had their differences.

And this is precisely what happened in the 1980s, as a vocal movement of (often Southern) "paleoconservatives" (as they came to be called) dissented from the prevailing conservatism of Ronald Reagan's America. Writing in the thirtieth-anniversary issue of *National Review* in 1985, the emerging paleoconservative writer

Chilton Williamson, Jr., asserted bluntly that Richard Weaver would not have been "comfortable" with the "new breed" of "boisterous," optimistic conservatives, "entirely devoid of the tragic sense," who had come to prominence in the Reagan era. No, said Williamson, Weaver had seen "more deeply" than "the GOP boosters of the Eighties" the "socially and morally destructive aspects of that form of industrial capitalism we call the West."[136]

The deployment of Weaver's writings as artillery in sectarian strife intensified in the late Eighties and Nineties during the bitter ideological war between paleoconservatives and neoconservatives, a controversy in which one of Weaver's staunchest admirers, M. E. Bradford, was a protagonist.[137] As the neoconservative ideology of "democratic capitalism" gained popularity, becoming the semi-official creed of the Reaganites, embattled paleoconservatives turned to what they called the Old Right for countervailing intellectual ammunition. And no one on the Old Right seemed more useful than Weaver. If Irving Kristol was the "godfather" of neoconservatism, Richard Weaver seemed to acquire a comparable stature among paleoconservative champions of the "Old Republic."[138]

From a paleoconservative perspective, the enlistment of Weaver in their army made sense. What could be more glaring than the gulf between the stern antimodernism of *Ideas Have Consequences* and the cheerful American exceptionalism of Ronald Reagan? What could be more antithetical to Reagan's "supply-side economics" than what Eugene Genovese claimed was the "deep anticapitalism" of Weaver's conservatism?[139] Indeed, had not this gulf existed since the infancy of the postwar conservative revival? In the 1950s, in the very years that Weaver was questioning such "god terms" as "progress" and "science,"[140] Reagan had been a spokesman for General Electric, whose corporate motto was: "Progress is our most important product." No wonder, then, that in 1996 a Southern devotee of Weaver argued in *National Review* that Weaver's conservatism had "nothing in common" with the defense of capitalism.[141]

In appropriating Weaver for their purposes in this way, the paleoconservatives were relying almost exclusively on the early Weaver—the scourge of "progress" and "bourgeois capitalism" in *Ideas Have Consequences*—not on the Cold War conservative who had heaped praise on American capitalism in 1959 and 1962. It was Weaver the cultural declinist whom they quoted, not the conservative activist who openly identified his cause with middle America in the late 1950s and early 1960s. Of course, few conservatives of any stripe appeared to realize that by 1959 Weaver had begun to attenuate, in some respects, the cultural pessimism he had adopted so fervently in the 1940s when he had felt "condemned" to live in "darkest Chicago."[142] But perhaps it would not have mattered if they had. For *Ideas Have Consequences* was a powerful book, and by 1963 it had taken on a life of its own.

And then, in the 1990s, just as Southern traditionalists and others were reaffirming Weaver's status as an "intellectual saint,"[143] a surprising twist in the Weaver saga occurred. For the first time, Weaver himself came under significant fire from the Right.[144] In 1992, in a book portentously entitled *The Conservative Crack-Up*, R. Emmett Tyrrell, Jr., accused Weaver of encouraging "a sense of political futility" among conservatives after World War II. If Weaver was right that the "dissolution of the West" had begun with the acceptance of nominalism in the fourteenth century, then—Tyrrell asked with exasperation—"what the hell could be done about it?" Tyrrell conceded that Weaver's "dismal scholarship had its virtues": it directed readers to "important things, the nature of man, the quality of men's souls." Unfortunately, said Tyrrell, Weaver's writings were "more likely to move his readers to political despair than to enthusiastic, back-slapping political action."[145]

Tyrrell's frustration was echoed a year later by Samuel Francis, a Southern paleoconservative disciple of James Burnham. In an essay pungently entitled "Ideas and No Consequences," he asserted that modern American conservatism was a failure. One large reason, he declared, was that the movement's intellectuals, including Weaver, had been guilty of an "abstract and abstruse intellectualism" which had helped to doom their cause to "irrelevance." Men like Weaver, Eric Voegelin, and Leo Strauss, said Francis, had practiced a "formalistic and normative approach" to political theory, an approach "reluctant to admit that some things, even ideas, fail." The Old Right, charged Francis, had been "too uxoriously wedded to Weaver's principle that 'Ideas Have Consequences.'" It had too often responded to "the civilizational crisis it perceived" by indulging in "a pretentious medievalism," attraction to "archaic social and political forms such as the antebellum South," and other brands of "romanticism" and "archaism." "Ideas do have consequences," Francis acknowledged, "but some ideas have more consequences than others," in part because "some ideas serve human interests and emotions...while other ideas do not." The Old Right "intelligentsia" had fallen short, said Francis, because American culture contained "no significant set of interests to which its ideas could attach themselves." Lacking a social base from which to resist the "managerial revolution," the "hyperintellectualism of the Old Right" had collapsed in futility.[146]

As if these blows to Weaver's iconic status were not enough, in 1996 Jeffrey Hart delivered another. Hart's target was not *Ideas Have Consequences* but the Southern Agrarian vision that undergirded it. To Hart, this was precisely Weaver's weakness: his "Southernness" had rested upon just that—a vision, a dream, "an abstraction from historical reality." Rejecting the argument that "capitalism" and "tradition" were irreconcilable, Hart retorted that the conservative, antebellum South so cherished by Weaver had itself been "capitalist" at its core. The very "essence" of the early nineteenth century Southern economy had been "trade and money." Clearly Hart had little patience with Weaver's oft-quoted contention that the Old South had been a feudal society, *"the last non-materialist civilization in the Western World."*[147] To Hart, Weaver's "polarizations" between the South and North, between "traditional community and capitalism," were "abstractions masquerading as actual entities." Although Hart did not criticize *Ideas Have Consequences* overtly, he suggested that its author, leading a life of "isolation," "seemed to forget what lived, non-abstract social existence is like." For Hart, Weaver was "an uncertain guide to a fully imagined American conservatism."[148]

The unexpected emergence of a critique of Weaver's thought from within the Right raised many questions.

Fifty years after the publication of *Ideas Have Consequences*, was its reign as a conservative classic finally ending? Had Weaver (at least the early Weaver) been too abstract and formalistic, too imbued with Platonism, too convinced of the primacy of ideas? Had his interpretation of the decline of the West stretched conservatives' mental horizon too far, to the point of neo-medieval archaism and irrelevance? During most of his career Weaver had been a determined standard-bearer for two powerful intellectual traditions: cultural pessimism about modernity and (the other side of the coin) the philosophy of Southern Agrarianism. Had he perhaps been too devoted a paladin? In his quest for a true and coherent "metaphysical dream," did his own "dream" become a confining ideology?

As conservatives celebrated *Ideas Have Consequences'* fiftieth anniversary, few could deny that much of Weaver's worldview seemed more remote than ever from the "lived, non-abstract social existence" of late-twentieth century America: his admiration for "the chivalry and spirituality of the Middle Ages,"[149] for instance; his unqualified assaults upon science and technology; his celebration of a regime of "distinction and hierarchy"; his blasts at the middle class. As Americans, including conservative Americans, logged on to the Internet, invested in the stock market, and anticipated the third millennium, few gave any sign of repudiating the institutions of modernity. If an antimodernist revolution of this magnitude had been Weaver's objective, his cause seemed truly lost.

And yet, as Russell Kirk remarked in the mid-1950s, Weaver's writings, "once read, ferment in the mind."[150] As the Cold War abroad yielded in the 1990s to "culture wars" at home, the perception of cultural disintegration and decline, to which Weaver in 1948 gave classic expression, appeared to be making a comeback on the Right. If true, the life of *Ideas Have Consequences* was not yet over. In 1996 Robert Bork produced a telling volume in this vein under the title *Slouching Towards Gomorrah*; it was a national best-seller.[151] In the late 1990s the American conservative community seemed divided between "optimists," who believed the future of Western civilization to be promising, and "pessimists," who judged the West's moral foundations to be collapsing with frightening speed. For conservatives of the latter persuasion, *Ideas Have Consequences* had lost neither its persuasiveness nor its punch.

What a remarkable book *Ideas Have Consequences* had turned out to be. In the 1940s an unknown English instructor at the University of Chicago had set out to be a diagnostician of the decadence of the West. If, fifty years later, certain elements of his book appeared antiquated, its power to provoke seemed undiminished. Too much of its account of the consequences of moral and epistemological relativism had proven to be almost eerily prescient. In *Ideas Have Consequences* Weaver warned: "We approach a condition in which we shall be amoral without the capacity to perceive it and degraded without means to measure our descent."[152] In the America of the late 1990s, many conservatives felt that Weaver's prophecy had come true.

As *Ideas Have Consequences* started its second half century in print, there was every reason to believe that it would be read for a long while yet.

ENDNOTES

1. For a sampling of tributes to Weaver soon after his death, see: Russell Kirk, "Richard Weaver, RIP," *National Review* 14 (April 23, 1963), 308; Kendall Beaton [Weaver's brother-in-law], "Richard M. Weaver: A Clear Voice in an Addled World" (typescript, August 5, 1963), copy enclosed with Beaton to Louis H. T. Dehmlow, August 11, 1963, Richard M. Weaver Collection, Division 1, File 4, Hillsdale College, Hillsdale, Michigan; Ralph T. Eubanks, "Richard M. Weaver: In Memoriam," *Georgia Review* 17 (Winter 1963), 412–15; Wilma R. Ebbitt, "Richard Weaver, Teacher of Rhetoric," *ibid.,* 415–18. Eubanks called Weaver "one of the ablest cultural critics of our times."

2. Nisbet's comment was printed on the front cover of the paperback edition of *Ideas Have Consequences* published by the University of Chicago Press in 1984.

3. Henry Regnery, "Richard Weaver: A Southern Agrarian at the University of Chicago," *Modern Age* 32 (Spring 1988), 111–12.

4. Eugene Genovese, "Ideas Had Consequences," *New Republic* 214 (June 17, 1996), 36.

5. Joseph Scotchie, *Barbarians in the Saddle: An Intellectual Biography of Richard M. Weaver* (New Brunswick and London: Transaction, 1997), x.

6. *New York Times,* June 2, 1983, C13.

7. The three books published by Weaver in his lifetime were: *Ideas Have Consequences* (Chicago: University of Chicago Press, 1948), *The Ethics of Rhetoric* (Chicago: Henry Regnery, 1953), and *Composition: A Course in Writing and Rhetoric* (New York: Henry Holt, 1957). The four that appeared between 1964 and 1970 were: *Visions of Order: The Cultural Crisis of Our Time* (Baton Rouge: Louisiana State University Press, 1964), *Life Without Prejudice and Other Essays* (Chicago: Henry Regnery, 1965), *The Southern Tradition at Bay: A History of Postbellum Thought* (New Rochelle: Arlington House, 1968), and *Language Is Sermonic: Richard M. Weaver on the Nature of Rhetoric* (Baton Rouge: Louisiana State University Press, 1970).

8. George M. Curtis III and James J. Thompson, Jr., eds., *The Southern Essays of Richard M. Weaver* (Indianapolis: Liberty Press, 1987).

9. Richard M. Weaver, "Up from Liberalism" (1959), reprinted as a Heritage Foundation *President's Essay* (Washington, D.C., 1987), with a Foreword by Edwin J. Feulner, Jr.

10. Richard M. Weaver, *Visions of Order: The Cultural Crisis of our Time* (Bryn Mawr: Intercollegiate Studies Institute, 1995). Since the publication of this volume, its publisher has relocated to Wilmington, Delaware.

11. A recent bibliographic search yielded doctoral dissertations by Jing-Ling Jenny Lin (Ohio State University, 1991), Brenan R. Nierman (Georgetown

University, 1993) and Fred Douglas Young (Georgia State University, 1994), as well as master's theses by Phillip Roy Ballard (East Texas State University, 1987), Christopher Todd Carver (Texas Tech University, 1993), Robert J. Drumm (Texas Tech University, 1995), Edward C. Reilly (University of Maine, 1990), and Lisa Jane Tyree (University of Arkansas, 1989). The two biographies of Weaver that have been published so far are Fred Douglas Young, *Richard M. Weaver, 1910–1963: A Life of the Mind* (Columbia and London: University of Missouri Press, 1995), and Joseph Scotchie, *Barbarians in the Saddle* (already cited). A relevant monograph is Bernard K. Duffy and Martin J. Jacobi, *The Politics of Rhetoric: Richard M. Weaver and the Conservative Tradition* (Westport: Greenwood Press, 1993). An excellent anthology of appreciative essays is Joseph Scotchie, ed., *The Vision of Richard Weaver* (New Brunswick and London: Transaction, 1995). Two recent articles of note are George A. Panichas, "Irving Babbitt and Richard Weaver," *Modern Age* 38 (Summer 1996), 267–76, and R. V. Young, "Juliet and Shakespeare's Other Nominalists: Variations on a Theme by Richard Weaver," *Intercollegiate Review* 33 (Fall 1997), 18–29.

12. E. Victor Milione, "The Uniqueness of Richard M. Weaver," *Intercollegiate Review* 2 (September 1965), 67. See also Willmoore Kendall, "How to Read Richard Weaver: Philosopher of 'We the (Virtuous) People,' " *ibid.*, 77–86. According to Kendall, Weaver was "much eulogized but seldom if ever subjected to analysis and, what is more important, seldom if ever really listened to" (p. 79).

13. Russell Kirk, *The Sword of Imagination* (Grand Rapids: William B. Eerdmans, 1995), 173.

14. "In This Issue," *National Review* 14 (April 23, 1963), 303.

15. Eliseo Vivas, "Introduction" to *Visions of Order*, ix.

16. Clifford Amyx, "Weaver the Liberal: A Memoir," *Modern Age* 31 (Spring 1987), 106; Thomas Landess, "Is the Battle Over...Or Has It Just Begun?" *Southern Partisan* 3 (Spring 1983), 19; Eliseo Vivas, "The Mind of Richard Weaver," *Modern Age* 8 (Summer 1964), 307, 310; Edwin J. Feulner, Jr., "Foreword" to his 1987 *President's Essay* cited above, p. 1; Eugene Davidson, "Richard Malcolm Weaver—Conservative," *Modern Age* 7 (Summer 1963), 229.

17. Eugene Davidson and Henry Regnery both spoke of Weaver in these terms. Davidson, "Richard Malcolm Weaver—Conservative," 227; Regnery, "A Southern Agrarian," 112.

18. The friend was Bernard Iddings Bell. Kirk, *Sword of Imagination*, 174.

19. Ralph T. Eubanks, "Richard M. Weaver, Friend of Traditional Rhetoric: An Appreciation," in Weaver, *Language Is Sermonic*, 4; Donald Davidson, "The Vision of Richard Weaver: A Foreword," in Weaver, *Southern Tradition at Bay*, 15.

20. Eubanks, "Richard M. Weaver, Friend of Traditional Rhetoric," 4.

21. Eugene Davidson, "Richard Malcolm Weaver—Conservative," 229–30.

22. Richard M. Weaver, "Up from Liberalism," *Modern Age* 3 (Winter 1958–1959), 23.

23. Eugene Davidson remarked that "everything Weaver did evidenced his patient, stubborn battle on behalf of this core of values that he taught and by which he lived." Davidson, "Richard Malcolm Weaver—Conservative," 227.

24. Landess, "Is the Battle Over...?" 19.

25. Eugene Davidson, "Richard Malcolm Weaver—Conservative," 227; Henry Regnery, *Memoirs of a Dissident Publisher* (New York and London: Harcourt Brace Jovanovich, 1979), 191–92; Fred Douglas Young, *Richard M. Weaver,* 166; Ted J. Smith III (Weaver's biographer) to the author, June 21, 1998.

26. Richard H. King, "Anti-Modernists All!" *Mississippi Review* 44 (Spring 1991), 194.

27. Walter Sullivan, *In Praise of Blood Sports and Other Essays* (Baton Rouge and London: Louisiana State University Press, 1990), 28.

28. Regnery, "A Southern Agrarian," 111; Feulner, Foreword to his 1987 *President's Essay,* 4; R. V. Young, "Juliet and Shakespeare's Other Nominalists," 18.

29. Nisbet comment on the cover of the 1984 paperback edition of *Ideas Have Consequences.*

30. Richard M. Weaver to Cleanth Brooks, January 28, 1948, Cleanth Brooks Papers, Box 15, Beinecke Rare Book and Manuscript Library, Yale University.

31. Weaver, Foreword to paperback edition of *Ideas Have Consequences* (Chicago, 1959 and 1984), v; list of reviews of *Ideas Have Consequences* provided to the author by Professor Ted J. Smith III.

32. Weaver to Donald Davidson, February 28, 1948, Donald Davidson Papers, Special Collections, Heard Library, Vanderbilt University.

33. *Ibid.*

34. Eliseo Vivas, "Historian and Moralist," *Kenyon Review* 10 (Spring 1948), 346.

35. Willmoore Kendall in *Journal of Politics* 11 (February 1949), 261.

36. Kirk, *Sword of Imagination,* 172; Kirk, "Ten Exemplary Conservatives" (lecture at the Heritage Foundation, Washington, D.C., December 11, 1986: Heritage Lecture 83), 8.

37. Russell Kirk, *Beyond the Dreams of Avarice* (Chicago: Henry Regnery, 1956), 80.

38. *Ibid.,* 81.

39. Kirk, "Ten Exemplary Conservatives," 8.

40. Kendall in *Journal of Politics* 11 (February 1949), 260.

41. Frank S. Meyer, "Richard M. Weaver: An Appreciation," *Modern Age* 14 (Summer-Fall 1970), 243, 244.

42. Tillich's comment was printed on the jacket of the original hard cover edition of *Ideas Have Consequences* and on the back cover of subsequent paperback editions.

43. Weaver, *Ideas Have Consequences*, 1.

44. *Ibid.*

45. *Ibid.*, 2–3.

46. *Ibid.*, 94.

47. *Ibid.*, 98.

48. *Ibid.*, 85, 89, 91.

49. Whittaker Chambers's essay about Toynbee was the cover story of the March 17, 1947 issue of *Time*. Chambers's piece is reprinted in Terry Teachout, ed., *Ghosts on the Roof: Selected Journalism of Whittaker Chambers, 1931–1959* (Washington: Regnery Gateway, 1989), 141–49.

50. Arnold Toynbee, *Civilization on Trial* (New York: Oxford University Press, 1948).

51. Whittaker Chambers to William F. Buckley, Jr., August 5, 1954, printed in William F. Buckley, Jr., ed., *Odyssey of a Friend: Whittaker Chambers' Letters to William F. Buckley, Jr., 1954–1961* (New York: Putnam, 1969), 67–68.

52. George R. Geiger, "We Note...The Consequences of Some Ideas," *Antioch Review* 8 (Spring 1948), 251–54; Dixon Wecter, "Can Metaphysics Save the World?" *Saturday Review* 31 (April 10, 1948), 7–8, 30–32; Herbert J. Muller, "The Revival of the Absolute," *Antioch Review* 9 (March 1949), 99–110; S. I. Hayakawa, *Symbol, Status, and Personality* (New York: Harcourt, Brace & World, 1963), 154–70. The epithet "Divine Doctors of the Great Books Movement" was Hayakawa's.

53. Hayakawa, *Symbol, Status, and Personality*, 155, 158–60.

54. Weaver's master's thesis was entitled "The Revolt Against Humanism." He completed it at Vanderbilt University in 1934. See Fred Douglas Young, *Richard M. Weaver*, 56–58, for a discussion of the thesis.

55. Weaver, *Ideas Have Consequences*, 62, 130.

56. Willmoore Kendall, in his *Journal of Politics* review cited above, remarked that Weaver "on a number of counts...invites comparison" with Ortega y Gasset. One of Weaver's biographers has written that *Ideas Have Consequences* was "similar in both its theme and structure" to *The Revolt of the Masses*. Scotchie, *Barbarians in the Saddle*, 44. Weaver was undoubtedly familiar with Ortega's book. In Weaver's introduction (p. 33) to *The Southern Tradition at Bay*, which he wrote shortly before *Ideas Have Consequences*, he discussed Ortega's concept of the "spoiled child" psychology and specifically mentioned *The Revolt of the Masses*.

57. For Weaver's conversion to Southern Agrarianism and to what he called "the poetic and ethical vision of life," see his autobiographical essay "Up from Liberalism" (cited above) and the biographies by Scotchie and Young.

58. One historian of the South has written of Weaver: "What was he saying in *Ideas Have Consequences* that Ransom, Tate, and Davidson had not said in *God Without Thunder, I'll Take My Stand, Who Owns America?* and *The Attack on Leviathan?*" Fred Hobson, *Tell About the South* (Baton Rouge and London: Louisiana State University Press, 1983), 326.

59. John Crowe Ransom, for instance, directed Weaver's master's thesis.

60. Weaver, *Ideas Have Consequences*, 10.

61. Weaver to Donald Davidson, February 28, 1948.

62. The terms "cultural pessimism" and "declinist" come from Arthur Herman, *The Idea of Decline in Western History* (New York: Free Press, 1997). See especially pp. 7–9, for his distinction between them. Herman's treatment of post-1945 "cultural pessimism" focuses on its manifestation on the Left, where, he argues, the "antimodern chorus in America today" has its "leading voices" (p. 8). Herman does not mention Richard Weaver or (except in passing) other right-of-center declinists and cultural pessimists of the post-World War II period.

63. Weaver, *Ideas Have Consequences*, 1.

64. E. Victor Milione, "Ideas in Action: Forty Years of 'Educating for Liberty,'" *Intercollegiate Review* 29 (Fall 1993), 56.

65. Muller, "Revival of the Absolute," 106–7.

66. Weaver, *Ideas Have Consequences*, 162–63.

67. *Ibid.*, 4.

68. *Ibid.*, 52.

69. The text of Young Americans for Freedom's manifesto, known as the Sharon Statement, is printed in John A. Andrew III, *The Other Side of the Sixties* (New Brunswick and London: Rutgers University Press, 1997), 221–22.

70. Weaver, *Ideas Have Consequences*, 53, 21.

71. *Ibid.*, 36.

72. *Ibid.*, 131.

73. *Ibid.*, 2.

74. W. E. Garrison, "Unraveling Mr. Weaver," *Christian Century* 65 (May 5, 1948), 416.

75. W. A. Orton, review in *Commonweal* 48 (May 14, 1948), 126.

76. Wecter, "Can Metaphysics Save the World?" 31; John Lewis, "Ideas and Consequences," *Science and Society* 14 (Winter 1949–50), 68–76. Weaver himself asserted in *Ideas Have Consequences*: "The way was prepared for the criteria of

comfort and mediocrity when the Middle Ages abandoned the ethic of Plato for that of Aristotle.... In Thomism, based as it is on Aristotle, even the Catholic church turned away from the asceticism and the rigorous morality of the patristic fathers to accept a degree of pragmatic acquiescence in the world" (p. 119). It should be noted that comfort and pragmatism were not terms of approval in Weaver's vocabulary.

77. Ted J. Smith III to the author, June 21, 1998. In his eulogy of Weaver, Russell Kirk asserted that Weaver attended Episcopal church services in Chicago just once a year (Kirk, "Richard Weaver, RIP," 308). Without a doubt, Weaver's churchgoing in Chicago was infrequent. Although raised in the Methodist/Disciples of Christ tradition, Weaver did not belong to a church in his Chicago years. According to Professor Smith, Weaver once told a University of Chicago colleague that *if* he joined a church it would be the Episcopal church.

78. John P. East, *The American Conservative Movement: The Philosophical Founders* (Chicago and Washington, D.C.: Regnery Books, 1986), 46–52. Of original sin, for example, Weaver wrote that "there is no concept that I regard as expressing a deeper insight into the enigma that is man" ("Up from Liberalism," 29).

79. A number of commentators have noticed this. See, for example, East, *American Conservative Movement*, 46; Jeffrey B. Gayner, "The Critique of Modernity in the Work of Richard M. Weaver," *Intercollegiate Review* 14 (Spring 1979), 99; Fred Douglas Young, *Richard M. Weaver*, 102, 167.

80. Fred Douglas Young, *Richard M. Weaver*, 20, 34, 102. Weaver once wrote: "Literalism is the materialism of religion...." He claimed that his native region, the South, had "shunned" this materialism, "except in the crudest exhibitions of Fundamentalism." Weaver, *Southern Tradition at Bay*, 43.

81. Among the leading conservative intellectuals after World War II who converted to Roman Catholicism were Russell Kirk, Willmoore Kendall, and Frank S. Meyer, all of whom admired Weaver. I have found no evidence, however, that *Ideas Have Consequences* had any direct influence on their decisions to convert.

82. Weaver, *Ideas Have Consequences*, 3.

83. George H. Nash, *The Conservative Intellectual Movement in America Since 1945* (rev. ed. Wilmington: Intercollegiate Studies Institute, 1996), 42–49.

84. Weaver, *Ideas Have Consequences*, 129.

85. *Ibid.*, 1. Man is "free," said Weaver here, and "those consequences we are now expiating are the product not of biological or other necessity but of unintelligent choice."

86. Weaver, *Southern Tradition at Bay*, 394.

87. Weaver, *Ideas Have Consequences*, chapter 7. The quotations occur on pp. 165 and 166.

88. *Ibid.*, 69.

89. *Ibid.*, 53.

90. *Ibid.*, 62.

91. *Ibid.*, 37–38.

92. *Ibid.*, 107.

93. *Ibid.*, 74–75, 110.

94. *Ibid.*, 75.

95. *Ibid.*, 105.

96. *Ibid.*, 116, 105.

97. As an instructor at Texas A&M University in the late 1930s, Weaver (as he later put it) "encountered a rampant philistinism, abetted by technology, large-scale organization, and a complacent acceptance of success as the goal of life" ("Up from Liberalism," 24). It was, by all accounts, an unhappy time in his career, and it led directly to what he himself described as a conversion experience (*ibid.*). Already exposed to anti-corporate, anti-Republican, and Socialist thinking as a college student (he became a Socialist in the year he graduated), Weaver then discovered another strand of anti-modernism in the Southern Agrarians at Vanderbilt. In 1940 he left behind Texas A&M University—and all it stood for in his mind—and immersed himself in the literature of the postbellum South. This great turning in Weaver's life was, in the words of Donald Davidson, "the experience of a change of heart, of mind, of life" (Davidson, Foreword to *Southern Tradition at Bay*, 15). See also Fred Douglas Young, *Richard M. Weaver*, 61–67.

98. Weaver, *Ideas Have Consequences*, 132–33.

99. *Ibid.*, 134. One reason Weaver opposed "finance capitalism" was that its "aggregation of vast properties under anonymous ownership" was "a constant invitation to further state direction of our lives and fortunes" (p. 133).

100. *Ibid.*, 134, 135.

101. Weaver to Donald Davidson, February 28, 1948.

102. Richard M. Weaver, *The Ethics of Rhetoric* (Chicago: Henry Regnery, 1953).

103. Weaver was an enthusiastic supporter of *National Review*. Weaver to William F. Buckley, Jr., June 14, 1956, William F. Buckley, Jr., Papers, Box 4, Yale University Library.

104. Weaver to Cleanth Brooks, March 30, 1944, Brooks Papers, Box 15.

105. See Scotchie, *Barbarians in the Saddle*, 151–55, for a list of Weaver's contributions to *National Review* and most of his other published writings.

106. Weaver to Buckley, March 9, 1961, Buckley Papers, Box 17. See also Weaver to Buckley, September 14, 1962 and October 31, 1962, *ibid.*, Box 23.

107. For Weaver's contributions to *Modern Age*, see Scotchie's bibliography.

108. Weaver to Donald Davidson, September 7, 1960 and October 5, 1961,

Davidson Papers; Weaver to Robert Ritchie, March 30, 1963, Weaver Collection, Division 1, File 3; Regnery, "A Southern Agrarian," 112.

109. Weaver to Donald Davidson, September 7, 1960.

110. Information supplied by the Intercollegiate Studies Institute, March 10, 1998. Weaver remained on the board until his death.

111. The pamphlets were *Education and the Individual* (1959), *Relativism and the Crisis of Our Time* (1960), and *Academic Freedom: The Principle and the Problems* (1963). A fourth Weaver essay—originally a 1962 speech entitled "The Role of Education in Shaping Our Society"—was published by ISI several years after his death. For more on Weaver's work with ISI, see his correspondence with E. Victor Milione, Don Lipsett, and other ISI representatives, 1959–63, in the Weaver Collection, Division 1, File 3.

112. Weaver to Charles H. Hoeflich, April 19, 1961, Weaver Collection, Division 1, File 3. See also Weaver to Don Lipsett, January 23, 1962, in the same file.

113. Weaver to E. Victor Milione, March 14, 1963, Weaver Collection, Division 1, File 3.

114. Weaver to Robert Ritchie, March 30, 1963.

115. E. Victor Milione to Weaver, January 29, 1959, Weaver Collection, Division 1, File 3.

116. Information supplied by the Intercollegiate Studies Institute, March 10, 1998.

117. Weaver, Foreword to 1959 paperback edition of *Ideas Have Consequences*, vi. At about this time, Weaver had completed the first draft of another book of cultural criticism, the posthumously published *Visions of Order*. It had many similarities in perspective with *Ideas Have Consequences*, particularly in its view that the West had suffered an undeniable cultural decline in the past half century. Weaver, *Visions of Order*, 3–5.

118. Nash, *Conservative Intellectual Movement*, 383–84.

119. Weaver, *Ideas Have Consequences*, 181. Weaver wrote here: "Individualism, with its connotation of irresponsibility, is a direct invitation to selfishness, and all that this treatise has censured can be traced in some way to individualist mentality."

120. Weaver to Hoeflich, April 19, 1961.

121. Masthead of *New Individualist Review*, April 1961–Spring 1963. Weaver was much admired by the journal's young editors and contributors. See "In Memoriam: Richard M. Weaver," *New Individualist Review* 2 (Spring 1963), 2.

122. Richard M. Weaver, "How to Argue the Conservative Cause" (typescript of a speech before an ISI group in Chicago, September 22, 1962), copy in Weaver Collection, Division 3. This is an abridged and slightly variant version of a public lecture, "The Conservative Cause," which Weaver first presented at

the University of Wisconsin, under the auspices of the Wisconsin Conservative Club, on April 22, 1959. Audio recordings of the 1959 speech are in the Weaver Collection at Hillsdale College. Both versions (1959 and 1962) made the same points discussed in my text.

123. Richard M. Weaver, "The Southern Phoenix," *Georgia Review* 17 (Spring 1963), 6–17. In early 1963 Weaver was preparing to teach at Vanderbilt University in the academic year 1963–64 (and very possibly longer). Fred Douglas Young, *Richard M.Weaver,* 175–76; Scotchie, *Barbarians in the Saddle,* 15.

124. Kirk, "Richard Weaver, RIP," 308.

125. Scotchie's bibliography is the best introduction to this expanding literature.

126. Frank S. Meyer, ed., *What is Conservatism?* (New York: Holt, Rinehart and Winston, 1964), dedication page.

127. Kendall, "How to Read Richard Weaver," 77–86.

128. *Ibid.,* 80.

129. For Weaver's principal articles on Southern themes, see Curtis and Thompson, eds., *Southern Essays of Richard M. Weaver.* See also Weaver, "Integration is Communization," *National Review* 4 (July 13, 1957), 67–68, and Weaver, "The Regime of the South," *National Review* 6 (March 14, 1959), 587–89.

130. Lewis P. Simpson, "The Story of M. E. Bradford, " *Southern Literary Journal* 26 (Spring 1994), 103.

131. M. E. Bradford, *Remembering Who We Are: Observations of a Southern Conservative* (Athens: University of Georgia Press, 1985), 88. See also Bradford, "The Agrarianism of Richard Weaver: Beginnings and Completions," *Modern Age* 14 (Summer–Fall 1970), 249–56.

132. Landess, "Is the Battle Over...?" 17.

133. Documentation on this effort may be found in the Weaver Collection, Division 1, File 6.

134. Scotchie, *Barbarians in the Saddle,* 155; Landess, "Is the Battle Over...?"

135. For example: Hobson, *Tell About the South,* 323–35; George Core, "One View of the Castle: Richard Weaver and the Incarnate World of the South," *Spectrum* [School of Arts and Sciences, Georgia State University] 2 (June 1972), 1–9; William C. Havard, "Richard M. Weaver: The Rhetor as Philosopher," in Mark Royden Winchell, ed., *The Vanderbilt Tradition* (Baton Rouge and London: Louisiana State University Press, 1991), 163–74.

136. Chilton Williamson, Jr., "Richard Weaver: Stranger in Paradise," *National Review* 37 (December 31, 1985), 96, 98, 100.

137. For a brief summary of the controversy, see Nash, *Conservative Intellectual Movement,* 337–39.

138. See Scotchie, *Barbarians in the Saddle,* particularly chapters 3 and 8, for a

good expression of this point of view.

139. Eugene Genovese, *The Southern Tradition: The Achievement and Limitations of an American Conservatism* (Cambridge and London: Harvard University Press, 1994), 35.

140. Weaver, *Ethics of Rhetoric*, 212, 215.

141. Ben C. Toledano, "Up from Capitalism," *National Review* 48 (January 29, 1996), 64–65.

142. Richard M. Weaver, "The Meaning of Name and Place" (address at the Weaver family reunion, August 10, 1950), printed in a pamphlet entitled *Two Unpublished Essays by the Late Richard M. Weaver* (Glendale: Foundation for American Education, 1978). This essay was reprinted in the Spring/Summer 1981 issue of the *Southern Partisan*. In this address Weaver wrote: "I have been condemned for the past six years to earn my living in that most brutal of cities, a place where all the vices of urban and industrial society break forth in a kind of evil flower. I sometimes think of the University to which I am attached as a missionary outpost in darkest Chicago. There we labor as we can to convert the heathen, without much reward of success. But of course we learn many things about what is happening to this country."

143. In 1996 the neoconservative editor Richard John Neuhaus called Weaver "an intellectual saint in the conservative cult called Southern agrarianism." Neuhaus immediately added: "We have had our problems with some who claim to profess that creed, but in Weaver's thought it is undeniably attractive, often compellingly so." Neuhaus thereupon reprinted an excerpt from Weaver's essay "Up from Liberalism" and hoped that some of its readers would be inspired to read *Ideas Have Consequences*, "a closely reasoned and elegantly argued conservative classic." *First Things*, no. 60 (February 1996), 87–88.

144. During his career Weaver occasionally had been criticized by fellow conservatives on a few issues, notably his interpretation of Edmund Burke and Abraham Lincoln. But he had never been subjected to a frontal assault.

145. R. Emmett Tyrrell, Jr., *The Conservative Crack-Up* (New York: Simon & Schuster, 1992), 33.

146. Samuel Francis, *Beautiful Losers: Essays on the Failure of American Conservatism* (Columbia: University of Missouri Press, 1993), Introduction: "Ideas and No Consequences," especially 1–4.

147. Weaver, *Southern Tradition at Bay*, 391.

148. Jeffrey Hart, "Dream Weaver," *National Review* 48 (March 25, 1996), 60–61.

149. Weaver, *Ideas Have Consequences*, 187.

150. Kirk, *Beyond the Dreams of Avarice*, 81.

151. Robert Bork, *Slouching Towards Gomorrah: Modern Liberalism and American Decline* (New York: Regan Books, 1996). Note the subtitle.

152. Weaver, *Ideas Have Consequences*, 10.

Ideas Have Consequences
as a Masterwork of Rhetoric

Lawrence J. Prelli

This essay derives from my interest in the history of thought about rhetoric, which Weaver's University of Chicago officemate, P. Albert Duhamel, defined as the art of "effective expression."[1] Weaver's place in the history of rhetorical theory is assured, as evidenced by the extensive discussion of his work in the scholarly literature.[2] However, professional rhetoricians have paid much less attention to Weaver's efforts as a *practitioner* of the persuasive arts. And, to my knowledge, no one has examined in detail his early historical and theoretical writings for qualities that mark them as specifically *rhetorical* discourses.[3] That is what I propose to initiate with respect to *Ideas Have Consequences* (hereafter, *Consequences*).[4]

I contend that a major reason we still celebrate this book is that it is a masterwork of rhetoric. Behind Weaver's critique of modern culture is a positive, holistic vision that readers can strongly sense. That vision, together with the timelessness of the points Weaver frames for our consideration, accounts in large part for the book's endurance.

So, I want to emphasize the *rhetorical* rather than strictly philosophical, or historical, or political qualities of Weaver's book. The key that unlocks that rhetorical understanding is Weaver's first written and last published book, *The Southern Tradition at Bay* (hereafter, *Tradition*).[5]

I will explore three ideas which, I believe, advance this position. First, both *Tradition* and *Consequences* advance rhetorical objectives that address metaphysical conflicts deep at the core of modernist culture's moral and spiritual poverty. Second, both books advance the idea that rhetorical efforts to restore a culture conducive to a rich moral and spiritual life must engage and restructure people's most fundamental sentiments so that they adopt an attitude of piety toward the world and other persons. Finally, Weaver's *Consequences* implements a structure of argument that requires his readers to choose between qualities of thought and conduct inherent in a cultural vision founded on rightly disposed, or pious, sentiments—a vision Weaver identified with the Old South in *Tradition*—and opposed qualities that perpetuate and reenforce the impieties of the decadent modernist culture they see around them.

I will start with the first idea concerning the rhetorical objectives of Weaver's first two books.

Tradition is explicitly rhetorical in its aim. Weaver sought in that book to present an "articulate tradition," to let those who lived in the South of 1865–1910 express in their own voices "the mind of a religious agrarian order in struggle against the forces of modernism."[6] And Weaver thought that Southern voice spoke to contemporary readers in a way that challenged them at the very foundations of their world view. That challenge was no less than "to save the human spirit by re-creating a non-materialist society." "Only this," said Weaver, "can rescue us from a future of nihilism, urged on by the demoniacal force of technology and by our own moral defeatism."[7]

But there was an obstacle. The voice of the Southern tradition was conspicuously reticent about the underlying standards of its culture. The Old South lacked an elaborated theory of reality, or metaphysics, that articulated the most fundamental standards that constituted its view of the world. As Weaver put it, "The South possesses an inheritance which it has imperfectly understood and little used. It is in the curious position of having been right without realizing the grounds of its rightness."[8] That is no small obstacle, since Weaver thought the Southern tradition could make its most telling challenges to modernist forces unleashed by the North at the metaphysical level. The struggle against modernism, at its root, is a struggle over the most fundamental assumptions about the nature of reality. That struggle must engage people at the deepest sources of their world view. Only then will people see clearly the impoverished consequences of a culture rooted in materialism and start to feel intuitively the strength of a non-materialist alternative.

Without a positive metaphysics, the Southern voice lacked the rational grounds to mount a direct challenge to the poverty of modernism—to take the offensive against its adversary. This absence explains why the Southern voice, in Weaver's view, all too often had a gratingly romantic pitch at its highest volume; it was narrowly defensive, overly sentimental, hypersensitive, in response to challenges that modernist dogmas mounted against its traditions.[9] Weaver thought that the absence of an articulated, positive metaphysics explained why modernist forces had so effectively put the Southern tradition at bay.

So Weaver, the rhetorician, sought to articulate the fundamental rational standards of rightness implicit in the Southern tradition. With those standards, the Southern tradition could then speak for all that makes a civilized culture viable, and for all that revolutionary modernism subverts.[10] With those standards, the Old South could help mount a coherent accusation that behind the wealth and sophistication of modernist culture is a spiritual wasteland. With those standards, the Southern tradition could challenge the spiritually ailing and unimaginative modern world with an alternative vision that finds meaning in transcendental ideas that fire the imagination, instill right sentiments, and clarify the grounds of right reason and right conduct.[11]

And Weaver believed there was an audience that would be receptive to this challenge: "The common man is now ready to discard his bastard notions of science and materialism," to turn away from that which is "symbolic of spiritual decadence" and toward that kind of world view which, historically, "inspired our best art and held together our healthiest communities." The Old South defended that alternative, keeping it alive "behind the barricades of revealed Christianity, of humanism, of sentiment."[12] Here, Weaver wrote, is the Southern tradition's rhetorical allure in the modern world:

> There is something in its heritage, half lost, derided, betrayed by its own sons, which continues to fascinate the world. This is a momentous fact, for the

world is seeking as perhaps never before for the thing that will lift up our hearts and restore our faith in human communities.... Victims of the confusions and frustrations of our time turn with live interest to that fulfillment represented by the Old South. And it is this that they find: *the last non-materialist civilization in the Western World*. It is this refuge of sentiments and values, of spiritual congeniality, of belief in the word, of reverence for symbolism, whose existence haunts the nation. It is damned for its virtues and praised for its faults, and there are those who wish its annihilation. But most revealing of all is the fear that it gestates the revolutionary impulse of our future.[13]

Weaver's correspondence as he neared completion of his revision of *Tradition* reveals his exhilaration at the prospect of publishing his *opus* on the South.[14] It must have been quite a blow to him when the book was rejected for publication.[15] Weaver, the rhetorician, who had worked so hard to make the Southern tradition metaphysically articulate, was left without a means of reaching his audience.

Now we can see more clearly that *Consequences* is the rhetorical counterpart to Weaver's first written and last published book. Behind his criticism of modernism is the same positive, metaphysical vision we find articulated explicitly in *Tradition*. Of course, Weaver's vision in *Consequences*, as others have noted, is "divested of its strictly fortuitous regional overtones in idiom and preoccupation."[16] For instance, the ruggedly independent Vermont farmer replaces the backwoods Southern agrarian. Even his discussion of chivalry fails to evoke Old

Southern culture in most readers' minds.[17] Donald Davidson, however, identified the most important rhetorical shift in emphasis. He wrote that although South-North issues are absent in *Consequences*, the book "could well be entitled 'The Northern Tradition at Bay' or 'The Tradition of Western Civilization at Bay.'" Davidson continued: "To 'Northern' or 'American' society in general Weaver puts the same fundamental questions and applies the same searching tests that he had used for the defeated but not reconciled South of 1865 to 1910."[18]

Davidson is right, but we can put the shift in emphasis between the two books even more sharply: *Consequences* is the refutative counterpart of the constructive case made in *Tradition*; it is *Tradition*'s promised challenge to modernism redeemed. *Tradition* articulates a positive cultural vision rooted in nonmaterialist metaphysics; it is the constructive case needed to repel the onslaught of Northern modernism. *Consequences* takes the offensive; its refutative case traces modernism's spiritual and moral poverty to a flawed materialistic metaphysics. The vision of the Southern tradition is precisely what shapes and constrains Weaver's criticism of modernism in *Consequences*. It is, for Weaver, the concrete exemplar of "true" culture. *Consequences*, then, is traditional Southern agrarian culture, incognito, mounting a metaphysical "challenge to forces that threaten the foundations of civilization."[19]

Weaver himself thought that the appeal of *Consequences* with readers was rooted primarily in its rhetorical qualities. We see this in his "Foreword" to the second edition of the book. Weaver acknowledges there that the book had mixed responses as a philosophical work that looked to trace the first cause of modern disintegration. The metaphysical analysis was required, says Weaver, but the book's success he attributes more to the "rhetorical note" it struck with readers: *Consequences* expressed readers' intuitive feelings that something was deeply wrong in modernist culture. His remarks are worth recounting in full:

> I have come to feel increasingly...that it is not primarily a work of philosophy; it rather is an intuition of a situation. The intuition is of a world which has lost its center, which desires to believe again in value and obligation. But this world is not willing to realize how it has lost its belief or to face what it must accept in order to regain faith in an order of goods. The dilemma is very widely felt, and I imagine this accounts for the interest of the book to many persons who would not be at all happy with the political implications of some of the conclusions.[20]

Weaver views *Consequences*, retrospectively, as a fitting rhetorical response to a situated problem in modernist culture whose existence his readers could *feel* deeply, but not articulate. His critique articulates the metaphysical source of that problem and, thus, furnishes a *rational* account that resonates with readers' deepest sentiments and feelings.

A troubled world view is experienced most keenly at the level of intuition, in a deep feeling that something is not right with the world: things no longer "hang together," expectations go unfulfilled, promises seem always to be betrayed. Central to Weaver's critique is a vision of culture that attracts people whose deepest sentiments are unsettled and ill at ease with the modern

world. At that level, *Consequences* makes its strongest
rhetorical challenge to modernist culture. Which brings
us to the second idea.

Consequences works rhetorically on readers' most fundamental sentiments, those that constrain and shape their
world view. The core of Weaver's program for cultural
transformation and change, as expressed in both
Consequences and *Tradition,* is to engage readers at that
deep level.

A world view is founded on fundamental sentiments
associated with what Weaver calls a "metaphysical
dream." He defines a metaphysical dream as "an intuitive feeling about the immanent nature of reality."[21] This
intuitive feeling is the ultimate source of evaluation for
ideas, beliefs, and conduct.[22] As such, the sentiments
associated with a metaphysical dream, according to
Weaver, are *prerational.* Any sense of "logic depends upon
the dream, and not the dream upon it."[23] If our fundamental sentiments are not properly disposed or
arranged, then all else becomes misguided: "If the disposition is wrong, reason increases maleficence; if it is right,
reason orders and furthers the good."[24] As an ultimate
source of evaluation, then, a metaphysical dream is the
common bond of spiritual community without which
people cannot live harmoniously together for any
extended period of time.[25]

Weaver thought that cultures define themselves by
"crystallizing" around those fundamental sentiments. He
explained this well in *Tradition:*

> These are feelings which determine a common atti-
> tude toward large phases of experience.... They

originate in our world view, in our ultimate vision of what is proper for men as higher beings; and they are kept from being sentimental in fact by a metaphysic or a theology which assigns them a function understandable through imagination. The propriety of any given sentiment will rest on our profoundest view of life: our attitude toward the dead, toward traditional institutions, toward the symbols of community life—all come from a metaphysical dream of the world which we have created, or have been taught.[26]

If foundational sentiments are wrongly disposed, the culture that crystallizes around them will necessarily encourage a world view that is wrong and false. Conversely, if a culture coalesces around rightly disposed sentiments, it will encourage a world view that is right and true. For Weaver, the Old South was a model for *true* culture that coalesced around rightly ordered sentiments, a culture expressive of a nonmaterialistic world view. Modernist culture is not a valid culture; its pervasive materialism is a function of wrongly disposed sentiments. Lost is an imaginative, transcendent metaphysical dream founded on rightly disposed sentiments that imbue life with spiritual and moral meaning.

Recall Weaver's "intuition" of the modernist situation expressed in the "Foreword" to *Consequences*. He talks there about a loss of center accompanied with widespread nihilism. That "intuition" of the modern situation has resonance with *readers'* intuitions and feelings that something is deeply wrong—that there has been a loss of center. Weaver's critique points to the cultural consequences of sentiments wrongly ordered, and readers can sense that underlying that critique is an alternative, holistic vision founded on rightly disposed sentiments. He therefore created a dilemma for his readers: They can *feel* the poverty of modernist culture and *feel* the attraction of the alternative vision, but they cannot bring about change from one to the other without first redisposing their own most fundamental attitudes toward the world. The site of the struggle with modernism is within their own deepest sentiments.

How do you distinguish rightly ordered from wrongly disposed sentiments? This is where a concept pivotal to both *Tradition* and *Consequences* becomes salient: Properly disposed sentiments coalesce around the attitude of *piety*. Weaver explains the idea: "Piety is a discipline of the will through respect. It admits the right to exist of things larger than the ego, of things different from the ego."[27] Those things are in themselves "sources of right ordering,"[28] of value, that are beyond the power of our own egos to create, control, and contrive. The proper conduct of the pious, then, is to act with self-restraint and self-control before those things. We piously accept the existence of sources of right ordering beyond ourselves, sources of value apart from our own narrow needs and selfish desires. We should respect, if not revere, those things; hence, piety is associated closely with those who have "accepted a dispensation."[29]

There are three existing things that we should regard with a spirit of piety. Only then, Weaver tells us, can we "bring harmony back into the world where now everything seems to meet 'in mere oppugnancy.'"[30] The three are "nature, our neighbors—by which I mean all other people—and the past."[31]

We are pious toward nature—"the substance of the world"[32]—when we recognize our limitations before the mystery of a created order that commands respect. In *Tradition*, Weaver explains:

> Piety comes as a warning voice that we must think as mortals, that it is not for us either to know all or to control all. It is a recognition of our own limitations and a cheerful acceptance of the contingency of nature, which gives us the protective virtue of humility.[33]

Similarly, in *Consequences*, Weaver writes that we hold a pious attitude toward nature when we believe that "creation or nature is fundamentally good, that the ultimate reason for its laws is a mystery, and that acts of defiance ...are subversive of cosmos. Obviously a degree of humility is required to accept this view."[34]

In *Tradition*, Weaver distinguishes piety toward nature from "ethics," which he defines as "the restraining sentiment which we carry into the world of our fellow beings"; as piety respects nature's mystery, so ethics "respects the reality of personality."[35] The culture of the Old South, Weaver tells us, appreciated the distinctive qualities that marked individual personalities and, thus, especially nourished an attitude of respectful restraint toward them:

> Its love of heroes, its affection for eccentric leaders, its interest in personal anecdote, in the colorful and dramatic, discounted elsewhere as charming weaknesses, are signs that it reveres the spiritual part of man. It has instinctively disliked, though it has by now partially succumbed to, the dehumanizing

influence of governments and factories. Individualism and personality are making a stand—perhaps a
Custer's last stand—in the South.[36]

In *Consequences*, Weaver replaces the term "ethics" with
"piety" to designate the restraining sentiment toward others. We are pious when we "credit the reality of other
selves," acknowledge the "substance" of other beings, and
"accept their right to existence."[37] Indeed, piety requires us
to acknowledge that other persons have the "right to self
ordering,"[38] that each possesses a distinctive character, or
personality, which cannot be reduced to some normative
"mass" standard.[39] Weaver alludes to chivalry, without
Southern associations, to exemplify that "the very foundation of human community" is an imaginative seeing "into
other lives" with pious realization that they, however different, exist as part of "beneficent creation."[40]

We are pious toward the past when we accept its existence, "credit" it with "substance,"[41] and acknowledge
"that past events have not happened without law."[42]
Weaver develops this idea fully in *Consequences*:

> Imagination enables us to know that people of past
> generations lived and had their being amid circum-
> stances just as solid as those surrounding us. And
> piety accepts them, their words and deeds, as part
> of the total reality, not to be ignored in any sum-
> ming-up of experience. Are those who died heroes'
> and martyrs' deaths really dead? It is not an idle
> question. In a way, they live on as forces, helping to
> shape our dream of the world. The spirit of modern
> impiety would inter their memory with their bones
> and hope to create a new world out of good will
> and ignorance.[43]

The modernist is fundamentally impious. Impiety takes shape in the hubristic attitude that denies the right to exist of any substance capable of exerting restraint on the free reign of one's own ego. As Weaver says in *Consequences,* the modernist "denies substance because substance stands in the way."[44] Modernists cannot give due regard to nature, to other personalities, or to the past, since doing so would acknowledge sources of right ordering independent of their own egoistic demands for continual satisfaction of volatile desires and appetites. The hubris of modernists reveals itself in their incapacity to accept mysteries beyond their reach and in the absence of restraints on their conduct before an order of reality that they did not create, contrive, or control.[45] This is what pulls moderns away from the integrative center and conduces to the fragmentation of modern culture. Weaver says of the modern, "His picture of the world will be changed profoundly if he merely has to take cognizance of the fact that he is dependent on the universe, as it in turn seems dependent on something else."[46] The battle, for Weaver, must be waged at the fundamental level of sentiment that shapes and defines our world view.

The rhetorical task is to redispose people's most fundamental sentiments so that they accept a nonmaterialist world view. Only that change can restore the necessary restraints of piety. We see this in both books. Weaver makes his rhetorical agenda clear in *Tradition*:

> The first step will be to give the common man a world view completely different from that which he has constructed out of his random knowledge of science. Without this the various schemes of salvation are but palliatives. What man thinks about the

world when he is driven back to his deepest reflections and most secret promptings will finally determine all that he does.[47]

In *Consequences*, Weaver expresses the need for a metaphysical dualism that fixes the points for decision
between alternative world views:

> The first positive step must be a driving afresh of the
> wedge between the material and the transcendental.
> This is fundamental: without a dualism we should
> never find purchase for the pull upward, and all ide-
> alistic designs might as well be scuttled. I feel that
> this conclusion is the upshot of all that has here been
> rehearsed. That there is a world of ought, that the
> apparent does not exhaust the real—these are so
> essential to the very conception of improvement that
> it should be superfluous to mention them. The open-
> ing made by our wedge is simply a denial that what-
> ever is, is right, which takes the form of an insistence
> upon the rightness of right. Upon this rock of meta-
> physical right we shall build our house. That the
> thing is not true and the act is not just unless these
> conform to a conceptual ideal—if we can make this
> plain again, utilitarianism and pragmatism will have
> been defeated.... The prospect of living again in a
> world of metaphysical certitude—what relief will
> this not bring to those made seasick by the truth-
> denying doctrines of the relativists! To bring dualism
> back into the world and to rebuke the moral impo-
> tence fathered by empiricism is then the broad char-
> acter of our objective.[48]

Weaver contrasts the contesting world views starkly,
and confronts readers with the consequences of a culture

founded on impious sentiments. How his arguments work to frame the decision between the two alternative world views is central to understanding why *Consequences* is truly a remarkable work of rhetoric. This brings us to the third idea: *Consequences* structures its critique so that readers must choose between a pious or an impious world view. On the one side are qualities of modernist culture rooted in materialism, which lets loose the unbridled impieties of egotism. On the other are qualities of an alternative cultural vision founded on transcendental belief in the primacy of ideals, an alternative that refines sentiments and restores self control and self restraint, an alternative which, in a word, restores piety.

Structures or patterns of argument were called in classical rhetoric *topoi* or *loci*; they are "topics," "regions," or "places" where orators can find lines of argument.[49] I have examined how Weaver's arguments in *Consequences* are structured. One important structure I found there is what Aristotle, in his treatise on the art of rhetoric, identified as the *topos* or topic of *opposites*.[50] According to that *topos*, you can develop a constructive argument for a proposition by considering the opposite of the thing in question to discern whether the opposite thing possesses opposite qualities. If it does, you can establish the proposition. If not, you can develop refutative arguments. In *Consequences*, the "thing" in question is *modernism* and its qualities and the opposite of modernism is none other than the Southern tradition and *its* qualities, which shaped Weaver's vision of nonmaterialist culture. We find at least three applications of that topic that put qualities of modernism in polar opposition to qualities of

Weaver's Southern tradition: (1) modernist immediacy is opposed to transcendental distance, (2) technological fanaticism is opposed to the centrality of moral ends, and (3) the hysterical optimist is opposed to those who see the world with a tragic vision. I shall discuss these three arguments in turn.

To follow applications of the immediacy-transcendental distance opposition we must first inquire into the meaning of the terms. The quality of *transcendental distance* is a virtue of the nonmaterialist world view, and fosters an attitude of piety toward nature, other persons, and the past. This involves reflection on the *ideas* that reveal the true nature of intelligible things. Such reflection requires distance. Immersion in or preoccupation with the immediacy of how things appear to us through our senses deflects attention from internal reflection on abstract ideas that constitute the true meaning of intelligible things.[51] Distance, of course, does not mean unrestrained reflection that retreats completely from the world as experienced through our senses; rather, we reflect on the idea as embodied within and, thus, as constrained by that which we have experienced.[52] Put otherwise, we quest for the transcendental meaning immanent in our concrete experiences of the world.

Weaver does not emphasize the term "transcendental" in *Tradition* as he does in *Consequences*, but he depicts the Southern way of life as one that fostered belief in transcendental ideas. For example, he describes how respect for other personalities requires standards that at once acknowledge a common nature while also affording opportunity for gradation and distinction. Accordingly, the "restraining sentiment which we carry into the world of our fellow beings" should be bound with an ethical code of religious origin, says Weaver, "so that its power to impress derives from some myth or some noble parable."[53] The purpose of such a code, he continues, "is to lead everyone to a relatively selfless point of view, and to make him realize the plurality of personalities in the world."[54]

In *Consequences*, Weaver emphasizes a spiritual, transcendental reality inherent in personalities. He writes:

> Personality in its true definition is theomorphic... that little private area of selfhood in which the person is at once conscious of his relationship to the transcendental and the living community. He is a particular vessel, but he carries some part of the universal mind. Once again it happens that when we seek to define "the final worth of the individual," as a modern phrase has it, we find that we can reverence the spirit in man but not the spirit of man.... There is piety in the belief that personality, like the earth we tread on, is something given to us.[55]

In *Tradition*, Weaver contends that the paramount purpose of an ethical code rooted in religion is to "insist upon the rightness of right and keep in abeyance the crude standard of what will pay."[56] This invites judgment and discrimination among the plurality of personalities who gather in society. Weaver extols Southern culture as one that sought to "grade men by their moral and intellectual worth."[57] The symbolizations of Southern cultural codes and conventions constrained interactions among the multiplicity of personalities within the societal hierarchy and did so without reduction of all to some indistinguishable "mass."[58] Put otherwise, the transcendental value of those "delicate arabesques of convention" is rooted in their "non-utility," in their "remoteness from practical concerns, which keeps us from immersion in the material world."[59] In a word, the symbolizations of cultural convention infuse actions with significance within an imaginative world of *ideas*. Accordingly, here is how inhabitants of that imaginative cultural world viewed those from the North:

> Southerners who belonged to the tradition thought they saw in the levelling spirit of the North, in its criteria of utility, in its plebeian distrust of forms, in its spirit of irreverence...a kind of barbarian destructiveness, not willed perhaps, but certain in its effect.[60]

Opposed to transcendental distance is the modernist drive for immediacy, which values the proximate and ready-to-hand over distant, elusive, transcendental meaning. The drive for immediacy reveals an impious disposition toward nature, other persons, and the past. For instance, the modernist sees other personalities as indistinct at their core, and looks to see who people "really are" through stripping away all cultural veils and trappings that conceal their most private persons. The "honest" person is then one who reveals the most intimate and meanest details about himself and, thereby, shows equalitarian solidarity through low level sameness with all others. Once the quest for immediacy is unleashed on personalities and reduces them to a coarse or even animal core, the only standard of valuation—of distinction—that remains is a function of the materialist calculus of utility and commercial gain.

The opposition of the modernist quest for immediacy and the quest for transcendental ideas structures some of Weaver's most penetrating criticisms in *Consequences*. With this oppositional structure, Weaver distinguishes cultured persons who possess properly refined sentiments from modernist "barbarians" whose sentiments are disordered precisely because they lack the refinements of a true culture. Weaver uses the example of the frontiersman to display the vice of immediacy so typical of the modern. The frontiersman, Weaver tells us, is "impatient of symbolism, of indirect methods, and even of those inclosures of privacy which all civilized communities respect."[61] The frontiersman, in a word, is impatient of culture. He flees to the wilderness to get emancipated from the conventions and codes that restrain him. Weaver quotes de Tocqueville to describe the drive to reveal the stark material reality behind whatever the symbolism of culture conceals:

> As it is on their own testimony that they are accustomed to rely, they like to discern the object which engages their attention with extreme clearness; they therefore strip off as much as possible all that covers it, they rid themselves of whatever separates them from it, they remove whatever conceals it from sight, in order to view it more closely in the broad light of day. This disposition of mind soon leads them to condemn forms, which they regard as useless and inconvenient veils placed between them and the truth.[62]

In direct contrast, the cultured person wants transcendental meaning, the *idea*. The cultured person "avoids the relationship of immediacy; he wants the object somehow depicted and fictionalized...he wants not the thing but the *idea* of the thing."[63] In this regard, the veils and cloaks of culture are essential to the reality of the idea that attracts the cultured person. As Weaver puts it, "the reality which excites us is an idea, of which the indirection, the veiling, the withholding, is part. It is our various supposals about a matter which give it meaning, and not some intrinsic property which can be seized in the barehanded fashion of the barbarian."[64] Consequently, the cultured person becomes "embarrassed when this thing is taken out of its context of proper sentiments and presented bare."[65] That is "sacrilege," since "the forms and conventions" represent at one stroke the ordering "ladder of ascent" and the restraints needed to maintain pious regard for others.[66]

What are the consequences for moderns caught up in the quest for immediacy? Weaver tells his readers to look around. See how the modern acts impiously toward others. Obscenity—"that which should be enacted off-stage because it is unfit for public exhibition"[67]—is so abundant due to the pervasive influence of institutions of mass publicity that it becomes almost unrecognizable. Indeed, the modernist goes so far as to make a "virtue of desecration,"[68] and confuses obscene display with extension of freedom. Consider Weaver's vivid rendering of the modern social scene:

> Picture magazines and tabloid newspapers place before the millions scenes and facts which violate every definition of humanity. How common is it today to see upon the front page of some organ destined for a hundred thousand homes the agonized face of a child run over in the street, the dying

expression of a woman crushed by a subway train, tableaux of execution, scenes of intense private grief. These are obscenities. The rise of sensational journalism everywhere testifies to man's loss of points of reference, to his determination to enjoy the forbidden in the name of freedom. All reserve is being sacrificed to titillation. The extremes of passion and suffering are served up to enliven the breakfast table or to lighten the boredom of an evening at home. The area of privacy has been lost; there is no longer a standard by which to judge what belongs to the individual man. Behind the offence lies the repudiation of sentiment in favor of immediacy.[69]

Consider next the "technological fanaticism-centrality of moral ends" opposition. In *Tradition* Weaver uses this argument to frame a principal rationale for conducting that study. Southern culture, he says, is the last center of resistance against the "false messiah" of science and its concrete technological manifestations; it has avoided becoming completely "engrossed in means to the exclusion of ends."[70] This is so because its tradition incorporated moral ends as central to a civilized life. For instance, the sense of internal moral restraint that its people exhibit in their interactions with each other exemplifies precisely what the modern world so sorely lacks. Weaver describes this feature of civilized culture as follows:

We must see first of all that the kingdom of civilization is within. We must confess that the highest sources of value in life are the ethical and aesthetic conceptions with which our imagination invests the world. We must admit that man is to be judged by the quality of his actions rather than by the extent of his dominion. Civilization is a discipline, an achievement in self-culture and self-control, and the only civilizing agent is a spirit manifesting itself through reason, imagination, and religious inspiration, and giving a sort of mintage to acts which would otherwise be without meaning.[71]

Pious regard for others acknowledges them as moral agents and, thus, as subject ultimately to discrimination and judgment on moral grounds. Moral hierarchy, therefore, is compatible with qualities that distinguish personalities.[72] Moral distinction, however, is lost with standardization, with the "surrender to criteria of uniformity and objectivity."[73] That is the reason Weaver opposed ostensibly equalitarian arguments that look to judge people according to "ability." As Weaver puts it, the technological world of specialization immediately reduces that term's meaning to "some special skill, aptitude, or ingenuity at an isolated task."[74] The consequence? Personalities are gauged by the standard of efficiency, a standard more appropriate for machines than for civilized people. In contrast, Weaver tells us, "ability must take account of the whole man: his special competencies plus his personality and his moral disposition, even his history. It is well that people are not ranked for measurable efficiency as engines are for horsepower, but rather for the total idea we have of them."[75] Civilized people are complex, self-ordering, moral personalities; therein is the source of distinction.

We also see this argument pattern in *Consequences*. Opposed to the civilized person who keeps moral ends central to his life is the technological fanatic. Fanaticism is described "as redoubling one's effort after one's aim has been forgotten," which links with the "fallacy of technology" that concludes "because a thing can be done, it must be done."[76] "Means absorb completely," and people become so "blind to the very concept of ends" that all meaningful thought about ends is correlated with the availability of means.[77] What proceeds, then, is a fanatical interest in technology that Weaver characterizes as "psychopathic because it involves escape, substitution, and the undercurrent of anxiety which comes of knowing that the real issue has not been met."[78] The technological fanatic's personality is deeply disordered. "Sanity is a proportion with reference to purpose," Weaver says, so "there is no standard of sanity when the whole question of ends is omitted."[79]

When moral ends are no longer central to life, conduct toward nature and other people becomes irredeemably impious. The substance of nature, the very matrix of our existence, is reduced to mechanical principles of its operation. Lost is the mystery of nature as creation.[80] The technological fanatic also fails to acknowledge that personalities are self-ordering moral agents; rather, they become instruments of variable technical utility whose ultimate worth is measured against the standard of efficiency, usually with respect to advancing commercial demands and interests.

The final argument applies the "hysterical optimist-tragic vision" opposition. The two outlooks adopt mutually opposed assumptions about the human condition. The tragic vision sees infusing all human efforts to impose technological control and to advance grand projects for social change the enduring tragedy of the human condition. Fundamentally, nature and humanity are not malleable and, thus, cannot be altered and perfected to fulfill egoistic desires. Our projects for worldly success and happiness are often undone by events. Yet, those who have tragic vision still acknowledge the goodness of creation even when confronted with a world so obviously full of evil. To see the world with tragic vision tempers expectations without being blinded by cynicism and despair.

The view of the hysterical optimist is a variant of what we might generally call the Utopian vision.[81] The Utopian sees nature and humanity as malleable and, therefore, in principle, perfectible. The Utopian is impious, perhaps more so than any other modern, since he sees the order of nature, of other self-ordering beings, and of the past, as rearrangeable according to his own prescriptions, wants, and needs. The hysterical optimist is a variant of the Utopian and, when frustrated, becomes the focus of one of Weaver's most illuminating criticisms of modernism.

In *Tradition*, Weaver turns to the Old South's agrarian way of life as one that fostered habits of character and outlook that captured what I here call the "tragic vision." Weaver describes that vision as follows:

> The agrarian South, close to the soil and disciplined in expectation,...has suffered more afflictions than Job but has continued to call God and nature good. It accepts the unchangeable and hopes that it is providential. As a result, the backwoods Southern farmer does not feel as sorry for himself as the better healed, better padded, and more expensively tutored Northern city cousin. This acceptance of nature, with an awareness of the persistence of tragedy, is the first element of spirituality, and a first

lesson for the poor bewildered modern who, amid the wreckage of systems, confesses inability to understand the world.[82]

The tragic vision contrasts sharply with the disposition of frustrated Utopians who languish within the artificial environs of urbanized living. Urbanized moderns, Weaver tells us, have lost the sense of the difficulty of things, and act as spoiled children:

> Their institutionalized world is a product of toil and discipline: of this they are no longer aware. Like the children of rich parents, they have become pampered by the labor and self-denial of those who went before; they begin to think that luxuries, though unearned, are rightfully theirs. They fret when their wishes are not gratified; they turn to cursing and abusing; they look for scapegoats. If the world does not conform to our heart's desire, some *person* is guilty! So runs their tune.[83]

The urbanized modern, then, "is in a constant state of vexation over the unmalleability of the world."[84]

We find this argument structure applied in a major critique of modernist culture in *Consequences*. The tragic vision is opposed to the outlook of the hysterical optimist,[85] which I take to mean a type of Utopian who clings tenaciously against all evidence to the contrary that the world is getting better and better in linear fashion. This Utopian "has been given the notion that progress is automatic, and hence he is not prepared to understand impediments; and the right to pursue happiness has not unnaturally translated into a right to have happiness, like a right to a franchise.[86] But the truth of the tragic vision

periodically breaks through and when it does the hysterical optimist becomes frustrated, and acts as a spoiled child:

> But the mysteries are always intruding.... No less
> than his ancestors, he finds himself up against toil
> and trouble. Since this was not nominated in the
> bond, he suspects evildoers and takes the childish
> course of blaming individuals for things insepara-
> ble from the human condition. The truth is that he
> has never been brought to see what it is to be a
> man. That man is the product of discipline and of
> forging, that he really owes thanks for the pulling
> and the tugging that enable him to grow.... This cit-
> izen is now the child of indulgent parents who
> pamper his appetites and inflate his egotism until
> he is unfitted for struggle of any kind.[87]

This frustrated Utopian is incapable of the primal feeling of piety. Insulated within an urbanized environment,
he has forgotten "the overriding mystery of creation" and
"lost sight of the great system not subject to man's control."[88] His optimism is hysterical, denying all evidence
and experience that contradict claims to complete self sufficiency and total control. Weaver puts it this way:

> It is the city-dweller, solaced by man-made com-
> forts, who resents the very thought that there exist
> mighty forces beyond his understanding; it is he
> who wishes insulation and who berates and perse-
> cutes the philosophers, prophets and mystics, the
> wild men out of the desert, who keep before him
> the theme of human frailty.[89]

If only the modern could restore "the primal feeling of
relatedness" and acknowledge "the presence of some-

thing greater than self," Weaver comments, then even the denizens of cities might remain unspoiled.[90]

Hysterical optimists, then, confront the same difficulties as those moderns who quest for immediacy or become fanatically preoccupied with technology. All must redispose the deepest sentiments to redirect their world view. Moderns must acquire a primal level of feeling conducive to an attitude of piety to find meaning amidst the spiritual wreckage of modernist culture and to restore faith in a faithless world.

Weaver, the rhetorician, accomplished in *Consequences* what he sought to achieve in *Tradition* with an important shift in rhetorical emphasis. Both books articulate and give rational form to intuitively felt sentiments underlying world views. *Tradition* furnishes rational grounds for Southerners' intuitive feelings that their defense of a declining cultural tradition was right regardless of the fact that the cause was lost on the field of battle. *Consequences* evokes standards that make its readers' intuitive feelings that something is deeply wrong at the core of modernist culture articulate and rational. *Tradition* gives a model of culture founded on sentiments rightly disposed toward the nonmaterial and *Consequences* presents the opposite features of a culture founded on sentiments wrongly disposed toward the material. The positive standards extracted from the concrete historical exemplar of the Old South, then, are the mirror image of major negative features exposed in the critique of modernism, or the triumphant Northern tradition now writ large as modernism throughout American culture.

The Old South, I have said, appears incognito in

Consequences. The contrast of that book with *Tradition* displays Weaver's rhetorical virtuosity in selecting persuasive means suited for a broader, less sectarian readership. Rather than express the positive standards of an alternative cultural vision in terms of religious, agrarian Southern society, Weaver employs the philosophical nomenclature of metaphysics. He traces the fragmentation and nihilism of modern culture to the fourteenth century and William of Occam's denial of the reality of universals.[91] Throughout the work, we encounter philosophical language without detailed and systematic exposition of the sort one finds in academic essays dealing with metaphysical or theological questions. Readers sense resemblances with ideas extant in the history of philosophy—"That passage reminds me of Aquinas, this seems reminiscent of Plato"—but the relationships seldom are developed, let alone treated definitively, in Weaver's text. This might strike academic philosophers and theologians as weak scholarship,[92] but Weaver deploys those arguments primarily for reasons of rhetorical effectiveness. Appeals to "transcendentals," "universals," "truth," and so on, stand in for concrete historical depictions of the Southern tradition; both "philosophical" arguments and historically grounded examples are alternative *rhetorical* adaptations of Weaver's holistic vision of a culture founded on sentiments rightly disposed toward a nonmaterialist world view.

"Transcendental," "universal," and related philosophical terms still attract rhetorically. Modernism has yet to drain them completely of meaning. That language, it would seem, furnishes Weaver with a vocabulary that impresses readers with the strong sense that behind his critique of fragmented modernist culture is an alternative, integrated, holistic vision. Those philosophical terms evoke the guiding presence of a spiritually rich and morally centered idealism behind his critiques and, thus, make it possible for him to "articulate" readers' "intuitive feelings" about what is wrong with their culture and to furnish them with standards that make those critiques incisive and rational.

The *topos* examined in this essay relates impoverished qualities of modernist culture to opposite standards founded on dispositions conducive to an idealistic, non-material culture. Weaver's criticism induces readers to bring qualities of modern decadence into relationship with qualities inherent to his positive vision: modernist immediacy is contrasted with transcendental distance, technological fanaticism is opposed to the centrality of moral ends, and hysterical optimism conflicts with the tragic vision.

Notice how arguments structured with the "opposites" *topos* focus points for audience decision. Opposites admit no moderating middle ground; they explicitly exclude the middle, so there is no lurking about or hiding out there. One must choose. Weaver's arguments structure points for decision starkly, without prospect of compromise. One either is caught up in the quest for immediacy or reflective about transcendental meaning; one either is a technological fanatic or a moral agent who makes ends central; one either holds the view of an hysterical optimist or sees life with tragic vision.[93]

Recall the high stakes involved in this decision. The decision reveals readers' piety or impiety with respect to nature, to others, and to those who have passed from temporal existence. The choice is between a world view rooted in materialism and a world view inspired imaginatively and spiritually with ideals. The consequence is either to collaborate with modernist dogmas that culminate in fragmentation and nihilism, or to pursue Weaver's alternative, holistic idealism that returns them to a stabilizing center with its promise of spiritual and moral meaning. That is the dilemma Weaver leaves his readers after he has articulated and made rational the grounds for their felt uneasiness about the modern world surrounding them. Weaver, the rhetorician, raises the question whether they will confront the struggle within themselves to exercise self-control and self-restraint, to redirect and rightly dispose their own deepest sentiments, to choose a life of piety amidst the spiritual and moral wreckage of a decadent modern culture. And therein lies the rhetorical effectiveness and enduring appeal of *Ideas Have Consequences*.

ENDNOTES

1. P. Albert Duhamel, "The Function of Rhetoric as Effective Expression," *Journal of the History of Ideas*, 10 (1949), 344.

2. For examples, see Donald P. Cushman and Gerard A. Hauser, "Weaver's Rhetorical Theory: Axiology and the Adjustment of Belief, Invention, and Judgment," *Quarterly Journal of Speech*, 59 (1973), 319–329; Sonja K. Foss, Karen A. Foss, and Robert Trapp, *Contemporary Perspectives on Rhetoric* (Prospect Heights: Waveland Press, 1985); Richard L. Johannesen, Rennard Strickland, and Ralph T. Eubanks, "Richard Weaver on the Nature of Rhetoric: An Interpretation," in Richard L. Johannesen (ed.), *Contemporary Theories of Rhetoric: Selected Readings* (New York: Harper & Row, 1971), 180–195. For a recent book-length analysis, see Bernard K. Duffy and Martin Jacobi, *The Politics of Rhetoric* (Westport: Greenwood Press, 1993).

Weaver's theoretical writings about rhetoric are deep and extensive. For those unfamiliar with this work, three essays are good points of departure and are conveniently reprinted in Richard L. Johannesen, Rennard Strickland, and

Ralph T. Eubanks (eds.), *Language is Sermonic: Richard M. Weaver on the Nature of Rhetoric* (Baton Rouge: Louisiana State University Press, 1970). The essays are "The *Phaedrus* and the Nature of Rhetoric," 57–86; "The Cultural Role of Rhetoric," 161–184; and "Language is Sermonic," 201–225.

3. Commentators who knew Weaver acknowledge the heretofore unexplored rhetorical character of his early work, as well as his primary standing as a rhetor rather than a philosopher. See George Core and M. E. Bradford, "Preface" to Richard M. Weaver, *The Southern Tradition at Bay: A History of Postbellum Thought* (New Rochelle: Arlington House, 1968), 9–10; and Donald Davidson, "The Vision of Richard Weaver: A Foreword," in Weaver, *Tradition*, 14–15.

4. The edition used here is the 1984 reprint of Richard M. Weaver, *Ideas Have Consequences* (Chicago: University of Chicago Press, 1948).

5. Richard M. Weaver, *The Southern Tradition at Bay: A History of Postbellum Thought* (New Rochelle: Arlington House, 1968).

6. *Ibid.*, 44.

7. *Ibid.*, 391.

8. *Ibid.*, 388.

9. *Ibid.*, 389–390.

10. *Ibid.*, 388.

11. *Ibid.*, 391–394.

12. *Ibid.*, 392.

13. *Ibid.*, 390–391.

14. See in particular the letter from Richard M. Weaver to John Randolph, August 24, 1945.

15. See Donald Davidson, "Foreword," 16.

16. Core and Bradford, "Preface," 10.

17. Compare *Consequences*, 33 and 175, with *Tradition*, 35, 59–72.

18. Davidson, "Foreword," 16–17.

19. *Consequences*, "Foreword," vi.

20. *Ibid.*, v–vi.

21. *Consequences*, 18.

22. *Ibid.*

23. *Ibid.*, 21.

24. *Ibid.*, 19.

25. *Ibid.*, 18.

26. *Tradition*, 40.

27. *Consequences*, 172.

28. *Ibid.*, 171–172, 181–182.

29. *Ibid.*, 182.

30. *Ibid.*, 172.

31. *Ibid.*

32. *Ibid.*

33. *Tradition*, 32.

34. *Consequences*, 172.

35. *Tradition*, 34.

36. *Ibid.*, 35–36.

37. *Consequences*, 175–176.

38. *Ibid.*, 181–182.

39. *Ibid.*, 180–181.

40. *Ibid.*, 175.

41. *Ibid.*, 176.

42. *Ibid.*, 182.

43. *Ibid.*, 176–177. Weaver does not develop the concept of piety in relation to the past in *Tradition* as he does in *Consequences*, but he expresses there a view of history that illustrates the concept elaborated in the latter work quite well. Weaver claims in *Consequences* that "A *pietas* toward history acknowledges that past events have not happened without law" (p. 182). His *Tradition* is no less than an effort to go beyond "the waywardness of events" and show that "behind all there must be a conception which can show the facts in something more than their temporal accidence" (p. 388). Put otherwise, the aim is to extract a law-like conceptual pattern from the particularities of the Old South's struggles against the North that can furnish *moral* guidance in contemporary circumstances. Weaver put it this way (p. 388):

> In this research...I have attempted to find those things in the struggle of the South which speak for something more than a particular people in a special situation. The result, it may be allowed, is not pure history, but a picture of values and sentiments coping with the forces of a revolutionary age, and though failing, hardly expiring.

For Weaver, then, *Tradition* is an effort to look toward the past for a source of right ordering, of value; it exemplifies, rather than conceptualizes, pious regard toward the past.

44. *Consequences*, 183.

45. *Ibid.*, 183–184. Also see *Tradition*, 32–33.

46. *Consequences*, 184.

47. *Tradition*, 391.

48. *Consequences*, 130–131.

49. For an introduction to theory of rhetorical topics see Lawrence J. Prelli, *A Rhetoric of Science: Inventing Scientific Discourse* (Columbia: University of South Carolina Press, 1989), chapter 5.

50. Aristotle, *Rhetoric,* trans. W. Rhys Roberts (New York: Random House/Modern Library, 1954), 1397a5 (p. 142).

51. *Consequences,* 27.

52. *Ibid.,* 173–74, 174–75.

53. *Tradition,* 34.

54. *Ibid.*

55. *Consequences,* 181.

56. *Tradition,* 34–35.

57. *Ibid.,* 35.

58. *Ibid.,* 36–37.

59. *Ibid.,* 41.

60. *Ibid.*

61. *Consequences,* 24.

62. Quoted in *Consequences,* 24–25.

63. *Consequences,* 26.

64. *Ibid.,* 26–27.

65. *Ibid.,* 26.

66. *Ibid.*

67. *Ibid.,* 27–28.

68. *Ibid.,* 28.

69. *Ibid.,* 29.

70. *Tradition,* 30–31.

71. *Ibid.,* 32.

72. *Ibid.,* 34–35.

73. *Ibid.,* 37.

74. *Ibid.,* 39.

75. *Ibid.*

76. *Consequences,* 60.

77. *Ibid.*

78. *Ibid.*

79. *Ibid.*

80. *Ibid.,* 5.

81. Janice Hocker Rushing and Thomas S. Frentz mention the Utopian and tragic visions among the dialectically opposed values that they believe struc-

ture American society. Resemblance of my treatment with their mentioned dichotomy is merely fortuitous, since I extrapolate meanings of the competing visions from Weaver's writings. This in no way contradicts the observation that my discussion here is consistent with their more general model for rhetorical criticism of social values conflicts and resolutions. See their "The Rhetoric of 'Rocky': A Social Value Model of Criticism," *Western Journal of Speech Communication*, 42 (1978), 63–72.

82. *Tradition*, 34.

83. *Ibid.*, 33.

84. *Ibid.*

85. *Consequences*, 11.

86. *Ibid.*, 114.

87. *Ibid.*, 114–15.

88. *Ibid.*, 115.

89. *Ibid.*

90. *Ibid.*

91. *Consequences*, v, 1–17.

92. Eliseo Vivas makes a similar observation in his otherwise sympathetic review of *Visions of Order* in *Modern Age*, 8 (1964), 309.

93. Weaver later authored two essays that stressed the importance of denying the "excluded middle" as a viable political position. See "The Middle of the Road: Where it Leads," *Human Events* 13 (March 24, 1956). Reprinted as an American Conservative Union Special Report, January 1966, and in James C. Roberts (ed.), *The Best of Human Events* (Lafayette: Huntington House, 1995), 23–25; and "The Middle Way: A Political Meditation," *National Review* 3 (January 20, 1957), 63–64.

Consequences in the Provinces: Ideas Have Consequences *Fifty Years After*

MARION MONTGOMERY

The year Richard Weaver published his *Ideas Have Consequences*, 1948, I was discovering myself an ignorant, green, naive freshman, caught up in readjusting. I was lately home from three years of army service and confused in response to a new chain of authority within the academic world, not knowing whether to salute professors or not. Theirs was a strangely familiar hierarchy, with office removed by degree from the ground struggle with entrenched ignorance, the programming of the illiterate (in varying degree) from Freshmen to Doctoral Candidates. For such labor, official rank. There were teaching assistants, instructors, Assistant and Associate and Full Professors, and presently (under the pressures of supply and demand in the academy) Chaired Professorships. There were Heads and Division Directors and many Deans and Vice-Presidents, leading up and away even unto a President. In sorting that hierarchy in the next few years, I was to discover myself, with one war behind me, unknowingly enlisted in yet another, a war which now after fifty years reveals itself to have been largely a civil war abroad in the body politic, ideologically fought for that body by proxy as it were, within the academy.

Though unknowingly, I had enlisted in that civil war, a naive recruit. I was yet blessed in being green in my desire to know. Meanwhile, in that larger world enclosing the academy, this was proving a period of euphoria to the popular spirit, itself largely unaware of its vulnerability to contentious ideologies concerned for power in the civil arena. Indeed, most of us I suspect felt we were emerging triumphant from what had been billed to us as a holy war, and so invulnerable at that moment of history. There was prospect of goods and services, reward for pleasures foregone during the war years between 1941 and 1945. The economy was beginning to boom, so that righteousness of sacrifice by the body politic was to have worldly reward. An almost martial music of the doctrine of progress, long since infecting that popular spirit in a trickle down consequence from doctrinal philosophy since Occam (as Weaver might put it)—that music everywhere encouraged economic quick step, in anticipation of fulfilling our growing desires for a good life just at hand. It was indeed a booming time, and the generation spawned in that spirit, who are now approaching or already reaching retirement, we still call with increasing nostalgia the "Baby Boomers."

As for myself at that time, I was waking to ideas increasingly important to me, though I could not at first decide what academic "major" to elect, never having heard either of the rapidly classical version of liberal arts education (then being more rapidly abandoned under the pressures of and so justification by exploding enrollment). Nor of President Charles W. Eliot of Harvard, who had begun its destruction almost a century before by forcing elective, specialized programs. These programs had, by the 1940s, devolved into "professional" education as paramount to the good of society. And so, what indeed, was I to "major in"? I knew by then that the center would be for me in a concern for words. But journalist? Teacher? What? My "profession" I could not know. What I did know was that the bright and opening world, though taken by the popular spirit as otherwise, was a dangerous place to such a naive spirit as myself. I knew this more intuitively than rationally, which means that I knew myself in some degree as less than *innocent*, though that is a term convenient to conscience as a substitute for *ignorant*.

Two or three years earlier, I had stood in snow outside a barb-wire fence in Germany, talking to a young SS lieutenant wounded on the Russian front, now waiting a disposal of his case, he grateful to be a captive of the U.S. Army rather than of the Russian. I was his formal guard, a soldier policeman, on the periphery of a drama then about to unfold, now called the Nuremberg Trials. This lieutenant assured me in a formal English far superior to my own that very soon he and I would be standing shoulder to shoulder to oppose the Russians. At that time clouds were already gathering heavy in the East, where not long after they would erupt in another police action, the Korean War, a war now remembered vaguely by most of us. But now in the late 1940s, before that eruption, finding myself responsible for policing my ideas in words, as a freshman at the University of Georgia, I struggled with strange ideas caught in strange words, continuing to write poetry (as I supposed it). With delight I began to discover Greece and Rome and their men of letters, often with a confused fascination which I might later have described as a sense of *déjà vu*. I was discovering intuitively known but rationally undigested things. And making lasting friendships through that struggle of recovery, with young and old persons, themselves devoted to encounter with that strange legacy called tradition. At that time the student body itself seemed rather more old than young, given the influx of veterans. I remember one day in a poetry class a fellow student, older than I, bursting out, "Well, I never heard of *that* before, Professor." To which the reply, which is still one of our family mottos, we having now raised children and observed grandchildren rising: "Stick around, Mr. Geslin. There may be two or three other things you never heard of." The words bore a gentle irony, from a man who was first my teacher, then a colleague, but always a kindly and encouraging friend, youngest brother of Donald Davidson, whom at that time I'd never heard of. William Wallace Davidson, steady witness to us ignorant students of the enduring inheritance in our poetry. Out of that witness he published a single volume of quiet, self-deprecating poems aptly called *Stubborn Clay*.

And so, these were the confusing and also intoxicating circumstances to me at the time when Weaver himself had at last journeyed up from liberalism toward his traditionalism, a traditionalism which proves gathered of many parts, sorting his own intellectual inheritance in ways that were to prove most friendly to my ambiguous but growing intellectual concerns. Increasingly, half-knowingly, I sought to discover a comfortable community beyond all wars perhaps (such is the persistence of naiveté); a community in which mind might be encouraged and the gift of a word to that mind improved and refined toward some unity of consent. Just when I first encountered *Ideas Have Consequences* I cannot say. But I know it at once became important to me as it did to a gathering of like-minded souls whom I was coming to know soon after it was published. I am prompted to this reminiscence, indeed, by having just had returned to me, in fact coincident to my invitation to join in this gathering, a first edition copy of the book, from the second impression, from an old dear friend from those olden days and battles long ago.

He sent me also two letters that I had written him dated at about the time I was at last finishing my undergraduate degree. I'd written him, after he had moved to Alabama to work for a newspaper. I was becoming famous to local friends as an associate at our university press and as "Business Manager" of the *Georgia Review* founded by one of the Agrarians, John Donald Wade. My job there was more nearly that of Managing Editor, as I discovered in discovering the proper relation of words to reality. As for my office as "assistant director" of the university's press, that, too, was a misnomer, since I was expected to deal with routine business detail—brochures and a few advertisements. I discovered my limit when I attempted to persuade my director-boss that the press should begin a reprint series, rescuing vital books, my proposed first title Donald Davidson's *Attack on Leviathan*. Judging from their catalogues, most university presses now have such series, and even Weaver's works are included. But it is that returned copy of Weaver which I have reread, along with my letters, to recall how much affected I was by Weaver. I am embarrassed, I confess, by those letters of mine, I too confident then of already having recovered from the naive, green beginning of 1948.

Weaver proved for me an inviting beginning of a very fundamental recovery—or so I now trust to be true. Indeed, this old copy of his book now returned was one of ten I had ordered when the book was discarded by the University of Chicago Press, or in their term "remaindered," at fifty cents a copy. Five dollars was a considerable matter to me then (and still no mean matter), so that my venture speaks something of the book's importance to me. I wanted the copies to lend, this one of them now returned to me forty-five years late, but with no late overdue charge. What happened to the others, save for my own original personal copy, I don't know, but I trust they may still be doing their good work. My library was growing, mostly with those textbooks I was reluctant to "remainder" to the local bookstore, though they could be returned for a feeding pittance in a lean time. *Ideas Have Consequences* was different though, a book sought after to hold, something quite other than those hastily gathered textbooks after the chaos of registration for new courses. It marked a progress in my concern to build a library, which I began while in the Army by the purchase of my first hardback book, *Reptiles of the World*. The titles juxtaposed—or so I am pleased to suppose now on reflection—suggests my intuitive desire for a metaphysical understanding of creation, embracing creation from reptiles to ideas. I had not at that earlier time heard of

Aristotle or Plato, and certainly not of Thomas Aquinas. And so I valued and still highly value that little book of Weaver's which set me more deliberately on my way. It was for me then, as I can now see more clearly, an apt prelude to my own intellectual journey which has brought me to this place at this time and with these words.[1]

And so now I can appreciate it more fully as a necessary and helpful prelude to my continuing journey. Revisiting my letters to that dear friend, now dead, I discover that by 1950 I had lost confidence that the United Nations could resolve our problems with the U.S.S.R. and China, and that I was all for hitting both in 1950, with everything we had. In part, this was in anger over my youth still suspended, since I remarked the likelihood of finding myself again in the Army. I also discover from those letters that I was beginning to recognize another kindred soul witnessing in words, T. S. Eliot. I said in one of those old letters that a mutual friend on the journalism faculty, charged with screening submissions for the Peabody Awards, had come upon a great recording of Eliot's *Cocktail Party*. I invited my absent friend from his Alabama exile back to Athens to hear it with our small community. Worth mentioning, since what I discover now is an important relation between Eliot's sometimes agonized journey up from Modernism and Weaver's intellectual journey up from liberalism, about which more anon.

Richard Weaver, in the opening words of his introduction to *Ideas Have Consequences*, speaks of his little book as yet another "about the dissolution of the West," an addition to a "growing literature."[2] But that literature of which he speaks is relatively recent, given that in the first half of our century the preponderance of critiques and prophecies is heavily dominated by Hegelian-Marxist advances under the banner of progress, supported by the latest sciences oriented largely around an orthodox Darwinian theory of nature, but pursued rather ruthlessly through logical positivism as the currently respectable philosophy descended out of Occam's Nominalism. This was the age of the triumph of ideas, and that term *idea* was a rather popular element of titles before World War II, from J. B. Bury's *The Idea of Progress: An Inquiry into Its Growth and Origin* (1924), with its introduction by that old Modernist Hegelian historian Charles A. Beard, down to R. G. Collingwood's *The Idea of History,* published two years before Weaver's book. In a review almost contemporary to Weaver's book, Leo Strauss takes Collingwood severely to task. And we remember that Strauss happened to be at the University of Chicago at that time along with Weaver. Now Strauss is one of our age's two principal political Platonists—the other Eric Voegelin—and the Platonic dimension in the early Weaver is itself consequential.[3]

As for *idea* reduced to *ideology,* as in the Hegelian-Marxist devotions of the intelligentsia of that moment between two World Wars, the term *idea* will become less popular after Eliot and Weaver. There was that shocking attempt by T. S. Eliot, the recent recipient of a Nobel Prize in literature, who in 1939 gave us his *The Idea of a Christian Society* and followed it with his modestly titled *Notes Towards the Definition of Culture,* the latter in the year of Weaver's warnings to us that, since ideas have consequences, bad ideas have bad consequences. Out of Eliot's and Weaver's efforts, aided by others, we began a recovery of idea to the perspective of human intellectual limits, as Eliot had been arguing necessary since his other notorious "notes" against Modernist heresy, his 1933 Page-Barbour lectures published as *After Strange Gods: A Primer of Modern Heresy*. Just how destructive bad ideas could be had also just been engaged by C. S. Lewis, whose own abiding little book, *The Abolition of Man*, had appeared in 1947. There was a beginning, then, of the endless sorting of the concept of idea which we inherit as our own task, an obligation to our intellectual inheritances in a stewardship of intellect itself.

Weaver recognizes, in the midst of a general euphoria of the popular Western spirit as it sees itself emerging triumphant from World War II, darker clouds than that spirit could see, and deeper at last than even the spectacle of war itself. And he recognizes that there is a growing body of disaffected intellectuals, himself among them, apprehensive of a spiritual calamity already underway. One well names some of the work which takes up his and Eliot's and Lewis's alarms, appearing increasingly in critiques of a growing failure of Modernism and its doctrines of progress so heavily infecting both the social and the hard sciences, which were themselves increasingly allied with each other in a dream of reconstituting human nature itself according to a Modernist, gnostic want. Many of these works counter to Modernism have a delayed effect upon the heresy of progress so generally held by the Western intellectual community. Indeed, many of them only now begin to enjoy a recovery to a community concern for the intellectual failures evident at this lag-end of our century. There was Bertrand de

Jouvenel's *On Power: The Natural History of Its Growth* in 1945. And before it, in a forewarning, Denis de Rougemont's *Love in the Western World*, in English by 1940 but only discovered in America in the 1950s. There was Eric Voegelin's *The New Science of Politics* (1952) and his essays of the 1950s drawn together as *Science, Politics and Gnosticism* (1968). There was Leo Strauss's *Natural Right and History* (1953) and Russell Kirk's *The Conservative Mind: From Burke to Santayana* in that same year, 1953. There was, in short, a reawakening of intellect underway, these being but a few titles signifying that reawakening now so conspicuous to hindsight as we reflect on the 1940s and 1950s.

Though these attempts to recall intellect to known but forgotten things did not and do not agree with each other to such an extent as to have allowed the emergence of a common metaphysical position to intellectual awakening, they do agree in opposing the reductionist intent of those Modernist doctrines triumphantly devoted to intellect as autonomous. For Modernism constitutes a new religion. In the next decade, of course, the gathering clouds collided as anticipated by Weaver. They erupted into political and social storms in the 1960s, in which decade is born that now famous resistance to some of Modernism called Neoconservatism, in which were gathered liberal converts to an umbrella alliance of "'conservative" causes. Thus their survival out of a dying intellectual liberalism, only to find themselves uneasy in their alliance with the older, so-called Paleoconservatives. Neoconservatism, we observe, is a movement now falling apart at the close of our century, its epitaph having been written by Norman Podhoretz in a recent issue of

Commentary.[4] There are interesting footnotes to these contentions among allies against Modernism. Indeed, among those Neoconservatives there are now discovered what is being characterized as a Theoconservative movement such as Father Richard John Neuhaus speaks for in his *First Things*. What seems evident in these late eruptions of alliance is a return to those earlier beginnings in the 1940s, beginnings to be rediscovered in Bertrand de Jouvenel and C. S. Lewis and T. S. Eliot and, of course, in Richard Weaver, for all of whom Christian orthodoxy was important. It is a return to the necessity of a recovery, not only of what Leo Strauss calls "the natural horizon of human thought," as he opposes a reductionist historicism in Collingwood, but a recovered orientation, beyond that immanent horizon of history in an affirmation of the transcendent, despite a reluctance of consent to that recovery of the transcendent by such anti-Modernists as Leo Strauss.[5]

What these diverse "conservative" prophets share, then, is not a common vision but a common opposition to the dominant spirit of our age. From a diverse, and sometimes *ad hoc*, resistance to Modernism, these uneasy alliances developed. As for that increasingly dominant spirit of our age, at first passively subscribed to by the popular spirit and then actively sustained, Allen Tate addressed it in 1945 at the close of World War II, in an essay called "The New Provincialism." A few words from his argument well characterize the bankruptcy of the dominant intellectual community at the end of that war. It was a failing enterprise discovered as in collapse by Richard Weaver, though not without some agony to his own liberal inclination, forcing his move "Up from

Liberalism," as he names it in one of his essays. For he, too, held humanitarian sentiments, only gradually discovering how easily perverted they might be by Modernist ideology in its pursuits of power.

Tate's essay appears in the *Virginia Quarterly*, about a decade after Eliot had given at that University his little "Primer of Modern Heresy," his *After Strange Gods*. Tate no doubt remembers even as he writes his old friend Eliot's defense of Christian society, concurring with it. "When the regional man, in his ignorance...extends his immediate necessities into the world, and assumes that the present moment is unique, he becomes the provincial man." That is the theme central to the consequences of such an idea as progress decreed unfettered by transcendent obligation, against which Weaver will presently take a stand. In a distinction central to these "conservative" prophets rising against Modernist doctrines, Tate adds: "Regionalism without civilization—which means, with us, regionalism without the classical Christian culture—becomes provincialism; and world regionalism becomes world provincialism. For provincialism is that state of mind in which regional men lose their origins in the past and its continuity into the present, and begin every day as if there had been no yesterday."[6]

Thus we discover a "difference between two worlds: the provincial world of the present, which sees in material welfare and legal justice the whole solution to the human problem; and the classical-Christian world, based upon the regional consciousness, which held that honor, truth, imagination, human dignity, and limited acquisitiveness, could alone justify a social order however rich and efficient it may be; and could do much to redeem an order dilapidated and corrupt, like the South today, if a few people passionately hold those beliefs."[7] Tate's little essay is a primer as it were of distinctions which Weaver embraced in escaping the socialism which had for a moment engulfed him at the University of Kentucky, before he moved West to Texas to teach and then back to Louisiana State University as student to Tate's friends there, among them Cleanth Brooks and Robert Penn Warren. We need reminding as well that Voegelin was also there at L.S.U., from 1942 until 1958.

What a way we have come since the two Wars' ends. From Ideas as saving ideologies, to an alarm over the provincialism inherent in ideology, to an end of an era in the 1990s reflected in this decade's titles. There is recently Francis Fukuyama's *The End of History and the Last Man* (1992). There is David Lindley's *The End of Physics: The Myth of Unified Theory* (1993) relevant to some of Weaver's concerns with empirical science, as is Steven Weinberg's *Dreams of a Final Theory: The Scientist's Search for the Ultimate Laws of Nature* (1992). Most recently, there is that controversial symposium edited by Richard John Neuhaus, *The End of Democracy? The Judicial Usurpation of Politics* (1997). The sense of an ending seems more and more pervasive of the intellectual community as it reels before the intellectual egalitarianism now destroying the academy under the battle flags of the "Politically Correct," with "Multiculturalism" a theme pleasing to the sentimentality required as dogma of the moment.

And all this, or so I contend, is our exasperated circumstance because of our inattention to the necessity of a metaphysical understanding of the givenness of creation, including the limited givenness of man himself. That is an implied necessity underlying almost every point of our conflict with those enemies of the transcendent whom Weaver would oppose. But lacking metaphysical vision, our resistance reduced to contending with the dominant physical vision—the materialistic vision of existence which Weaver opposes—we yet lack an intellectual consistency in support of our resistance. We lack a common, positive authority beyond the immanent, bubble world of self-sufficient consciousness. That is, lacking an understanding beyond the spectacle of this present moment and place as provincially defined by a still-dominant Modernism, our actions of resistance, however heroic, too often prove only *ad hoc.* That means that we contend on the grounds chosen by the radical antagonists of being itself, whereby (the transcendent denied) attention must be focused upon the immanent, upon a closed world. The prophets among our opposition are often fascinating and seductive in championing this closed world we know. We need only name a few of the famous: Darwin, Freud, Jung, Marx, Bergson, Sartre. A selective naming, the point of which is that these seem to speak more hopefully to the disoriented popular spirit than we in Weaver's tradition have done, seducing spirit to an acceptance of the immanent as the ultimate. The public spirit is affected by the trickle-down effect of their ideas, making generally acceptable an illusion to replace the true nature of our human existence as created intellectual soul incarnate, our existence as *person.*

Meanwhile, it appears more and more evident to some of us that ours is a civilization riddled in its structures and institutions by intellectual termites acting collectively, their hidden presence most evident in the public arena again and again, where there is a popular support of untenable ideas constituting and defining a new common principle necessary to accumulate power. They possess residual sentiments of an older vision through such terms as *academy* or *government* or *science* or *society* or *democracy.* Collectively anarchic, however, their object is an object of intended destruction of the old vision of *being* itself, as Voegelin warns us.[8] Thus the program of what I call a new evangelical religion, Modernism, requires intellectual provincialism as dogmatic faith, a principle to be subscribed to increasingly under penalty of law. As a secular fundamentalist religion, its guiding principle is that each intellect is autonomous and therefore sovereign, an independent nation unto itself, out of which faith devolves a destructive pragmatism whose end is the satisfaction of appetitive desire—whether the appetite for abstract power or for material indulgence. The sacrificial victim to this end, the victim of this termite destruction: *whatever is.* But the anarchic necessity to this sovereign intellect is that the object to be overwhelmed is *whatever is not its own autonomous consciousness.* Thus creation becomes the unexamined provender to the appetitive sovereignty of the alienated person. In a summary term from an old tradition that object under destruction (or in a Modernist term of camouflage *deconstruction*) is the *body of creation,* which body includes nature and nations, things and persons.

And so it is to this concern for our metaphysical weakness as traditionalists that I now turn, taking Richard Weaver's "Introduction" to his little book as apt point of departure. It is apt, in that Weaver there recognizes evidences of the imminent collapse of Western civilization, speaking passionately on that evidence. What would he say now, given his anticipatory pathological analysis of our pending collapse, which prophecy he made in the 1940s? Or, again figuratively, were he to see the current landslides of a civilization he sought to buttress against the prevailing winds of the Modernist *El Niño,* what hope would be left him?

I trust he would not be dismayed beyond continuing the task we now inherit from him. For, as T. S. Eliot reminded us, lest we escape responsibility through dismay, there is no such thing in this world as a lost cause, because in this world there is no such thing as an eternally won cause. What is required of us is that, in such pauses in our labors as this one here on a quiet, friendly campus as we gather to pay Weaver tribute, we look to our equipment, knowing, with Eliot, that at each venture we are always at a new beginning, requiring of us as he urged a "raid on the inarticulate" in the knowledge that we do so—such is our limited effect in this world—while yet burdened with "shabby equipment always deteriorating" as we use it. Given also that our equipment—our words—is complicated in us by "the general mess of imprecision of feeling" as we attempt to command "[u]ndisciplined squads of emotion." These are words from Eliot's *East Coker* (1940), where he reminds us as well that there is "only the fight to recover what has been lost/ And found and lost again and again," though now seemingly "under conditions/ That seem unpropitious." There is for us, he cautions, "only the trying" for the "rest is not our business."[9] That is, it is not our business, insofar as we believe in the overarching and permeating grace we associate with the transcendent God.

And so to that equipment necessary against those opposing weapons of false ideas established by Modernism—ideas themselves *partially* dependent upon truth, but transformed by ideological partiality into absolute ideology. Gerhart Niemeyer, one of Weaver's successors in these continuing raids on the ultimately inarticulable Absolute Truth, defines ideology for us in his essay "The Terrible Century." He says:

> Ideology is the name for that kind of disorder which consists in substituting for philosophical questions about what is given a set of assertions about what is not given. What is not given includes the historical future, particularly when one "inquires" about it in order to control the "destiny of mankind." What is given but not accessible to the type of knowing suitable for *things* in this world is the divine reality, above and beyond that of the cosmos and of human history. When speculation of the mind begins to criticize being as such, when it aims not at understanding the "constitution of being" but at its control by the human will, the result is not philosophy but ideology.[10]

Now one of those desirable ideas easily made to seem false by the ideologist, we must be careful of, lest we make of it but a counter ideology. I do not mean here that portmanteau term hiding so many burglary tools used against being, *liberalism,* or its counter term with similar characteristics, *conservatism.* Instead, my concern here is with an even more popular term, flourished as either a pejorative whip or raised as if itself a sign of the cross against barbarian invasions. The term: *tradition.* Certainly it seems a term suited to describe those soldiers in

Weaver's camp intent on raids upon the inarticulate with weapons forged largely from tradition. But the difficulty is that these good soldiers do not always recognize it is possibly a self-wounding sword if not carefully repaired for each encounter. It is in *traditionalism*, as Eliot suggests in his *After Strange Gods*, that one makes a beginning at a viable recovery of community, a recovery of the *person* threatened with becoming one of Tate's provincials instead of a regional person. Here is the ground in which must be recovered what I myself hold necessary to the viability of traditional man—that *person* seeing before and after but also seeing within and above. That Eliot recognizes this necessity of both horizontal and vertical vision needs only our revisiting his *After Strange Gods*, lectures never again republished after 1934 but carrying important argument to our recovery of the term *tradition*.[11] It is in a recovery of this term—or so I contend—that we make a beginning toward an eventual recovery of a metaphysical vision necessary to an order of community as a body of persons, members one of another.

Now Eliot begins those lectures warning us against the pursuit of strange gods by addressing the Agrarians, some of them (particularly Allen Tate) already known to him as friends. Hence, it is suitable then to recall here that Weaver is decidedly of that Agrarian company though biding in Chicago in the 1940s, being only recently there from his studies at Louisiana State University—the fruit of which retreat as student into the academy was to be his posthumous *The Southern Tradition at Bay: A History of Postbellum Thought* (1968). But Eliot was speaking soon after the publication of *I'll Take My Stand* (1930), and he has as his initial concern a fear that these (somewhat) younger poets, those

Fugitives turned Agrarian turned polemicists, might not be sufficiently oriented, under the pressure of their concerns, to the necessity that *tradition* be recovered through *orthodoxy.* The relation of those two concepts is Eliot's central theme.[12] Tradition, he says, is "a way of feeling and acting which characterises a group throughout generations." It is "of the blood," being often "unconscious," so that consequently it "has not the means to criticize itself." It is a matter of "good habits," but it may easily become victim to the latest tradition—even to Modernism and a pursuit of strange gods. For certainly Modernism has at our century's close become the dominant tradition to our popular spirit, though it is a tradition largely ignorant of its descent to us at least since Occam, as Weaver would say. Thus a necessity of orthodoxy, "which calls for the exercise of all our conscious intelligence." Through orthodoxy, let us say, our concern must become paramount that tradition orient itself to the *truth of things* beyond mere tradition taken as the current residue in intellect, carried in the blood of "feeling" but unpurified by thought. For "good habits" are good insofar as they are oriented by the ultimate truth of things, which for Eliot, as it would be presently for Weaver, requires a vision of the immanent in relation to the transcendent.[13]

It is through orthodoxy, then, that community in the world maintains "a consensus between the living and the dead," and so stands witness to whatever truth may be thus rescued, an inheritance we are to bequeath to those not yet born.[14] That is why I have come to value Thomas Aquinas's reminder: "The purpose of the study of philosophy is not to learn what others have thought, but to learn how the truth of things stands."[15] In the light of this guiding truth, we may more effectively lament a recent academic tradition, increasingly dominant after the end of World War II. It is known in that infamous phrase, "publish or perish." In the interest of the mechanical efficiency of academic programs, statistics as abstract facts may be used to persuade legislators and hard-pressed academic administrators in their resolving financial and promotional problems with faculty. Thus the validity of academic study was gradually subverted, especially when turned over to growing departments of "public relations" specialists within the academy. The reaction to this perversion, which had proved so successful in maintaining an illusion of academic order, has ended in the overthrowing of that doctrine. But it has not thereby purified the academy, since the triumphant reaction was not validly grounded in intellectual integrity as the governing principle to the academy, a devotion to the recovery of the truth of things. Hence we have, as now dominant in the academy, those new and suspect doctrines, proscribed to intellect within the academy and defined by the "politically correct" agenda, made generally popular through a sentimentality ravenous for what is now celebrated as "multiculturalism." Thus an intellectual anarchy has triumphed, whereby the subjective desire of the disoriented, individual intellect is self-authorized to define its acceptable object as whatever proves most convenient to its own isolated, sovereign desire. What "I" desire justifies my intellectual action, and that action in turn defines what is true.

Such is the pit which intellect has dug for itself by the end of our century in following the Nominalistic philosophy, an end anticipated by Weaver. For when "Logic became grammaticized" at the time of Occam, he said, the dislocation occurs whereby definition determines truth itself.[16] Definition follows upon the sufficiency of political power in the moment, since signs no longer attach to realities but ultimately only to intentional desire. Thus the "letter" of the law, independent of reality itself, requires our general consent to actions destructive of the truth of things. Intellectual integrity is the sacrifice now made to political expediency in pursuit of desired power disguised by signs, though those signs may residually carry a lingering tradition older than the moment's expediency. For there is, after all, a reality called "the common good," however much reduced as shibboleth that phrase has become. Predictably a destruction of community has spectacularly occurred in our century, always under the banner of the "common good." And most spectacularly, of course, we have seen it in lessons not yet sufficiently learned, the general slaughter of millions of persons under Stalin's and Hitler's definitions of the common good. But now most subtly and, ultimately I fear, with a more fundamental destructiveness to community, it bides in a general justification of the common good as *individual, sovereign desire,* whose most destructive shibboleth has been the term *democracy* in one of history's ironies planted in the popular mind in the 18th century.

And so the necessity of recovering that principle to intellectual integrity, thus to recover as well a viable intellectual community. That principle does not have, as if its final end to our intellectual journeying, simply the knowing of "what men have said," though that is a mediate responsibility to intellect. Rather, what is required is a devotion to the truth of things as the measure of the validity of those things we say. And if in this cause I appeal most often to Thomas Aquinas, I quickly add that, alas, I suspect that sometimes Thomas himself is used in what Eric Voegelin might call a gnostic way, as if Thomas's words were in themselves divinely absolute. That is a mode in deference to him which would surely sadden Thomas. Such a use by eager Thomists can but give Thomas and his own devotion to the rescue of the truth of things a bad name, especially in some careless intellectual quarters, one of which quarters may prove, indeed, in Weaver's own early arguments. It is the danger Plato has also suffered almost from the beginning, as St. Augustine cautions us in his *City of God*.[17] For there developed out of Plato a diverse spectrum of Platonisms, perhaps most recently familiar to us academics in that English school associated with the name of Bishop Berkeley, for whom (in another of the ironies of history) we have named a California city now made famous since the 1960s for anti-intellectual riots. The Platonic "shadow" world was seen by the good Bishop to be a nonexistent order, declared by much rhetorical unfolding as consequent to a subjective idealism which was more immediately out of Descartes than out of Plato. (We academics may also remember Samuel Johnson's "I refute Berkeley thus," thereupon kicking a large stone.)

If there are many Platonisms, then, there are also many Thomisms. And that returns us to our present concern, namely that we must take care that there not be too many *Ideas Have Consequences*, through devoted imitations of Weaver, as opposed to a devoted concern to honor his attempt to recover the truth of things by an attention of intellect to the truth of things. Therefore my epigram is apt to our concern: ours must be a concern for the truth of things, to which I add a gloss by that most careful Thomist, Etienne Gilson, from his essay "The Realist Beginner's Handbook": "It is not in St. Thomas or Aristotle [or, we add, in Plato] but in things, that the true realist sees everything he sees. So he will not hesitate to make use of these masters, whom he regards solely as guides towards reality itself." For it is "much better to deck oneself out in truths which others have handed down, as the realist, when necessary, is willing to do, rather than like the idealist, refuse to do so and go naked."[18] Such then, the intellectual prudence necessary to the rescue of such a term as *tradition*.

We are born traditionalists, like it or not. Or, in Tate's terms adapted to our point, we are born original and regional, though we may make ourselves provincials in false pursuits of self-declared originality. To resist that deconstruction of our natural gifts as created intellectual soul incarnate, we must first of all accept responsibility for those gifts. The traditionalist, this is to say, has as his abiding responsibility the winnowing of his historical and natural inheritance in a continuing rescue of those permanent things of which Eliot spoke. In that devotion, through a piety recognizing the givenness of his particular existence, he will not so easily become an intellectual victim to Modernism; he will not become provincial. He will become neither obsessed by nostalgia toward his historical and social inheritance nor become victim to utopian dreams through his presumptions of an autonomous power of intellect to be exercised nominalistically on the mere authority of his own will, whereby he mistakes himself as the agent of grace to his own unqualified desires. Incidentally, I cannot here refrain from observing yet another of history's ironies. The Southern Agrarians were characterized by the liberal and radical left establishment of the 1930s as exhibiting a romantic nostalgia, wishing to turn back the clock. In the 1990s, the remnants of that old liberal establishment so antipathetic to them increasingly are devoted to a nostalgia for the 1930s, a judgment easily supported by reference to memoirs published in the past decade.[19]

Such an approach as ours here, let us be reminded, requires of us not only a most resolute rejection of such omnipresent threats to us as gnostic Modernism. It requires as well a careful attention to the inherited weaponry to be used against such continuous threats to intellectual integrity. Thus we must, while honoring and holding with a pious reverence such heroic stands at historical points of intellectual crisis as Weaver's *Ideas Have Consequences*, submit as well to the necessity of refurbishing whatever equipment bequeathed us by him for intellect's continuing resistance to false doctrines. The intellectually and spiritually debilitating doctrine continues for us to be Modernism's reduction of the final end of man to the confines of the immanent world—reducing man to a provincial by denying that regional ambience to experience which itself denies the horizon of the immanent as terminal to man.[20] That is the shocking possibility Eliot encounters and dramatizes in his "Gerontion," that little old dying man declaring "Think at last/ We have not reached conclusion, when I/ Stiffen in a rented house [the body]."[21]

It is with this obligation, accompanied with a continuing gratitude to Weaver, then, that I would have us look closely into our ally Weaver, beginning briefly at his "Introduction" to his famous book. I would do so by illustration, not in a judgmental rejection of Weaver as mentor. I do so particularly in relation to his incipient Platonisms which I believe at last a weakness, knowing even so that perhaps a case can be—and hope may be—made that Weaver himself comes to recognize difficulties and somewhat changes his own perspective after his early work. The Weaver of *Ideas Have Consequences*, the Weaver of 1948, would no doubt angrily reject my own perspective upon the virtues of tradition made from a Thomist position. But if one can make his way up from liberalism for a new beginning, as Weaver did in the 1940s, that new beginning is not necessarily his own final intellectual end. Therefore, the purpose of my concern becomes not at last with Weaver himself as thinker in his *Ideas Have Consequences* or *The Ethics of Rhetoric*, but with the dangers to us in our own initial enthusiasm over this first little book, which might tempt us perhaps to a careless consent to all its argument, as if it were the end of Weaver's argument against Modernist perversions of intellectual integrity rather than a signal beginning for a recovery of intellect from the deadly entanglements of Modernism's ideas.

I have come to the conviction, led to it in part by my first encounter with Weaver's *Ideas Have Consequences*, that without some metaphysical purchase in the nature of reality, the life of the mind can only be *ad hoc*, in response to the present moment's circumstances. That is why a communion between the living and the dead, in a continuing responsibility to the truth of things, is so necessary to me, as I believe it necessary to the good health of the intellectual community. This is to say that the life of the mind is a continuous conversation, more or less inclusive of both companionable presences and antagonistic presences, in a dialogue mutually concerned always for the truth of things. Not that under the pressures of the contingent moment of history to that dialogue there will not occur interruption or distraction. Indeed, these may become so intrusive as to make resistance necessarily *ad hoc*, though there is always the abiding presence of truth even then. We suggested that Eliot feared that the Agrarian's concern for tradition might overwhelm this larger obligation. Now with some reflection, I wonder whether Weaver's response to Modernism does not carry something of that *ad hoc* nature. Put directly, I wonder whether Weaver in his response did not too easily assume a Platonic position which he might with a reflective leisure have qualified in his concern for viable culture.

It is this concern that I address, then, and rather specifically a concern for the relation of consciousness to the created world as it seems present in his argument. Now, as I would not have been in the 1950s, I am uneasy with such statements as this from his "Introduction": Nature, he says, "had formerly been regarded as imitating a transcendent model and as constituting an imperfect reality." But with the coming of Nominalism and its intellectual aftermath, nature "was henceforth looked upon as containing the principles of its own constitution and behavior."[22] The problem here is that by this summary assertion, Weaver posits a Platonic shadow nature as if anciently accepted as our only intellectual tradition, antecedent to Occam, and it implies a former Platonic doctrine to be recovered. But in setting his argument characterizing Modernism's reading of nature, he characterizes as the Modernist's distortion of reality a position which in his terms is more clearly Thomistic than Modernist. It is as if he has not yet had the leisure of a conversation with Thomas Aquinas which might remind him that Occam's principal enemy was Thomas himself, not Plato. In the issue, what Modernism partially succeeds in doing is adapting Platonic idealism to its own species of idealism by limiting it to the immanent. What it does, or so I contend, is stand Platonic idealism on its head on the authority of its presumption of the specific human intellect as autonomous.

Thus the Modernist bent which is given to "universals" through Occam is *subjectivism* as the principal universal, justified by what is a species of intellectual shell-game. By its presumption of subjective authority over truth, it builds a new perspective of nature as shadow. For by the extension of the subjective as determinate, truth itself will become the creation of autonomous intellect, a central Modernist dogma. And all this it too easily accomplishes in the interest of its desire for gnostic power over being itself, over the fundamental reality of created nature. For it is a temptation common to our fallen nature to value subjective desire over the truth of things. Thus the Modernist dogma of subjectivity wins approval as an absolute, denying the independent, separate reality of existential things other than the autonomous intellect which is so fascinated by itself as object. It would deny actual things made real by an essential nature—as existing in fundamental respects inviolable to the subjective desires of finite intellect presuming its godhead over being. One current dilemma out of this impiety toward being is a general confusion in the public arena over questions of genetic engineering, especially the haunting questions associated with cloning, out of faint recollections of *Genesis*.

The Thomist such as Etienne Gilson or Jacques Maritain would insist that, by the reality of created things, those things bear in themselves principles revealing of their own constitution, revealing the ground to their nature as actual things in being itself. But Weaver by his statement as quoted attributes this aspect of reality to a distortion by Nominalistic gnosticism. It is in Gilson's response to the Cartesian distortions of epistemological reality of consciousness itself, through the instrumentality provided by Nominalism, that he remarks the problem here. "If we go deeper into the *nature* of an object given us, we direct ourselves towards one of the sciences, which will [or ought to be] completed by a metaphysics of nature." But if we go "deeper into the *conditions* under which the object is given us, we shall be turning towards a psychology, which will reach [or ought to reach] completion in a metaphysics of knowledge." As for science proportionately engaged by intellect, he says, "science is not a critique of common sense but of the successive approximations of reality made by common sense." Indeed, "every form of realism is a philosophy made by common sense," leading toward a metaphysical vision of nature and to an understanding of the *conditions* to intellectual encounter with nature by consciousness.[23] They are complementary addresses to the mystery of existence itself, in response to that first and last of all our wonderings as finite intellect: *why something rather than nothing?*

What is effected by Nominalism, as it is appropriated out of Occam's intricate arguments, is an instrument of power over nature justified on the authority of autonomous intellect, whereby the Platonic idea of the transcendent model is presumed a creation by autonomous intellect itself through its signs, as first divorced *from* but then in turn imposed *upon* nature. In the Christian tradition, nature is created and therefore both dependent *upon* and *from* its Creator. Hence my epithet of Modernism as an inverted Platonism, in which doctrine reality becomes dependent upon autonomous intellect itself. It follows at last from this gnostic assumption that truth itself is that which is decreed by intellect. By the power of autonomous intellect, then, such truth is made universal—according, of course, to the extent of power exercised by the particular universalizing, autonomous intellect. This is to say that a principle, subjectively authorized, becomes a dogma to be imposed as a limit against rival intellectual subjectivisms, an ideology to be established by force if necessary, providing only that there is a sufficient power for its enforcement. Such is the tendency of positive law itself once divorced from natural law by an intention to gnostic power over being.

We see this gnostic principle increasingly at work in our world since the Renaissance, whether we look to the arbitrary "kingship" as advocated by Hobbes in his *Leviathan*, or to Hitler's arguments in *Mein Kampf*. Or we may find the same principle advocated by committees of the empowered, whether located in the academy, at the state capital, or even in churches. Wherever one or two or three intellects are gathered together in a presumption of, and so pursuit by, an autonomous power sufficient to dictate "truth," we are likely to find distortions of truth itself as properly measured by reality. That is the concern which Eric Voegelin warns us of in saying that the secular gnostic intellect as agent of the secular religion of Modernism has as its end power over being itself. And how clever that autonomous intellect proves to be in spinning out its programs, whereby the program itself determines the truth of things. That, then, is the multiple burden upon truth itself which we discover in the variety of ideologies most noticeably rising to power in the post-Renaissance world.

In our concern for Occam's Nominalism as eventually effecting a disjunction of consciousness from the rest of nature, we well remember that doctrine's initial appearance, occurring before Occam. It first surfaces in the scholastic debate over the nature of the mystery of a sacrament, in the 11th century: the Sacrament of the Eucharist. To the ensuing controversy among the scholastics over "transubstantiation" Abelard attempted a reconciliation of Nominalism to realism. And Thomas, in his *Summa Theologica* and *Summa Contra Gentiles,* argues the problem in favor of a realism against a disjunctive idealism. He also argues it especially in two briefer treatises, *On the Unity of the Intellect Against the Averroists,* engaging the dangerous doctrines of Siger of Brabant which argue for a universal intellect of which the discrete person's is a *part.* This before Kant's modifications of this Averroistic attention in his own "Universals." Thomas, in *On Being and Essence,* lays the ground for a refutation of Occam, though it is Occam and not Thomas who subsequently proved acceptable to the bursting interests in power over being which at last permeates the Renaissance spirit.

Historical spectacles of this triumph we may see in the growth of nationalism, as if a nation were an extension of the autonomous self collectively enlarged, a "national" pursuit of power centering notably in such documents as Machiavelli's *The Prince* and Hobbes's *Leviathan*.

If one were to suggest a recent terminal illustration of Occam's success, we might cite closer home Ralph Waldo Emerson, who declared in the 1830s that he would no longer honor the Sacrament of the Eucharist in any church ceremony using bread and wine. Emerson's was a welcomed spirit, indeed, to one Charles W. Eliot when he became President of Harvard in 1869, from which position of power he set about establishing what he would call in his farewell address "The Religion of the Future." Emersonian ideas were made welcome by President Eliot, especially as they helped prepare the way for this new "religion," in which certain principles were declared by President Eliot as its Moses: as a religion it would not "'be based on authority, either spiritual or temporal," for the desirable "tendency toward liberty is progressive, and among educated men is irresistible." It will allow "no personifications of the primitive forces of nature," nor "worship, express or implied, of dead ancestors, teachers, or rulers." It must certainly have nothing to do with "the personal welfare or safety of the individual in this world or the other," for the individual exists primarily for "service to others, and...contributions to the common good."[24]

Of course a "common good" is to be dictated by the lords of power in charge of establishing this new religion. They must decree that it will not be "gloomy, ascetic, or maledictory," and most certainly "it will not be propitiatory, sacrificial, or expiatory," nor "perpetuate the Hebrew anthropomorphic representations of God."[25] In short, it is a religion of the future which by the 1940s was a reality increasingly apparent to Weaver, as it was to T. S. Eliot, C. S. Lewis, Etienne Gilson, Allen Tate, Donald Davidson and many others. For it had become oppressively present as the progressive religion in the post-World War II world. What wonder that in opposition a scattered remnant should react in more or less *ad hoc* actions in an intellectual guerrilla warfare, a civil war within the intellectual community, only to discover themselves burdened by what Eliot would speak of as "shabby" equipment long neglected. It was a valiant resistance nevertheless, and it gained for us some advantage to the continuing resistance, though we may ourselves at the close of our century feel so hard pressed as not to appreciate or take possession of a possible position beyond those *ad hoc* weaknesses we may ourselves now discover.

For myself, I should like to speak something of that advantage to me in my attempts to piece my own equipment together out of the general inheritance from those old warriors involved in this never-ending war. What is necessary is a recovery of the nature of nature, in which recovery lies our own reorientation. What of the *nature* of the *object*—the *thing* among things whose truth we seek, in relation to the *conditions* to our intellectual seeking in this concluding century of a millennium, to borrow Gilson's terms? How may we at least begin to recover a "metaphysics of nature" as complementary to "a metaphysics of knowledge"? Not an easy undertaking for our own word, or for many words, when the progressive religion of Modernism has so deeply affected disparate specializations of knowledge, especially through the fragmentation of the intellectual community into compartmentalized, specialized vocabularies. As many of you will know from experience, the attempt at a recovery of truth as the measure of our words is a dangerous one. In the killing fields of intellect at our moment—that is, in the intellectual killing fields of the academy—no creature is likely to be so dangerous as the specialist cornered by unfamiliar ideas. Ours is a world in which *experts in* have replaced *disciples of,* though only *nominally* so—only *nominalistically* so. In the reality of our intellectual circumstances, the intellectual community has been eroded by *disciples of* ideologies often popularly subscribed to, as their originators tend also to be self-honored as *experts in* limited specialties. The climate of this erosion of intellect is agitated by intentions to power by disparate ideologies, knowingly or naively supported by the popular spirit. Hence testimony before a congressional committee on farm problems by a recent star in a movie dealing with poverty-stricken back country folks. Especially so, insofar as "we the people" are devoted to subjective "universalizing" of our always limited purchase upon the truth of things, though often valid in the true limits of created reality.

If we may consider that idealism in its Modernist manifestation becomes reduced to ideology through intellect's illusion of its own autonomy, that does not mean that the ideologue may not be at least sentimentally attached to his ideology by good intention, of course. Thus we are anciently reminded that good intentions may pave a road destructive of reality. But the most proximate sufferer at last is the ideological mind itself. Common sense puts it aphoristically: the road to Hell is paved with good intentions. And as theology adds: in the light of eternity, it is the paver who reaches that destination most certainly. Again, Gilson in his argument against Cartesian idealism speaks to this point. He says that in idealism "the order and connection of ideas replaces the order and connection between things," thus isolating intellect from reality.[26] In the event, intellect becomes disjoined from the order and connection between things. It becomes isolated from nature by its own actions of a thought which is intent upon ideas as if themselves the ultimate reality.

That other Thomist, Maritain, complements Gilson by opposing Kantian philosophy. Kant by a devotion to his own species of universals largely succeeds in furthering the disjunction of intellect from that natural reality of things in themselves which is the proper food to the ordinate growth of intellect, as common sense reminds us. Maritain holds that the problem with Kantian universality is that it is "not of the norm, as Kant believed." It is rather "a consequence of the norm's rationality," the norm itself to be recovered only through our experiences of reality, rationally engaged in relation to actual existences. By his pursuit of "the Categorical Imperative," Kant disjoins "the universe of morality or of freedom" from nature itself, including human nature, thus making it an idea "completely separated from the universe of nature, since the content of the law must be deduced from its form and from the universally normative essence of pure practical reason."[27]

It is in this sense a Platonic refinement justifying the authority of finite rational intellect, preparing a way (through intellectual pride) to a conclusion of autonomous sovereignty independent of complex reality. The effect is to separate intellect from its sustaining food to intellectual action—namely, existential reality itself. And so persuasive this mess of intellectually generated pottage that birthrights are easily foregone. Hence, out of Kantian thought, "universalism" may too easily feed illusion of *comprehension*, which in the issue proves a Cartesian entrapment of the self enlarged into a "universal" entrapment obscuring the solipsism. That proved the dead-end T. S. Eliot reached as "philosopher," to be observed underway in his formal dissertation, *Knowledge and Experience in the Philosophy of F. H. Bradley*.[28] Lost to and through that exploration, increasingly dependent on sign divorced from reality, is intellect's self-evident experience of its own immediacy to the created world. In a rescue from that isolation, Eliot will turn toward a still-point, a recovery possible at the center of the "turning world," existential reality.

In this perspective toward intellectual recovery, one may appeal to the anecdotal remembrances of Kant himself in those halls and streets of Königsberg, almost an inconspicuous shadow among the lights and shades of that complex community. Given his theologically disturbing ideas within that community, he might well be encountered by locals as an eccentric. In response and from our distance we might conclude him a prophet without honor. But one might also take local response as reflecting a common-sense recognition, if only an intuitive one, of a dilemma inherent to his presence as person about Königsberg. For him a "pure" critique of reason itself may prove more sterilized than purifying of existential experiences, leaving him a shadowy presence almost alien in the community. Our musing extrapolation here seems consonant with one philosophical realist's engagement of Kant, Jacques Maritain's. Maritain finds in him dangers obscured by "form" as presumed rationally perfected, for that perfection is at the expense of the actual complex and intellectually *incomprehensible* reality (in both philosophical and theological sense) in Kant's response as finite intellect to reality itself.

It requires Maritain as philosopher to make more than anecdotal the Prussian king's request (in 1794) that Kant not disturb or alarm orthodoxy by publishing further books on religion, with which request Kant dutifully complied—except that his philosophical work itself proved widely destructive of theological orthodoxy. In Maritain's view, Kant's concern for ethics proves radically deconstructive of moral theology. Thus, says Maritain, in Kantian ethics "the specification of moral acts is freed from consideration of the *good*, of the goodness-in-itself of the object (that is to say of its conformity to reason by virtue of the nature of things)." Kant's procedure is "very logical," but it can be so only "since things in themselves cannot be grasped in Kant's system," because they are insufficiently understood as *things* by his imposition of logical *form*. It is, from Maritain's Thomistic position regarding Kantian ethics, "a perverted Christian moral philosophy" which results. It is this perversion that, for instance, leads to those dislocations of moral realities to the soul which one finds (says Maritain) in Spinoza, whom Weaver incidentally speaks of rather more kindly than would Maritain.[29]

Now what I have been here preparing to support is the argument that we find a line of descent from Occam through Descartes and Kant into our own intellectual arena, whose reigning religion has been described, if shockingly, by President Eliot of Harvard. It is a religion which logical positivism supports in a "scholastic" service, by justifying the erosive action of autonomous intellect which further separates intellect from nature in the name of a freedom which denies any givenness that cannot be explained by the agency of autonomous intellect itself as the giver. Of course, this new religion flourishes in a variety of sects. It underlies, for instance, the *Humanist Manifestos* no less than it does a puritanic Marxist theology of materialism. It is involved as well in the sentimental attachment, or attempted re-attachment, practiced in current New Age fads: the attempt to infuse nature with a conjured humanistically colored universalism through the contemplation of a crystal in a remote desert setting. Nor is it coincidence that, in the multitudinous attempts of Spiritualism, all these intellectual systems are largely Kantian in their points of departure. Madame Blavatsky, for instance, was initially a devout Kantian in her philosophy.[30]

This speculative trail into Spiritualism is not in digression from a philosophical line out of Descartes to Kant. Nor is it an isolated byway removed from the culmination of Nominalism in esoteric logical positivism, or pragmatic materialism. It is rather a reminder of but yet another segment in the widening trail that subjectivism makes, the ever broadening and flattening highway within the matrix of our intellectual community as it has struggled in the post-Renaissance world to establish intellectual autonomy as absolute. The struggling itself is often taken as evidence of triumph, as in our sentimen-

tal pleasure in the epithet "The Age of Alienation," which
we give ourselves with a pride in an imposed pathos
derived from self-pity. Intellect appears sometimes lost
and pathetic in its longings for recovery. But sometimes
it appears arrogantly intent on making the country of
intellect to exist by the authority of the imposition of
signs upon reality regardless of reality, as if by arrogance
it might console itself. Gilson speaks more largely to the
circumstances of this intellectual disorientation than simply by his opposing Descartes in his *Methodical Realism*.
He speaks as well of the continued splintering effect out
of Cartesian thought upon the intellectual community
which succeeds Descartes. And as for these more lately
grown idealists since Descartes, Gilson says, "the order of
connection of ideas replaces the order and connection
between things." Here lies the danger to our reflection—
to speculative thought if engaged from the idealist's fundamentalist subjective perspective as absolute in its
freedom. For it necessarily substitutes thought for reality,
else it must surrender its subjectively sovereign autonomy. In Gilson's phrases, it mistakes "its principles and
system" for "reality itself," thus setting aside, by reason
made pure through Kantian critiques, that actual reality
which is the proper measure of reflective intellect itself.

In the end we reach a curious circumstance to the idealist intellect. For now idealists become "people for whom
the normal can only be a particular instance of the pathological. When Descartes states triumphantly that every
madman cannot deny his first principle, 'I think, therefore I am,' he helps us enormously to see what happens
to reason when reduced to this first principle."[31] And we
add that when Kant builds upon this first principle,

which we might name the Closed Bubble of the Self—an enlargement of intellect in the name of a subjective universalism denying the natural—Kant must rest his faith in the possibility of occupying a noosphere inhabitable only by an intellect disembodied from reality. That, Thomas might conclude, is the heresy of angelism. It is the illusion of a separation by the will of the finite, created human person (this wayward idealist) from the context of the created world. Thereupon, assuming the divorce accomplished, it bears an illusion of self-justification, reassuring the "originating" intellect of the reality of its illusion as autonomous authority. It rests (if but a moment) in the illusion that by autonomy it actually inhabits an intellectual noosphere of abstract idea by virtue of its sovereign authority.

Thus may intellect conclude that it lifts itself by its own bootstraps above entangling creation—so long as it can ignore the reality of actual bootstraps experienced at morning in an isolated room enclosing an isolated consciousness. As Eliot is wrestling with the dilemma of knowledge as rationalizing agency solving the mystery of experience, intellectual response to historical consequences upon philosophy in the evolution of Cartesian idealism, he is also writing poems. One of them in particular ("Preludes") reflects the isolating effect of thought in response to circumstances to such thought. A consciousness, clasping "the yellow soles of feet/ In the palms of both soiled hands," struggles with the "thousand sordid images," the residue of its existential experiences, but a residue divorced from existential reality. Those images constitute the "soul" of that consciousness, which in its present moment projects that residue upon a flat world, a "ceiling" to consciousness in consciousness' sordid tenement, its decaying body.[32] But there are no reassuring correspondences of image to reality possible in such isolation as only a distant dream itself. It is this illusion of intellectual levitation to angelism that leads Maritain to remark of its Kantian articulation that Kantian ethics is "a perverted Christian moral philosophy"—perverted in that as moral agent intellect implies itself its own savior. But Eliot's "voice" in his poem hardly takes itself as saved. The "worldly" effects upon creation, manifest in the social and political aspects of community, will be as various in consequence as those crystal-centered meditations in the desert (nature simplified from its particularities in a refracted light, mesmerizing the self in an illusion of "transport") or most recently the engineering of prime genetic matter once believed created, in order to reinvent being in the name of a common good. But we might remember here awkward primitive engineering acts to such a species of the common good as those by Stalin or Hitler or Pol Pot. It might shadow somewhat the latest clever engineering of genes that brings us that world-famous sheep Dolly, and even promises us cloned "persons," to the titillation of the "public spirit" through obfuscation of common sense.

The fragmentation of community out of Descartes and Kant, initiated by a wedge driven by Nominalistic sign between the immanent and transcendent: that is one intellectual tradition. Why, then, should we take the fragmented ideologies as parts differing by the mere coincidence of their dispersal among a variety of persons? Logical Positivism, Spiritualism, New Age religion share in dreams of intellectually cloned persons. In a growing desperateness of our dislocation from the responsibilities of stewardship to reality, the popular spirit is promised the attractions of "Virtual Reality," a shadow of a shadow, a means of having our sensual cake without the threat of cancer or AIDS or such dangers in a final freedom C. S. Lewis would call the abolition of man. Thus, *person* may conclude himself but a dream within his dream, hovering suspended, disoriented from both the immanent and the transcendent in a safety beyond risk. For he has at last consented intellectually to the ideological principle that *person* is the initiating illusion in this new moment along the way to that abolition of man. In that old attempt at self-naming before Occam, an attempt now out of philosophical favor, we were believed governed by a prudence (or at least steadily *some* were). Prudence required acknowledging any created *thing* as actual in itself, known by the actual experiences of a person through his actually existing in an actual world. Thus one might well conclude through speculative thought governed by prudence that he existed because created. But the gift of common sense made such a person aware as well that he is created only by limit, by particularity.

By an orthodox anticipation to intellect, largely borne through tradition, we might define man, not as in that Modernist angelistic inclination derived from Plato which is the dominant tradition of our moment, but as *created intellectual soul incarnate.* We intend by such a naming, through prudential humility, to acknowledge that, despite such multiple terms in the naming, we are yet struggling to name a *simple* entity, a person, always going in fear of the divisiveness of terms themselves. How easily we separate body from soul, nominalistically, as if thereby naming separate natures and not, in reality, as responding as best we may, given our intellectual limits preventing comprehension, to the handicap of our discursive gift as intellect. *As best we may*, as intellectual soul incarnate. For we know intuitively that what we attempt to acknowledge in accepting our existence as a "self" is a simplicity created, a limited unity. We *are* as person. And we *are* in a mystery of simplicity which is beyond our own comprehension at last, since by *comprehension* we speak of a property of the Creator—in whose image we nevertheless believe ourselves created. From that "likeness" of relation between incompatibles, the "image" and its Cause, derives our delegated stewardship to creation, in an accord to gifts of particularity whereby we *are*. And precisely here lie the circumstances of intellectual prudence. This is a belief held by virtue of faith out of that Revelation which was and is, and is the only intercessory to our otherwise sad limitedness.

Only discursively—such is a particularity in our nature—may we pay tribute to such a simpleness as our own "self" which proves beyond its own absolute comprehension, since ours is not a property of Absolute Love, another of our names for Absolute Comprehension. Thus we speak of the proper exercise of a self-love charged to responsibilities in the world, in relation to our love of neighbor through an openness to creation—a love beginning with and returning to our own *person* through ordinate love. Thus derives that deportment proper to that always neighboring and multitudinous (because limited) creation, the deportment of stewardship toward the impinging world. Such is our proprietary responsibility as free-holders in this general "incorporation," this inclu-

sive *property* existing out of the act of Love Itself. Richard
Weaver engages this point in his term *piety*, and in relation to that metaphysical concept of *property* which he
would establish, though as we shall argue he does not
engage it precisely enough in his articulation of his recognition.

I come now to suggest a metaphysical perspective
toward reality with which Weaver's position is incompatible at points, though I believe he intended otherwise.
And so I am required to make juxtapositions to explore
the differences. I do so, observing that Weaver seems
again and again made uncomfortable by or suspicious of
nature itself, of that world adjacent to his consciousness
with which he seems to me sometimes to confuse the
sheer materialistic ideology he opposes that would reduce
"nature" to a raw, almost prime, matter as if accidentally
provided autonomous intellect for its unfettered uses. We
see this inclination in his argument when his own position seems threatened. His argument then almost
becomes a species of ideology itself, as in his *Ethics of
Rhetoric* when he is presenting Lincoln's mind to us. There
Weaver affirms that "The true conservative is one who
sees the universe as a paradigm of essences, of which the
phenomenology of the world is a sort of continuing
approximation." Thus, by implication, the world of
essences is made to appear separate from the created universe, which is only its paradigm. That such is the drift of
his thought is immediately seconded by his reformulating
his point: "to put this another way, [the true conservative
sees the universe] as a set of definitions which are struggling to get themselves defined in the real world."[33]

Now if this "true conservative" sees the universe as a set of definitions struggling for a union with the real world, the universe itself must be in some sense an unreal world, a shadow world. Rather inescapably, the philosophical position Weaver assumes here is Platonic, shadowed itself by a Kantian terminology evident in Weaver's repeated uses of *universal*. In that mode of thought, the world of intellect in its quest for the transcendent union is taken as the only "real" world. Thus he will say, in *The Ethics of Rhetoric* (the second of his two books published in his lifetime) that an intellectual act of love is "a desire to bring truth into a kind of existence, or to give it an actuality,"[34] as if intellect by its love occasions truth rather than that love is graced in its growing by truth precedent and always independent of finite intellect's assumed causal actions. Truth measures love at last, and is not brought by intellectual desire into "a kind of existence" whereby the "essences" are joined to the universe, which universe is somehow an independent shadowy paradigm such as Maritain explicates in Kant. It is as if Kant has had a surreptitious effect upon Weaver's argument. This is to say that we inescapably breathe within a Modernist environment, a circumstance to intellect which of course Weaver was acutely aware of. It is most difficult to free ourselves from it, since intellect in this world at this moment inhales willy-nilly a debilitating pollen of Modernism afloat in the intellectual environment. Indeed, Weaver's very awareness of this polluted intellectual environment is motive to his prophetic warning that ideas have consequences not always healthful.

In the implications of Weaver's argument *as here made*, therefore, the intellect itself may be taken as some sort of universal, a transcendent to "nature," whereby our own worldly nature as specific person may become reduced to a paradigm of that other worldly reality. Here lies a sort of fuzzy Platonism, affected more by Kantian arguments than perhaps Weaver (if engaged on the point) would allow. It is nevertheless a position dangerously inclined to those old Averroist dislocations of the particular created nature of intellect in this particular person, against which St. Thomas objected. And it further makes problematic any good as attending creation in and of itself. In relation to intellect, for instance, the body whereby the person is said to be *incarnate soul* in a simple existence as person, is endangered by a dualistic argument which threatens at last to conclude the body an enemy of the soul, that old Platonic dilemma against which St. Augustine cautions us. What is obscured, or lost, in this inclination is the problem of free will, which by its given freedom as the only discrete sovereignty (though in that sovereignty of will it be limited to the small compass of the discrete person) the will is given a sufficient power to practice evil upon both the body and soul. That is, the discrete simplicity of person is made victim to its own perversions of its simple nature by its own perverse will.

And so, counter to this dangerous adaptation of Platonic idea, affected at its root by Occam, Descartes, Kant, we would counter with a Thomistic perspective upon the reality of man in nature. Contrary to Weaver, Thomas would insist that natural reality is good. Existential reality is that within which we find ourselves as a made creature, as a part charged with stewardship by the act of love whose effect is our discrete creation as intellectual soul incarnate. For if our ultimate end is *beyond,* we must yet make our way from *within.* What by ambiguous collectivism of term we call *nature* bears in it what Weaver explicitly denies when he attributes to Modernism that view of nature which in his pejorative attribution to Modernism we argued more nearly the Thomistic than the Modernist view of that "nature." The *thing* in itself bears for Thomas (but not for the Modernist) "its own constitution and behavior." It does so for Thomas by virtue of its being created *this thing.* The quoted phrase here is Weaver's, not Thomas's, spoken against the Modernist, and he speaks in denial of what he sees as the Modernist's insistence upon an independently constituted existence of *nature* containing within itself (consequent to that independence) all the causes of its behavior.[35] His objection has a valid center, but it is not presented in terms so carefully put as not to allow confusions of Modernist and Thomistic positions.

What is at issue is Modernism's strategy of denial, whereby existential reality is divorced from any orientation to a cause transcendent of nature itself. Thus to speak of existential reality collectively as *nature* serves as a reductionism from its older orientation, still residually echoed in that more resonant term *creation*—more resonant, that is, because implying "nature's" dependence in parts and as a whole as created, as opposed to being merely and even more mysteriously *independently* constituted. But even to speak of *independent constitution* in the Modernist reduction implies an inherent dependence upon *something* other and so antecedent *to,* for it is independent *of* or *from.* It is a term (*independent constitution*) setting aside by term one thing from another, so that what is occurring seems rather a rejection through

Nominalist agency of the older and more inclusive concept of dependence upon some transcendent, in order to arrive at a positive by a negating intellectual action. At some deep level of this intellectual action there is a perversion of reality intended. And indeed, this is the intellectual step allowing *nominally,* as perhaps opposed to any *actuality* in itself, a closed so-called *nature* dictated by Nominalism. Thus nature may be declared "independently constituted," so that nature's behavior must then be allowed explication only by reference to its own independent, internal behavior as nominalistically declared by the independence of intellect itself, removed from its own experiences of reality. But, alas, as our recent history in nature grotesquely reveals, that nature is enslaved by—determined by—imposition of Nominalistic will.

In the intellectual issue, then—that issue intended by the most subtle of Modernist intellects—a forced conclusion is presumed effected by a nominalistic strategy. This independent constitution of a so-called *nature* we encounter through an undeniably existing consciousness which undeniably responds to the multitudinous things (including ideas, incidentally). But the existence of such things (including the encountering consciousness itself) by such Nominalistic reckoning can only have as cause sheer *accident,* in the most radical sense of that term *accident,* whereby any antecedent cause is denied. That is, if one thinks of *nature* as a closed totality accidentally evolved into discrete actualities, into discretely existing independent *things,* that closing is already itself a "setting aside" which would deny to *accident* any precedent. But without a precedent *something,* accident itself could not occur. What we are left with is a very strange mystery in this secular religion we call Modernism: *self-creation ex nihilo,* the self-creating god being the individual consciousness itself, upon which faith in its own autonomy holds that all else depends for cause—upon this momentary consciousness itself.

That is the nature of the intellectual presumption which Weaver would oppose, a presumption more pervasive of the popular spirit at the close of our century than it was when he began his objections. It is a presumption absorbed more by osmosis into the popular spirit than arrived at by thought. In the interest of self-justification, to establish the authority of self-creation *ex nihilo,* Modernist scholastics quickly recognize the necessity of a consolation to those ossified intellects less sophisticated than the scholastic himself, lest these deprived (insufficiently evolved?) intellects prove potentially resistant to the proposed new religion of the self, which above all requires a rejection of the more normal common-sense responses to reality. On the one hand, then, there is celebrated as a palliative, thus wooing our consent, the broadening range of appetitive pleasures through things accepted as accidental in their natures and so indifferent to programmed manipulation—justifying appetitive gluttony which we speak of euphemistically as "Consumerism." On the other hand, in response to a lingering, intuitive desire to worship the source of things and the end of things, the Cause of causes, an alternate strategy must concentrate, must intensify, the concept *nature* itself through personification, making it an immanent spirit suited to naive worship. And indeed, this is the point for our attention to what must be declared at last the diabolic in this Modernist strategy.

For it at once recognizes this necessity of adoration as speaking a *something* beyond the self as inherent to human nature—as speaking a reality unaccountable in a nature declared independently constituted. It recognizes its own endangerment by that inherent necessity unless it supplies a surrogate god. For always there arises a desire in the person to a perfection of being through a turning out of the self in adoration of something beyond the self.

This is a circumstance most complicating to that intended gnostic program of the Modernist scholastic, the principle of self-creation *ex nihilo*. Marx recognized as much, and his remark that religion is the opiate of the people camouflages his own substitution of materialism to replace the Christian God as an acceptable opiate, a surrogate god, in his version of a new religion. Modernism requires therefore a palliative to the more highly gifted intellects, perhaps *materialism* as idea. Thus as an idea the world is reduced and may fascinate such intellects—flatter them as inhabitants of a universe of ideas beyond the sordid actualities of the material world. Dostoevsky's *Crime and Punishment* dramatizes this necessity to Raskolnikov, and his consequent collapse as intellect. But Modernism must as well fascinate the lesser intellects, the *ordinary* on behalf of whom Raskolnikov commits his crime as justified because he is among the *extraordinary*. Among such *ordinaries* Modernist ideology recognizes that it may fascinate the lowly by making nature a something answering their inherent (if unexplained) desire to adore. It is in response to this Nihilistic distinction abroad among the intelligentsia that Chesterton wittily reminds us that Nature is not our "Mother" but our "Little Sister," thus speaking implicitly to that obligation to stewardship we have affirmed. And in this respect, Raskolnikov in his prison exile begins the long learning of this reality, supported in his labor by his own Beatrice to his quest, Sonya.

And so nature personified becomes one of our recent opiates. In this age of ecological alarm (much of it quite justified by Christian concerns for a proper stewardship of creation), it has come to seem more acceptable to worship nature than to worship the God of nature through an ordinate reverence toward creation, *proportionate* to the mercy of God's continuous creation—his act of Love whereby things are. In the manufacture of an object for adoration—an idol suited to idolatry as a control of the *ordinary* in the interest of power disguised as order—the Modernist ideologue must palliate the *extraordinary* intellect also, lest it discover propensity to adoration within itself. There grows an elaborate rationalization of this residual inclination to adore which is undeniably present in the *ordinary,* breaking out in them from time to time in a religious fundamentalism variously colored in the social world. Anthropological and biological sciences join, supported by psychology, in service to palliating the intelligentsia, in our moment none more persuasive as an object for intellectual adoration than the latest discoveries of genetic determinism.

Dostoevsky, we have recalled, is attuned to this tendency, taking a wicked delight through his surrogate spokesman in the matter, his minor devil in *The Brothers Karamazov.* Ivan Karamazov, a more fascinating complication than Raskolnikov in respect to his Romantic Modernism, his self-valuation as extraordinary, encounters no Grand Inquisitor as ally to his attempts to save the "ordinary" through his sense of his own "extraordinary" nature. Instead at a point of collapse he must deal with a tormenting devil, a "paltry, trivial devil" who can exhibit no "scorched wings and thunder and lightening" but only banal arguments justifying himself as abused victim of both God and man—reflecting to Ivan undeniably at last himself as but a paltry creature whose intellectual refuge as accidentally extraordinary collapses about him. The little devil declares himself "an X in an indeterminate equation," as if arrived there by victimization through Ivan's rationalistic diminution of evil as accident. That devil sighs in sadness: "In our day what's retrograde is believing in God, but I am the devil, it's all right to believe in me." In such a self-righteous belief he is devil minor, destructive accident strangely at odds with Modernist intentions. He feels unappreciated, having served Ivan secretly as justification of his *extraordinary* nature in its pursuit of the good at whatever cost. Ivan defends the Karazamov "baseness," allowing him to declare that "Everything is permitted" by his intent to create good out of accidental evilness, a self-appointed task which Ivan sees God as having neglected, though his own inescapable dependence on a God he declares nonexistent torments him.[36]

Contrary to Ivan's doctrine of God's unjustness (given that evil exists) some Christian mystics witness to the proper "ecological" responsibility—Dame Julian of Norwich, or the voice in *The Cloud of Unknowing*, or St. John of the Cross, for instance. Interestingly, these particular mystics appear on the historical scene at that mensurally resonant point in time as we turn from the

Medieval to the Modern world, at that point of an increasing philosophical cacophony which Weaver associates with Occam. And if one doubts this new cultivation of our intuitive need to worship by turning us to nature itself as worshipful idol, one need only listen carefully to the developing political agendas issuing from Washington, D.C., in the final decade of our century, in relation to a term even more ambiguous than *nature—the environment.*

In that older and more resonant term *creation,* existential reality may be recovered to its transcendent dependence, as Dame Julian does in holding a hazel-nut on her open palm. That is surely a fundamental concern to Richard Weaver, though it tempts him toward a dangerous dualism at nature's expense. Thus our concern: we may by an *ordinate* relocation, however, recover a *proportionate* reverence for creation's multitudinous and discrete Many in relation to that Transcendent One in whom we live and breathe and have our being, but not by intellectual commitment to dualism either ancient or modern. Such a recovery is especially diametrically opposed to the convenience of any reductionist collectivity, a closed reduction of the Many to that self-contained One, the Modernist consciousness, which is then declared intellectually accountable only to accident. For when the inescapable actuality of things—experienced by consciousness in response to the truly discrete constitution of and behavior of things, each in itself—when that actuality becomes dislocated, the necessity of reconciliation to things becomes the more pressing upon us, giving rise to an intellectual disquiet, diverse in its manifestations through the diversity of ideologies. That is the circumstance to our current political and social chaos, which makes it crucial that we approach with caution Weaver's appeal to dualism in order to counter Modernism.

It is in response to this intellectual disquiet that *nature*—things actually existing by virtue of limit itself, *created* by limit—is proposed by Modernism as accountable to accident as if thereby to still the disquieted among us. Thus it would have accident as the only ground, which is not a real ground but only an intentional principle willfully directed against existential reality. This is the dualistic shell-game Nominalistically practiced by Modernism through turning Platonism upside down, whereby *accident* replaces *being* itself as the only acceptable ground to the discretely existing things of creation. The independent constitution of nature and of its actions are thus to be declared the effect of cumulative accident. If that doctrine is accepted, it must follow that intentional intellect is therefore freed to reconstitute accidental things according to the intentional desire of the self-constituted intellect. *Voilà:* the Age of Alienation, evidenced in that trickle-down effect of this bad idea in the dissolution of family and community everywhere apparent in the 1990s.

What is required, as Weaver knew, is a recovery of *nature's* origins in respect to the constitution and behavior of existing things as discrete entities properly called *creations,* existing independent of mythical accident, but independent as well of the intentional violations of creation by the presumed autonomous independence of gnostic intellect itself, which desires to reconstitute being. That intellect proves diabolic, however much supported by inconspicuous minor devils (*pace* Ivan Karamazov) through its struggle to reconstitute being, out of a faith resting in the enunciation of Milton's Satan, a figure hardly minor in our literature: "The mind is its own place, and in itself/ Can make a Heav'n of Hell, a Hell of Heav'n." Even in so remote a country village as the Karamazov's Skotoprigonyevsky, Ivan imagines such possibility. It is this false recovery that Thomas Aquinas attempts to resist, seeing it an inherent danger in Occam's Nominalism. That resistance is evident in Thomas's devastating critique of the Averroist manipulations of Platonism in respect to universals. Thomas by reason disposes of the "universal" intellect within which the Averroist would locate each person's intellect as dependent and as lacking therefore its own *essential* nature as particular. That is why a Platonic world or pseudo-Platonic world divorced from the actual constitution of specific, limited creation must prove a false divorce, whereby intellect attempts to posit *essence* as separate from the actually existing thing. Thomas will argue that the person's initial movement as simple person (*created intellectual soul incarnate*) is toward God. But this is a move, he says, made necessarily according to the limits of the person's actual and discrete nature as created. That is, the initial move is made intuitively through our senses in response to existential reality—our first movement as *homo viator* toward God—in an initial response to particularly existing things, which are themselves separate from (independent of) our moving consciousness as person.[37]

It must follow from this Thomistic view that the materially existing world is good in itself, inasmuch as it *is*. For in its diversity of *things*, within which actual and poten-

tial being resides, that world is dependent from and sustained by a continuous creation. Thus it does not "fall to
naught," as Dame Julian of Norwich discovers in her
reflection on the hazel-nut lying on her palm, that little
round world.[38] That nut is actual beyond mere paradigm,
and it is known as actual by intellect. Further, what is
intuitively known (though not rationally *comprehended*) in
this initial action of intellect in a communion with the
actual hazel-nut is the abiding essence of the thing itself,
whereby it is the very thing it is. Its limited actuality and
potentiality is to be referred to its comprehensively creating Cause, whose continuous love prevents its falling to
naught. That is why, though a fascination with essence
may dissolve into that perversion of science called scientism, even the brain of a leech may speak to the wonder
of its Creator. And independent of those leeches or hazel-
nuts, Thomas argues, each person is possessed of a simple intellect, *simple* in relation to that absolute simplicity
we ascribe to God. In our approaching a vision of that
simplicity, an understanding of our existing (in a popular
term) as a discrete *self*, we engage the limits of our given
nature. We must divide with concept, in the pursuit of an
understanding, beyond mere *knowledge*, which understanding may be the more readily shared communally
out of common experiences of things in themselves. This
is the behavior of intellectual creatures in one aspect of
that mystery whereby we are said to be created in God's
image, so that our simple intellect moves variously,
moves intuitively in response to its own nature in a
response to the natures in creation itself. But intellect
moves as well *rationally*, not simply intuitively, though by
that signal gift of existing in the image of God we are eas-

ily tempted to a desire stirred by intuitive knowing to resolve our ambiguous desires *precipitately*. That is the beginning of our becoming lost in a dark wood called creation through the growing illusion of self-sufficiency— the first temptation to godhead shared since Adam.

Given the peculiar nature of our gift of intellect as enabled to move toward fulfillment both intuitively and rationally, we are prone to a temptation to accelerate desire's resolution. We wish resolution to our questions, an end to our intellectual desire, and so we prove easily disoriented from our final end. Put another way, because of anticipation, we wish for an intellectual or spiritual beatitude without the tedious necessities to the journeying toward that perfection which is an implicit necessity to us as *homo viator*, limited by our created nature. By presumptions of angelism, therefore, we would storm heaven prematurely. Dante dramatizes this inclination at the outset of his *Divine Comedy*, when his lost Pilgrim Dante, beginning to come to himself in a panic of intellect in the dark wood of the world, attempts to rush up the mountain directly to the sun, only to be forced back to that ominous cave opening, over which the ominous inscription: "Abandon hope, all ye who enter here." With a courage of desperation, he accompanies Virgil to the lowest depth in a modulated intellectual re-education. That is, Virgil is a symbolic mentor to the rational responsibility that is ours, a responsibility which cannot be obviated by wishful attempts at intellectual angelism—by our precipitous direct assault upon the sun as a demanded or desired sanctuary on the instant, whereby we dream of bypassing the givenness of the enclosing world. Especially what we would escape is that most problem-

atic little world, our self as person. Much later than
Dante, Flannery O'Connor will remark this inclination in
us from her Thomistic perspective. In her "The Grotesque
in Southern Fiction," she looks at this temptation as it
affects the expectations of her Modernist reader, who
when he reads a novel, she says, "wants either his senses
tormented or his spirits raised." Having forgotten "the
price of restoration," he "wants to be transported,
instantly, either to mock damnation or a mock inno-
cence." That is an ancient "native" inclination, but it is
one she knows with immediacy as exacerbated not only
in her contemporary readers but as well by our writers
since the Renaissance, the inclination often designated in
our recent literature as "Romanticism."[39]

In our moving, more or less sustained by our carnate
nature on that journeying, we encounter *things,* individual and specific. And by *specific* (as Thomas enlarges the
concept of *species* out of Aristotle in relation to the creating acts of God) we know the thing by an intellectual
response to its essential nature. It follows for Thomas that
what is known is the truth of the thing according to its
nature, though finite intellect cannot know that nature
comprehensively. We know it, to rescue Weaver's phrase,
according to, in an accordance with, "its own constitution
and behavior." That fullness of knowing which we
would designate as *comprehensive* is possible only to the
unlimited, loving, sustaining act of Mercy whereby this
particular thing exists as the thing it is and consequently
does not fall to nothingness. That is why, in this context
to consciousness in its communion with discretely existing things (St. Augustine and Thomas remind us) intellect
however far it may pursue in memory its initial act of

knowing, discovers that at every point it is already possessed of a limited knowing of some things, and especially (as St. Augustine affirms long before Descartes)
knowing itself as actual existence, as a reality.

That which is known, which is held by intellect, is a
truth independent of the act of knowing, which act cannot be that truth's *primal* cause. *Essence* in the thing,
according to its actuality and potentiality, is known to
finite intellect as *truth*, then. And it is in a pursuit of
understanding beyond knowing, sustained by such
truths held, that intellect makes its way toward its proper
end, toward that ultimate Truth, the Truth of all truths.
Initially consciousness moves intentionally (by preve-
nient grace, Thomas would say) in response to already
known truths out of the experience of its waking desire.
It moves through a communion in a willed openness to
creation between its own actual existence and those
actual existences—those things intellectually experienced. This is to speak of a fundamental, an *elemental*,
knowing which requires no rationalized justification of its
actuality such as Descartes thought necessary out of the
intellectual panic which, eschewing "common sense,"
possesses him in terror of the illusion to consciousness,
the terror that consciousness itself is perhaps an empty
bubble, isolated into itself. St. Augustine engages the
Sophists of his day on this Cartesian dilemma in *The City
of God*, though the bubble he burst has reconstituted
itself through Modernist sophistry until increasingly it
haunts Western philosophy since Descartes. "Without
any delusive representation of images or phantasms," St.
Augustine says, "I am most certain that I am, that I know,
and that I delight in this. On none of these points do I fear

the arguments of the skeptics of the Academy who say: What if you are deceived? For if I am deceived, I am."[40]

We have here touched, however much on its surface, upon Thomistic epistemology, which for Thomas explains the person's mode in a proper orientation to created reality as a gift to human intellect as graced by that intuitive knowledge whose complement is rational knowledge. A separation of the intuitive and the rational is destructive of the simple nature of intellect itself. It is by such separation that the Rationalist would elevate the rational, the Romantic the intuitive, in a distortion whose effect T. S. Eliot speaks of in respect to our post-Renaissance literature as the "dissociation of sensibility," though he subsequently discovers this to be the problem to a troubled heart and head deeper than literary symptoms, a troublesome spiritual dualism unhealthy to the person which is as ancient as Adam. Attempting to reconcile his inclinations as rationalist philosopher and intuitive poet, Eliot comes to experience a spiritual crisis, then popularly called a "nervous breakdown." Not a difficulty of our own invention, this dissociation, since it is spoken of as mythical in relation to the ancient temptation in the Garden of Eden, since which fall by Adam the struggle has continued ever since to build or rebuild Eden through misunderstandings. Advocates of the rational intellect and advocates of the intuitive often set themselves against each other across the range of intellectual history, each in pursuit of this illusion of restoration. But it appears a rather more daunting impasse to our own age, perhaps because we happen to be living at this moment. Still, it is a problem which rational intellect in its recovery of the intuitive can reveal to us as exacerbated by our age's devotions to the illusion of person as a Closed Bubble of the Self, a new myth out of Occam, Descartes, Kant (to put the descent summarily). Most proximately underlining this supposed new religion widely embraced by the intellectual community is that "Religion of the Future" which President Eliot of Harvard proposed to his theology students, against which Irving Babbitt and George Santayana rebelled as "humanists," with a subsequent opposition to it from their own disciples Paul Elmer More and T. S. Eliot, who declared themselves Christians in a denial of humanism as sufficient to resist the rapidly growing "Religion of the Future."

Gilson, observing our circumstances, remarks that modern philosophy "presents the appearance of a field of battle where irreconcilable shadows are locked in a struggle without end; thought against extension [the Bubble against the *other*, against "nature"]; subject against object; the individual against society." Such are the conjured circumstances to intellect as it attempts to explain and justify itself as separate from reality. Thus it would alleviate desire by "the analytical solvent of thought," which thought "vainly tries to integrate" a systematic paradigm commanding reality through the will of the finite intellect. It is as if we should attempt by sheer will to mix paint remover with paint to make a magic potion with which to paint both consciousness and the world, as if thereby to perfect our ideal color for reality. And in this frustrating dilemma to Modern philosophy, we become entangled in ever more subtle epistemological conundrums, increasingly suspicious of common sense, which as Gilson insists is the beginning of true philosophy: common sense in response to actual experiences of creation itself.[41]

We must, Gilson insists, "free ourselves from obsession with epistemology as the pre-condition for philosophy," whereby we may thus be freed of the danger of concluding that idea in intellect is the determiner of truth.[42] As St. Augustine and St. Thomas recognized, determinism implies an act which, in some degree, is a specific reduction and subjugation of an other. Determinism as a principle, presumed by and wielded by human intellect, can only end in a diminution of any specific (*i.e.*, created thing) as if thereby human intellect *comprehended* a thing in that absolute sense properly reserved by finite intellect to the Creator through an ordinate piety. The act of creation, whereby any *thing* exists *ex nihilo*, beyond its "natural" history and thereby exempting *nothingness*, is the only deterministic act dependably believed by intellect through faith. That is the only act acceptable as unfettered *determinism*. Gnostic intellect (raising its head first in that old garden) recognizes such a deterministic absolute as necessary, even though not *comprehensible* in the mystery of our always gnawing wonder: why something rather than nothing?

What a pitiable solution, then, the Modernist substitution for Absolute Love: *accident* as the absolute cause of existential reality. That is at once the ashy fruit to us and the ancient curse hidden in Nominalism, within a secret desire to be as the gods. It becomes a substitute for, rather than a vision of, the only Determinator. For the creative act, in respect to any *thing*, justifies that centering verb to our knowing: *is*. The thing *is* by a loving act of limit, whereby it is and can only be the thing it is. In short, it exists out of its very givenness. It is only the gnostic intellect, self-justified increasingly since Occam, that will presume itself the originating agent of absolute givenness, which illusional givenness it then speaks of as if ultimate *truth*. Thus it would impose will as truth upon the thing by that same presumptuous will. By that address, there develops the perversion of the responsibility of man as steward to existential reality, which the history of our decline from responsibility seems rather effectively to reveal, alas, especially in our attitudes toward that "metaphysical right" which Weaver calls the right of "property" in his *Ideas Have Consequences*, to which we shall now turn.

But in that turning let us first remark a peculiar deployment of the Modernist idea of determinism, an idea made rootless in the one True Determinator by gnostic excavations. We see it become largely pervasive of our intellectual community these past three or four hundred years in the devotion to the apotheosis of autonomous intellect. But now in our day it affects Raskolnikov's and Ivan Karamazov's *ordinary* intellects by a trickle-down effect from the *extraordinary* intelligentsia. Both natural and historical determinism as articles of faith to the Modernist religion prove persuasively convenient replacements for the reality of Original Sin. For this new species of deterministic "sin," reduced to existence as accidental, allows intellect its denial of personal responsibility. Something is lost: how inconvenient not to have a God to blame for such an inhospitable world to *homo viator*, the circumstance to Ivan's thought which leads to his "brain fever." That absence complicates any Ivan Karamazov by preventing a worthy antagonist, leaving such an intellect only himself as a minor inexplicable devil. How disappointing to be forced to rest that always gnawing recognition to intellect itself that evil exists in such unheroic shadow of itself, denied a Grand Inquisitor.

It is out of the thought of the Agrarians in part that Weaver concludes the "right of property" a metaphysical principle, a right transgressed by the extremes of Marxism on the one hand and by those of Adam Smith's Capitalism on the other, insofar as Capitalism tends to become divorced from its obligations to stewardship. As we remarked earlier, it was Eliot's fear that the Agrarians themselves, despite an appropriate concern for tradition, might nevertheless have lacked a sufficient respect for the complementary necessity of orthodoxy to tradition. His was a fear, in our present terms, that in their fierce defense of tradition they might neglect the spiritual obligations of the stewardship of "nature," of creation largely taken. In Weaver's argument, his early antagonists are Hobbes and Locke, who considered their positions built unshakably through applying "reason correctly upon evidence from nature." But the proper rejection of such argument requires our showing their positions wrong precisely because they do not reason correctly, since they distort their evidence to suit ideological inclinations. What is most immediately required is a rescue of a manner toward nature itself as a sacramental deportment in the concern for "property." And that requires the ordinating support of orthodoxy to tradition.[43] That approach aids our riddling of the concept of property as it derives from the realities of nature, a riddling coming at last to rest upon our obligation to recover a responsible stewardship to the created world.

After my first enthusiastic encounter with Weaver's lit-

tle book, and as I began to learn more about him, I began
also to wonder why Weaver, who was from a little mountain town in North Carolina, could abide Chicago. With
his growing reputation, he might easily have found what
I supposed more congenial "natural" surroundings than
those of the Windy City. I could understand why Leo
Strauss was there, though even he moved to St. John's
College at Annapolis. I have come to conclude pretty
much that Weaver could remain where he was largely
because his was the life of a mind rather more indifferent
to the contextual world than I at first supposed. Indeed,
his arguments near the end of his book emphasize the
importance to him of a studied separation from the
world, which seems to include even a separation from
what is popularly termed "nature." But the natural world
was to the Agrarians a necessary context to their own
intellectual pursuits. That this is so is reflected in the
imaginative figures used in their own intellectual arguments but especially evident in their poetry and fiction.
Donald Davidson sets as first in his *Poems: 1922-1961* his
"Ninth Part of Speech," which is concerned with
"Problems that flare out like a comet's tail" in our experiences of the world, "Unsolved equations, surded with
bane and bale" beyond resolution by "a printed gram-
mar's reach." Thus the importance to intellect of parsing
beyond the schoolhouse, to "some parleying among birch
boughs/ With beaver, deer, and the neat scurrying
grouse," so that from them we may learn a "ninth part of
speech/ That never yet was parsed or paradigmed." (It is
a part of speech Eliot will himself recover, perhaps, in
"Ash-Wednesday" when the "lost heart stiffens and
rejoices" in a response to lost lilac and bent golden-rod

and the cry of quail and the whirring wings of plover—
the senses at last recovered more ordinately for Eliot himself to "the salt savour of the sandy earth.")[44] That the
path to understanding is made *through* our sensual
engagement of the world created as good is everywhere
under recovery in the Agrarians' poetry and fiction.

Perhaps Weaver's desires seemed to require of him a
separation, though he made filial visits to family reunions
back in Weaverville, north of Asheville. On one occasion
he spoke in tribute to the family patriarch, an old man
thoroughly rooted in that lovely place in nature.[45] Out of
this wondering of mine about "nature's" immediacy to
Weaver, then, a reflection on Weaver's response to the
analytical scientist whose interest is specialized to a limited analytical address to classes of things in the world.
The danger to such a scientist is that he may succumb to
scientism, unable to see the leech in his lab because of his
denaturing abstraction of its brain. We see Weaver in a
moment of intellectual passion on this concern, prefer-
ring to such a scientist the virtue found in that intellect
possessed by "the philosophical doctor and his secular
heir, the gentlemen." Theirs are the "correct" virtues. For
the analytical scientist "demands an ever more minute
inspection of the physical world," by which pursuit he
makes "an ideal of specialism," reminding Weaver of
Nietzsche's "figure of the scientist who spends his life
studying the brain structure of the leech." What is
required by the philosophical doctor and by the gentleman (though perhaps not by the "country" gentleman)
as "the highest knowledge" is quite other. Respectively,
they respond idealistically to "the relation of men to God
and the relation of men to men." Thus Socrates in the

Phaedrus requires of such a philosophic teacher "that he learn not from the trees of the country but from the men of the city," Socrates thereby (in Weaver's conclusion) "exposing the fallacy of scientism." Through scientism it soon becomes "a banality that the scholar contributes to civilization by adding to its dominion over nature. It is just as if Plato's philosopher had left the city to look at the trees and then had abandoned speculative wisdom for dendrology."[46]

One may at once quite agree with Weaver in the condemning of scientism, and yet regret in him a tendency to reject as well the natural world, which speaks at every hand that question to intellect—that mystery: "Why something, rather than nothing?" And this something includes even trees with bark, in whose natural course appears such philosophical concerns as those of teleology, leading one of our great poets to speak of tongues in trees, books in babbling brooks. For that poet Shakespeare, in such reflection lies the discovery of the givenness of things as necessarily a certain good, to be found in every *thing*, perhaps even in the brains of leeches despite any reductionist scientism. Certainly the abuse of things by scientism which sets Weaver's own rhetoric on an anathematic edge is flush with intellectual and spiritual dangers. But the danger lies not in trees or leeches' brains, but in the scientist's will to power through gnosis, at the ultimate expense of intellect itself. One may be somewhat alarmed, then, by Weaver's summoning of Nietzsche as ally to his condemnation of scientism, for Nietzsche is notorious as philosopher precisely for his corrupting speculative intellect through which he would elevate the will to power over nature. The issue of Nietzschean thought is that new idol, man as Superman: man as the only acceptable god, as he specifically declares.

Now the problematic element in Weaver's position comes to a focus when, near the end of his little book, he is at last prepared to suggest remedy to our Modernist dislocation. It has appeared evident along the way that he maintains a decided preference for Plato over Aristotle among the philosophical doctors in the Western tradition. Thus Plato is a good Christian, for his

> pursuing virtue until worldly consequence becomes a matter of indifference, stands in contrast [to Aristotle]. Aristotle remains a kind of natural historian of the virtues, observing and recording them as he observed techniques of the drama, but not thinking of a spiritual ideal.... In Thomism, based as it is on Aristotle, even the Catholic church turned away from asceticism and the rigorous morality of the patristic fathers to accept a degree of pragmatic acquiescence in the world. This difference has prompted someone to say that, whereas Plato built the cathedrals of England, Aristotle built the manor houses.[47]

Weaver, we might say figuratively, is fearful of the manor house as a source of corruption, a corruption he suspects Aristotle of having bequeathed us in respect to an ethics derived from classical (Aristotelean) empiricism through definitions that for Weaver are suspiciously relativistic in their relation to the transcendent absolute proper to virtuous man. And, with Thomas inclined to Aristotle over Plato, that virtuous way subsequently becomes problematic through Thomas's influence. "The way [to our decline] was prepared when the Middle Ages abandoned the ethic of Plato for that of Aristotle," he

says. "The latter's doctrine of rational prudence compelled [Aristotle] to declare in the *Politics* that the state is
best ruled by the middle class. For him, the virtuous life
was an avoidance of extremes, a middle course between
contraries considered harmful." He insists against
Aristotle that virtues "like courage and generosity" are to
be pursued by an extremism "to an end at which man
effaces himself." Aristotle's argument rather "prescribes
for a prosperous worldly career," not that of the gentleman he speaks of but perhaps for that "country" gentleman associated with manor houses.[48]

Now surely Weaver misrepresents Aristotle here, in
that Aristotle's deepest concern is not for the worldly
career of middle class rulers at all. The highest good to
man he holds to be the exercise of intellect in pursuit of
and contemplation of truth. It is to be a contemplation of
truth according to the principles of knowing derived
from the pursuit of experiences to an understanding of
those experiences. For him intellect's proper intent is to its
own perfection. That, of course, will not be sufficient to
Thomas in his understanding as supported by
Revelation. For in this respect Aristotle is limited, implying perhaps a self-sufficiency to intellect, unaccommo-
dated to that grace necessary to the perfection of
discretely existing things (including Aristotle's own intellect) which have their origin in the Transcendent God
revealed to us in the Incarnation. For Thomas, Aristotle's
is an intellectual beginning *toward* that Revelation, a
removing of intellectual obstacles to encounter, reflecting
for Thomas that paradox or mystery whereby he will say
that our first responses to created things through our
senses are our first movements toward the transcendent

God, both sustaining interiorly and encompassing existential reality. Such is the intellectual movement toward God through the grace of our created limits as intellectual creatures, *incarnate.*

It needs remarking that, though Aristotle's explication of his concept of virtue involves the argument of a mean discovered as lying between antipathetic extremes, his is an explication which one might describe as a rhetorical strategy of necessity, especially so given our experiences of some persons who seem easily settled in extremities away from virtuous action as a center to spiritual balance. Cowards on the one hand, rash and foolish heroes on the other. These speak toward a virtue by their very excessiveness. Definition of a mean is a rhetorical strategy appealing to rational accommodations of experiences of the world, in the interest of a concept difficult to articulate—the concept of virtue. For surely Aristotle is concerned for positive virtue pursued through a rigor of logic. The clarification of his concern for valid positive virtue will be more persuasively developed by St. Thomas. Nor am I at all comfortable with Weaver's summary conclusion that the Catholic Church turned away from that asceticism and rigorous morality which is present in the patristic fathers, a turning in the interest of pragmatic acquiescence in the world, and Thomas's own life speaks the contrary. Weaver's is a conclusion almost as extreme as Dostoevsky's insistence that *atheism* is an idea used deliberately to infect Western man, created and promoted in the Western mind by the machinations of the Catholic Church through the Jesuits. We need only turn to Thomas's own prayers and hymns to be shown otherwise.[49]

Aquinas engages the Aristotelian concept of virtue by reorienting it through being and as *being* is dependent upon that Absolute Being, Whose adoration is for Thomas the end proper to all knowledge. It is in this advance beyond Aristotle's understanding of man's ultimate end which proves, not a rejection of Aristotle as Weaver is inclined to do, but a recovery of an incomplete, an insufficient (because incomplete) purchase upon the abiding nature of virtue itself as virtue is possible in nature and indeed is supported at last by the goodness of nature itself. For Thomas, virtue is possible through nature, whereby one speaks of man searching for beatitude as *homo viator*. Nature rightly taken is supportive of that virtuous journeying, and not antipathetic in itself to it, however complicating to that necessary journey. There is a suspicion of nature just below the surface of argument for Weaver, however, out of which suspicion comes his insistence upon a rigorous asceticism denying the world. And this is an ancient single-mindedness which has so often led acute intellectuals into Manichaean rejections of creation itself. From the Thomistic rejection of this inclination, the virtue of courage is not to be taken as a *product* of cowardice on the one hand and rashness on the other, as Weaver seems to read the Aristotelean mean, as if reason might thereby sum dangers and discover in summed dangers a positive good, a positive virtue. Aristotle nevertheless touches upon recognizable tendencies to excess, presenting them as tensional poles to intellectual pursuit of the truth, a consideration not easily gainsaid given our experiences of ourselves and others in action in the world. In doing so, then, he surely calls attention by negations of excess to arrive at a positive virtue, to be intellectually cultivated by eschewing the corruption of dividing by dualistic extremism. Aristotle's is a concern for virtuous deportment toward complex reality which Thomas will explore as in the keep of a right will to an understanding of creation as good.

In building upon the Aristotelian version of virtue, Thomas recognizes the positive virtue as tempted to polarized deflections toward excess, given that man is originally fallen. As a great dramatist will know, tensional poles tempting to extremes of action provide the spectacle of a good play, the spectacle speaking actions of the protagonist's intellect. Aristotle was concerned with the point, the defection from humility in Oedipus, for instance. Or there is a dramatic countering of bravado and cowardice in a comic pathos binding Falstaff and Hotspur in Shakespeare. The advantage to man is his resistance to a deflection in excess made possible to him by what Thomas calls "natural law," abiding in intellect as a gift to its limited and so vulnerable nature.[50] Hence generosity cannot be concluded an effect of an amalgam of stinginess and prodigality as originating causes. What one fears is that Weaver holds a deep suspicion of the Thomistic "rational prudence" as the enemy to an insufficiently qualified idealism, the effect of which suspicion is that his argument tends to an implied disjunction of man and nature, which in his articulation becomes overt. In that line we must ultimately conclude, however, a disjunction of body and soul which our experience as person denies. As Christian apologist against Modernist secularism, therefore, Weaver avoids (it seems to me) the Christian mystery which declares that through Christ there is both anticipated and provided to man a rescuing propitiation. And through that rescue lies a hope of the resurrection of body and soul in a perfected simplicity.

Weaver would set aside the manor house in favor of the cathedral, as if thereby to disjoin the manor and its people from those actualities of history whereby the manor and its people through a stewardship of nature, however imperfect, effected through a festival labor the great cathedrals in celebration, no less than the celebratory establishment of manor houses. Theirs was an action of celebration (again, however imperfect) through giving of creation toward the transcendent in such festivals of labor that Josef Pieper defines with emphasis in his *In Tune with the World: A Theory of Festivity*: "*To celebrate a festival means: to live out, for some special occasion and in an uncommon manner, the universal assent to the world as a whole.*" That is a deportment much changed by the time John Winthrop, in his *Model of Christian Charity*, declares the Puritan dream of founding in New England a "city upon a hill." "We shall find that the God of Israel is among us, when ten of us shall be able to resist a thousand of our enemies; when he shall make us a praise and glory that men shall say of succeeding plantations, 'the lord make it like that of NEW ENGLAND.'"[51]

In Henry Adams we find a troubled engagement of this disparity between the Medieval and Reformation visions of the relation of man's city to the City of God. In a sense, Adams finds himself both intellectually and spiritually disoriented, as a "last Puritan" intellect one is tempted to say, so that he must manage his intellectual survival as best he can through a Stoical pathos. And so Adams's concern may serve as a corrective complement to Weaver perhaps. As historian, Adams engages the

Weaveresque division of a speculative distinction of our dualistic inclinations, signaled in the terms of Adams's title to a chapter of his autobiography, "The Dynamo and the Virgin." And this spiritual dilemma is engaged in his autobiography in a very personal way, which he has pursued with rhetorical detachment centering upon the Medieval spirit surviving in the architecture risen out of that spirit.

In his *Mont-Saint-Michel and Chartres,* a prelude to his more famous *Education of Henry Adams*[52] (with its own rhetorical strategy of casting himself as persona, as if this were biography), the stones and glass rising toward Heaven allow a reflection upon the Western world's turning toward Modernism. He finds a festive spirit of awe and wonder reflected in the one cathedral, a spirit centering in St. Mary. That contrasts to an emerging and more militant spiritual energy reflected in the other cathedral, an inclination one suspects more acceptable to a John Winthrop as Puritan soldier than ever gentle Mary could be. To this point of contrast, let us recall that on occasion Andrew Lytle, that fiercely gentle man, used to remind us that the opposite of love is not hate, but power. It is this growing divergence between love (St. Mary) and power (St. Michael) that Adams as historian becomes uneasily aware of in his explorations of these two great cathedrals, the tensional suspensions no doubt all too personal. For he is one of the sons of Puritanism who, like T. S. Eliot as another of those sons, inclines to a skeptical refuge from resolving power through love. A way station to that refuge for intellectuals, especially American versions in this century, has been some species of Stoicism. But such retreat, as Eliot and Weaver both came to understand, can prove only a temporary stay against that intellectual confusion whose root cause is spiritual disorientation.

The gradual recognition of this spiritual concern for the tension between love and power was emerging in the 1940s, and has continued since then as a central theme in political and social issues, reduced to symbols of old knights as "Conservative" or "Liberal." And given Adams's recognition of the dilemma as so personally insistent, one well explores Bertrand de Jouvenel's adumbration of the theme from the late Middle Ages to the end of World War II, his *On Power: The Natural History of Its Growth*. His book was published in 1945, as Weaver is turning toward his own engagement of the theme in his *Ideas Have Consequences* and then subsequently to the rhetorical strategies addressing those tensional poles of love and power, his *The Ethics of Rhetoric*. It is the theme Weaver engages initially in seeing William of Occam as the "progenerator" of a Modernist intent to power over man and nature through Nominalism, a doctrine suited to the building of rhetorical fortresses against reality, as those great cathedrals had been for Adams.

It is as well a point Allen Tate dwells upon in his essay for *I'll Take My Stand*, lamenting the West's pursuit of a religion of the "half-horse," of horsepower divorced from the Cause of both horses and power, God.[53] That had been the troubling question to Adams, of course, in his pursuit of solution: thus his juxtaposing the Virgin Mary to the Dynamo. By Weaver's day, the dynamo has become pervasively established as Modernism's substitute for the Holy Ghost in the new religion, an *indifferent* power whose only grace is its submission to human will. The arresting acknowledgment: Stalin's ironic rejection of objections to his regime on spiritual grounds: "How many divisions has the Pope." But by the 1990s, in our exposition of this deportment to the world, it is not the dynamo or collective military divisions, but the computer chip upon which collective power turns in service to gnostic intellect. The spirit of the dynamo if taken as the Holy Ghost to immanent power troubles Adams, even as it fascinates him by its indifferent power as celebrated in spectacle in public exhibits at the Paris Exposition in 1900. Now figuratively at least, one encounters a dynamic energy of intent in Weaver himself in his proposal of an *intellectual* solution, an active dualism, to our *spiritual* difficulties, his metaphysical program partaking somewhat of mechanistic reduction. It is a proposal, however, in which I find little hope of new cathedrals.

Weaver's is a resolute advocacy of a dualism that had proved discomforting to Plato, with which Plato himself wrestled greatly. It is a problem to be subsequently engaged by Aristotle, and then by St. Augustine and St. Thomas, to mention only eminent minds confronting the problem of dualism as entangling intellect. As for Plato's engagement, there is a continuing irony of irresolution in his *Parmenides*, where he attempts to reconcile the One and the Many. The irony points toward *being* itself as a possible fundamental reality neglected by Plato. Irony emerges to reflection from a Thomistic view in the signs which Plato found inescapable to his attempt, most particularly in the verb *to be,* the "linking verb," which verb seems always haunted by multitudinous mystery in the attempt to link the Many toward a One. Thomas sought reconciliation of the One and the Many through a reality inclusive of the discrete particularities of existing things, in that concept he called *being* as naming the ground to reconciliation. In that attempt, he is concerned with distinctions to his concern for the mystery of being in relation to what he praises in hymns and prayers as that "Verity unseen," a Truth "veiled" in the mystery of that Scandal of particularity called the Incarnation, whereby the "Word is made flesh." Thomas deploys the rigors of reason through terms like *ens, esse, res,* knowing the attempt inevitably failing of a comprehension of mystery.[54] It is an attempt far more valiant intellectually than as merely a pragmatic acquiescence to the world through knowledge in a refusal of *understanding* because *absolute comprehension* by finite intellect is foredoomed. It is in the light of this valiant attempt, then, that I turn in conclusion to Weaver's own valiant but flawed attempt to propose a solution to our Modernist *dis-ease,* which we share with him in varying degrees of comfort and discomfort.

"The first positive step must be a driving afresh of the wedge between the material and the transcendental. This is fundamental: without a dualism we should never find purchase for the pull upward, and all the idealistic designs might as well be scuttled." Weaver adds, "The opening made by our wedge is simply a denial that whatever is, is right.... Upon this rock of metaphysical right we shall build our house. That the thing is not true and the act is not just unless these conform to a conceptual ideal."[55] Such is the rock of denial upon which Weaver would build his ideal city on the hill reaching toward heaven. It requires a division, a dualism which at its most fundamental level denies the good of creation itself. I say this, knowing that Weaver himself would deny such an intent, though it is evident in the signs he uses that the implication cannot be avoided.

Here, his is a voice we seem to have heard before, as already hinted. John Winthrop, setting out on the *Arrabella* to found the Massachusetts Bay Colony in 1630, declared "We shall be as a City upon a Hill, the eyes of all people are upon us. [W]e shall be made a story and a byword throughout the world." Those are still famous words, most popular now to secularist Modernism. What is less famous to us is the attitude toward creation reflected in Winthrop's grim reduction of stewardship, supported (sometimes ruthlessly) by many of the Puritan fathers. John Winthrop, that stern and somber governor of the Massachusetts Bay Colony, held that any festivity is automatically to be suspected. But knowing that some exercise of action in nature is necessary, he declares that both work and play are to be sober spiritual exercise— necessarily sober lest the person be too much taken with his sensual nature, either through his gains from work or from the pleasure of his play. What is required is a cautious suspicion of nature itself, the things of nature constituting a trap to the spirit whose most proximate ally is the body. Thus he writes, "I perceive that in all outward comforts, although God allow us the use of the things themselves, yet it must be in sobriety, and our hearts must be kept free, for he is jealous of our love."[56]

Weaver, in his justified concern to discomfort the recent heresies of utilitarianism and pragmatism, might well have discovered them to be a residue from such Puritan rejections of nature as the most dangerous enemy. Thus nature must be progressively subjected to ideas of the transcendent, subdued to "idealistic designs" by Winthrop. But nature once so reduced, when the transcendent end itself is at last rejected, becomes easy prey to gnostic heresies such as utilitarianism and pragmatism in a secular religion void of spiritual implications. Hence one is disquieted by Weaver's intentions to a new ideological church built on the heap of nature through dualism, the effect anticipated (Weaver says) being that destruction of utilitarian and pragmatic ideas. These "will have been defeated."[57] He confuses the heresies rampant out of Modernism with a proper virtue of intellectual prudence, that practical wisdom necessary whereby we recognize that our intellect is limited. It is prudence, for instance, which stands against the seductive argument of Nietzsche which otherwise makes us dream of leaping tall buildings at a single bound as Superman, in a disregard for the limits of nature, of that created world of which we are a part and in which we exist only according to the limits of our own created natures. One fears that in the excitement of the moment, in an opposition to an enemy I recognize as spiritual enemy as does Weaver, the temptation becomes to respond in kind, in grounds chosen by the enemy. That is, by a presumption that reality is measured by intellect, a growing tendency in Puritan thought, the intellect itself stumbles on that slippery slope of Nominalism. Thus Weaver's insistence that a "thing is not true and the act is not just *unless these conform to a conceptual ideal.*"[58] The relativist says very much the same thing, but that is a relativism against which Weaver intends his assault.

There is a great challenge in sorting ideas by anticipating their consequences, given the disjunction of terms from ideas, of ideas from intellectual concept, of concept from the realities of creation itself. And so with some trepidation in this challenge, I suggest, as John Milton is at last forced to declare in resisting his own Puritan party, that there is the danger of a "forcing protestant" mentality inimical to the truth of things from which Weaver does not quite escape.[59] It is a present danger, now secularized, inescapable in our current intellectual community, whether we declare ourselves *liberal* or *conservative*. I am speaking of a forcing of subjective truth by the presumption of the authority of a conscience dissociated from the transcendent orientation of conscience, but also freed from an obligation to sacramental stewardship in service to the body of creation. In the old Christian orthodoxy, conscience was understood to be oriented to God through the gift of intellect, whose action partakes in a sharing of providence appropriate to stewardship, as Thomas argues. There has occurred a secular reorientation, a substitution of a Modernist orthodoxy: the measure by the act of finite knowing is declared ultimate, the determiner of what is known. The truth of things is thus imposed upon by intentional subjectivity, decreeing things to the convenience of the knowing agent—the autonomous intellect. But this can be only at the expense of the truth of things in the devolution of the good inherent in creation itself.

And so the intellect's "participation" in "the eternal law" as proportionately "in the rational creature"—the *natural law* to which intellect is privy through specifying gift of likeness to God as the Eternal Law—is abandoned in the pursuit of technical power seized by abstractionism. That secularizing action—an abandonment of the sacramental office of stewardship—has therefore led to the reduction of law itself to the authority of subjective will, dictating the authority of autonomous intellect according to the dynamics of power as seized from nature, as Prometheus seized fire from heaven. The Nominalistic "letter" of the law is made supreme. Meanwhile, conscience as abiding witness to will, in respect to right and wrong action through will, becomes Nominalistically dislocated, though it still haunts consciousness.[60]

It is in the loss of checks and balances upon conscience, through intellectual virtues appropriate to intellectual actions, that a forcing "protestantism" has had its way for a span of time, so that when those virtues become finally divorced from their Christian orientation, there follows a triumph of ideologies whose scholastic justification proves some species of a logical positivism out of Occam, whether enacted in the political or academic realm as utilitarianism or pragmatism. Conscience unmodified by prudence and humility may make of the partial truth held by intellect an ideology, which then may easily become an idol of worship, though conscience itself maintains that it only intends a worship of the one true God. That was the danger threatening John Milton, evident in his prose polemics and I fear beyond Weaver's recognition of danger, as revealed in his treatment of "Milton's Heroic Prose" in *The Ethics of Rhetoric*. But it is also a danger one might fear buried already in *Ideas Have Consequences*, an endangering sliver agitating his general argument, so that for purposes of this concern, a brief look at its continuing presence as surfacing in the second of the two books Weaver published in his lifetime.

Weaver at points of his analysis of Milton's prose seems

to mistake Milton's militant advocacy based on the authority of his own conscience for a "richness of thought." Indeed, his close attention to the rhetorical strategy of adjectives and nouns rather underlines Milton as at least as much a talented name-caller as a persuasive rhetorician. We suggested that, as Plato discovers in the *Parmenides* in his attempt to reconcile the One and the Many, given our limits as discursive intellect, it seems the verb *to be* turns maverick, and thereby nouns and adjectives appear less mischievous to our pursuit of *idea* caught in *sign*. But by consort with such mischief within sign, a mind may join the conspiracy. It may declare that the mind is its own place, thus making *noplace* a place, an illusion. By sign-trickery, then, it wills heaven or hell in a negating action which—as Milton recognized—is fundamentally diabolic. One may grant a superlative gift of argument to Milton, then, but need not therefore consent to Milton's presumption that his conscience alone is the infallible echo of the absolute voice of God interior to intellect. For will itself may manipulate that "voice" to its conveniences in the beleaguered moment, a perceived danger to the limited intellect. Names skillfully deployed (adjectives and nouns) do not absolutely establish the object named (Heav'n or Hell) as either good or evil on the authority of the will's conviction that its act of naming is God's naming also. Indeed, in the interest of suppressing the monarchists, either as a group or individually, Milton deploys adjectives on occasion, assuming his signs purely on God's side. One sees him doing so in a passage where Weaver finds an "excellent pair" of adjectives deployed in "one of the most successful uses of his method": *timorous* and *flocking*.

The adjectives intend to make absurd those questions of principle antithetical to Milton, those words advanced by his chosen antagonists who (in his characterization) "would prognosticate a year of sects and schisms."[61] That Milton himself recognizes his own excess as a weakness is reflected at the end of the long passage Weaver quotes from Milton's *Animadversions upon the Remonstrant Against Smectymnuus*. Having italicized pejorative adjectives and nouns, some phrasal, to convict "any notorious enemy to *truth*," Milton concludes: "I suppose, and more than suppose, it will be nothing disagreeing from Christian meekness to handle such a one in a rougher accent, and to send home his haughtiness well bespurted with his own holy water."[62] That is a Miltonic tone we shall hear in *Paradise Lost*, put in a haughty mouth of that greatest theologian of all, fallen Lucifer, and with such a rhetorical effectiveness as to tempt us to conclude Lucifer the hero of that great poem, from which error C. S. Lewis attempts to dissuade us in his famous *Preface* to the poem.[63] Here in Milton's prose one becomes troubled, however, for if his is "Christian meekness" rather than a mean-spiritedness, one must tremble before such meekness. It seems rather a self-justification for an excessive rhetoric which well makes one fear that the term *meekness* is here used in a Nominalistic way to the convenience of the disputant. It is a set of mind in Milton which one finds also in Locke, though Locke is rhetorically more cautious.

It is as well a reflection of a set of mind such as we encounter in the Puritan divines and governors, from John Winthrop down through many generations—minds that share not only an antipathy to "Popishness" but to any deviations from the law as declared by

Winthrop and his successors on their own authority of conscience, they being regardless of will's subversion of conscience—particularly of their own, though seeing a Quaker conscience violently at odds with their own. Roger Williams and others were to discover as much, on occasion at bloody cost.[64] Milton in his resolute conviction of the rightness of his own conscience in defining "Christian liberty" will find enemy not only in "popery and idolatry" but in that Puritan Parliament summoned into session in January 1659. For what recourse of authority where private conscience is supreme? That Parliament in session subverts order, "forcing protestants" against whom Milton must then write his *Treatise of Civil Power in Ecclesiastical Causes*. One, with some reluctance at last, may conclude also that Weaver shares somewhat in this forcing protestant spirit evident not only in that special session of Parliament, but in Milton himself and in our country's New England Puritan forcers, in whom intentional will justified by conscience performs as if autonomous. That mind can only reject our challenge when confident of a private conscience sufficient to autonomous ends. But the sufficiency of private conscience, alas, is the principle used to justify gnostic power, and the political and social history of our own century is sadly strewn with consequences.

Where that "protestant" dislocation of terms leads us, if one looks at the problem from a Thomistic perspective, is to a somewhat disquieting address by Weaver which follows his wedge principle in *Ideas Have Consequences*, his defense of private property as a fundamental "metaphysical right."[65] For if a sufficient metaphysical vision is lacking to support that right, all will at last be lost, in that in the end sheer power determines right to property. That was Tolstoy's Manichaean position leading him to reject all creation. But there is an obverse species of "Manichaean" response to creation. Instead of rejecting creation in hope of heaven in that ancient Gnosticism, gnostically possessed "modern" man may reject heaven in hope of dominating creation. This is the secular Manichaeanism which Weaver would call the doctrine of *materialism*. But the one or the other species of gnosticism, from the Thomistic perspective, proves a religion in which the worship is of the "half-horse," to recall Allen Tate's argument. By such error, that great bumbling intellectual pacifist Tolstoy helped establish a principle which Lenin and Stalin would the more easily exploit in their own version of the "common good," all property common. Lenin in particular realized, when Tolstoy died (1910), that Tolstoy's sentimentalist address to property had inclined the popular spirit by vulnerable leanings suited to his own ideological intentions. The vague transcendent ideal of Tolstoy's tracts could be relocated as a religion of the State as god. What is lost in such "protestant" versions of the horse, seeing half as whole, is the metaphysical vision which orients intellect to nature. That involves a vision of the person as created intellectual soul incarnate who must recover and maintain himself in responsibilities as steward. It becomes lost in the rejection of the law of nature as under the law of God, a law available to the discrete intellect through a grace to that intellect called natural law. In its place rises the letter of the law, as we said, which is to say that the Nominalistic declaration of truth willed by autonomous intellect declares truth dependent from sign rather than sign dependent from the truth of things. That is why the Thomistic concept of natural law itself becomes a principle to be recovered, in an ordinate deportment to nature itself as good, a most crucial necessity. Nature is necessarily good as created, but it is as well both intricate and partial to both knowledge and understanding of a person at any moment of intellectual action in nature. Even in the leech's brain lies possibility of recovery, for it is a *thing* proper to our intellectual concern when that concern is governed by stewardship. Thus in this perspective, the leech's brain if rightly taken speaks something to human intellect of God's grandeur, "pied" though a person's vision of it may be. That was Gerard Manley Hopkins's discovery in his experience of dappled things, rose-moles in stipple on trout in the natural world or even discovered in trade's gear and tackle. Such vision is not impossible to the analytical scientist, nor to the idealist fearful of material reality, though it is difficult on either hand to deport intellect *proportionately* to creation with the reverence of St. Francis of Assisi, thereby *ordinately* celebrating the things of creation as the creatures of the Creator (see note 11).

Without this recovered responsibility of stewardship, the metaphysical right of property (which I quite agree with Weaver is such a *right*) will only be reduced to a right according to the letter of the law as maintained by sheer force. In such a world, the transcendent is already lost. One is trapped in a closed world—the world of the immanent as ultimate, between which and the transcendent our intellect has driven its wedge. In creation thus shadowed, as Matthew Arnold lamented, "ignorant armies," swept up in "confused alarms of struggle and flight," can but "clash by night."[66] It is an intellectual night, in that the divine light, both immanent and transcendent, informing and sustaining, has been resolutely denied.

From what I have been arguing, as my attempt to sort that intellectual inheritance from Weaver for which I am grateful, it must follow that my own concern for the beginning of a solution to our educational and social and political and theological chaos at the close of a millennium differs from Weaver's, though we share in a recognition of the problems confounding us, as we share a desire for remedy. And so I contend as the necessary "first positive step" an intellectual address differing from that dualism called for by Weaver, though I, too, subscribe to the necessity of a piety in that address such as he advocates. Rather than our "driving the wedge between the material and the transcendental," we should remove that old wounding wedge long since driven at that point— driven by gnostic intellect in its intent to a power over being itself, out of its presumption of material existence as neither good nor evil but only indifferent by its being accidental.

I hold it rather as necessarily good, in being created *ex nihilo* by a Supreme Good. With intellectual cleverness and wile and naiveté there has nevertheless been established a tradition of gnostic intellect dominant in our world. That intellect has driven the very wedge Weaver calls for as the "rock" upon which he would build his own metaphysical denial of this gnostic enemy of the transcendent. It is gnostic intellect which must insist that whatever *is* is not necessarily right. Whatever truly is, I asserted, is necessarily good, in that we name it as existing, as an *is*. But we can do so only by virtue of its *creation* and its continuing limited sustenance by an abiding loving act of creation. It is a relation annealed, bound, by love between the transcendent cause and the created effect which gnostic intellect would and must deny. It does so through a magic wedge—magic by virtue of intellect's ritualistic manner as gnostic, as alchemist—intending a transformation of essence by human will to satisfy a less than human desire. The gnostic manner is that of an illusion of intellectual autonomy, which we might describe in its recent history as an amalgam of ideas—often contradictory, though appealing to our illusionally inclined desire for autonomy.

We might name that amalgam of ideas the Occam-Descartes-Kant-Hegel wedge, to suggest but a few of the contributors to the collected consequential ideas involved constituently in forming a deadly shadow wedge. No accident, then, the deliberated chasm to intellect into which it increasingly collapses, discovering the dreaded but celebrated "Abyss" at its own center. And no prophecy of that inevitability of collapse more telling than the progressive rejection of the Incarnation as the annealing act of love, a propitiating act which President Eliot so explicitly rejects, whereby image man is drawn to Creator God. The shadow wedge, prying intellect from creation itself and thence closing upon its own "created" abyss, is made aptly evident in Emerson's thought. It is Emerson whom President Eliot woos to Harvard as a local god of intellect upon his ascension to office in the late 1860s. In the 1830s Emerson had declared he would no longer participate in sacramental worship, explicitly rejecting the bread and wine as proper creatures. And from that refusal, the growth of "Transcendentalism," a religion of angelism apotheosizing intellect, the gospel for which in the academy becomes Emerson's "The American Scholar."

A shadow cast upon the material world by illusional ideas—shadows themselves always necessarily dependent upon substantive truths implicit in creation itself, the proximate source to us of ideas. That shadow which we willfully cast proves *fascinating*, in the root sense of that word. It is especially so to the careless, naive popular spirit of any age, never more evident than in our own. What it destructively effects in that popular spirit, thereby generating a sufficient power for its support in maintaining the shadow as reality, is the seduction of the popular spirit to gnostic waywardness. For its point of departure is a partial view of reality which common sense acknowledges as a view of the real but may fail to recognize as only a partial view. That partial vision of human nature is made persuasively absolute through disorienting desire itself. That is, the appetitive dimension in our human nature is made the persuasive justification of the only "holy" desire to human nature, the fulfillment of its appetitive nature as the ultimate end. That fulfillment is colored by desire aroused and misdirected, so that the appetitive end may be declared man's ultimate end. That is the secularized reduction of beatitude, posited for fulfillment in time future by Edenic myths and always to be sought in the name of the "common good." The justification in the name of common good is so posited by the secular priests descended to us from Kant or Hegel or, in the most conspicuously ruinous visitation upon us at the moment, by Marx in our recent history. We must, under such destruction of community insofar as we would be that continuing body of which St. Paul speaks, be vigilant in our concerns for the health of that body. We must as we argued in the beginning be responsible to a sorting of inherited principles to that good health, to a continuity of the living and the dead in the light of truth. And above all, we must be aware of the limits of our seeing in that light, given the intensity of our concern at this dark moment of our history.

ENDNOTES

1. I have learned that another, more recent friend, appeared before an Atlanta priest, seeking instruction to enter the Church, under his arm a copy of *Ideas Have Consequences*.

2. Richard M. Weaver, *Ideas Have Consequences* (Chicago: University of Chicago Press, 1948), 1.

3. Leo Strauss, "On Collingwood's Philosophy of History," *The Review of Metaphysics* V (June 1952), 559–86.

4. Norman Podhoretz, "Neoconservatism: A Eulogy," *Commentary* 101 (March 1996), 19–27.

5. See Strauss, *op. cit.* He concludes his essay (586): "Historicism sanctions the loss, or the oblivion, of the natural horizon of human thought by denying the permanence of the fundamental problems. It is the existence of that natural horizon which makes possible 'objectivity' and therefore in particular 'historical objectivity.'" Strauss, of course, will not consent to the enlargement beyond that horizon by that most fundamental problem of all, the relation between the immanent horizon and its orientation to the transcendent, which is what Weaver is concerned with in his book. But the two nevertheless share in reaction to the closing off of intellect from that larger arena, the "natural horizon of human thought," accomplished by idea reduced to ideology.

6. Allen Tate, "The New Provincialism," *Virginia Quarterly* (Spring 1945), reprinted in his *Essays of Four Decades* (Chicago: Swallow Press, 1968), 535–46. Given the academic desert of the moment as the final refuge of intellectual Modernism, it is doubtful that Tate could publish his essay in the *Virginia Quarterly* in the 1990s. Or that Weaver could publish his *Ideas Have Consequences* with most university presses. Indeed, not long after the book's publication, William Couch as editor of the *Collier's Encyclopedia* commissioned an essay from Donald Davidson on "Regionalism" and an essay from

Weaver on "Propaganda." The American Library Association let him know that if he published either the edition would be blackballed and so not appear in most libraries. Weaver's essay is apparently lost, but Davidson's "lost essay" appears with my introductory note as "Regionalism," by Donald Davidson and Theresa Sherrer Davidson, *Modern Age* 37 (Winter 1995), 102–15.

7. *Ibid.*, 545.

8. See Eric Voegelin, *Science, Politics, and Gnosticism: Two Essays* (Chicago: Henry Regnery, 1968). See also his *From Enlightenment to Revolution,* ed. John H. Hallowell (Durham: Duke University Press, 1975).

9. T. S. Eliot, "East Coker," in *The Complete Plays and Poems, 1909–1950* (New York: Harcourt, Brace & World, 1952), 123–29.

10. Gerhart Niemeyer, "The Terrible Century," in his *Within and Above Ourselves: Essays of Political Analysis* (Wilmington: Intercollegiate Studies Institute, 1996). If we take Weaver's book as a prelude to that growing literature that has continued, we may well enlarge upon his sometimes cryptic summary observations of intellectual corruption since Occam in such works as this by Niemeyer. Indeed, Niemeyer's early study, *Between Nothingness and Paradise* (Baton Rouge: Louisiana State University Press, 1971) is an incisive critique of contributors to that intellectual decay since the Renaissance. And the titles to his last two collections of essays imply a metaphorical relation to Weaver's concern for the abandonment of the transcendent in favor of the limits of the immanent. *Aftersight and Foresight: Selected Essays* (Lanham: University Press of America, 1988) begins with an essay on "The Autonomous Man," these essays engaging past and future in prospect in the horizontal plane of our concern. In *Within and Above Ourselves,* the title suggests the importance of transcendence to worldly political concerns. The first two sections of these last essays have subtitles indicative: "History, Nature, and Faith" and "God and Man, World and Society," followed by "Beliefs and Structures" and concluding with a summary selection of essays, "Social Forces and Concepts of Order." The final essay: "On Authority and Alienation: A Meditation." In this line of thought, one reads as well Eric Voegelin's *From Enlightenment to Revolution.*

11. T. S. Eliot, *After Strange Gods: A Primer of Modern Heresy* (New York: Harcourt, Brace, 1934).

12. It is in this context to his argument that Eliot warns against the dangers to community of "any large number of free-thinking Jews," a phrase used to declare Eliot anti-Semitic by ignoring the qualification, *free-thinking*. It is seldom recalled that in these lectures he also speaks against "*Protestant* agnosticism" as equally destructive. I have engaged neglect of his lectures, along with misreadings of some of his early poetry, in answer to Anthony Julius's recent *T. S. Eliot, Anti-Semitism, and Literary Form* (New York: Cambridge University Press, 1995), my book (in manuscript) called "T. S. Eliot, Walker Percy, and the

Jews: The Spiritual Burden of Intellectual Lost Causes."

13. Eliot, *Strange Gods*, 30–31.

14. *Ibid.*, 31.

15. Thomas explores this concern in Question 166 ("Of Seriousness") and 167 ("Of Curiosity") in the *Summa Theologica*, II-II. It is, however, a prudential principle underlying all his work, as his always careful analysis of "what others have thought" reveals.

16. Weaver, 7.

17. Alfred North Whitehead suggests that all Western philosophy is a "footnote to Plato." Certainly as anciently as St. Augustine's *City of God* at the beginning of the fifth century, that great theologian recognized the necessity of Christianity's coming to terms with Plato in the attempt to recover an ordinate intellectual perspective upon the relation of the abiding City to the city of man. He did so at a time when Alaric the "Hun" sacked Rome, devastating that earthly city, at a time when the remnant of pagan intellectuals yet surviving the Roman Empire were insisting that the barbarian invasion was a judgment upon Rome because of its decadence, to be ascribed to the deserting of the old Roman gods for the Christian God by that false emperor, Constantine. And so St. Augustine, as he tells us, in writing his great book does so, not in reaction to the desecration by the Goths, but in response to those "worshippers of the many false gods, whom we are accustomed to call pagan." By their "attempt to blame this devastation on the Christian religion," they "blaspheme the true God with more bitterness and sharpness than usual." Therefore he writes his book "against their blasphemies and errors." Quoted by Etienne Gilson from St. Augustine's *Retractions* in Gilson's "Foreword" to *The City of God* (p. 20). See Vernon J. Bourke's abridged version of this 1950 translation by Walsh, *et al.*, a 1958 Doubleday Image book (D59). His intention is to recover by reason, in the light of revelation, the truth of things philosophically held. That is, his is a theological argument made with a philosophical authority which requires of him a sorting of pagan philosophy itself, whereby whatever truth resides in that philosophy is accommodated. Hence Plato proves a continuous presence to his argument, in whose arguments truth must be distinguished from error. Reason in those old philosophers, therefore, requires a sorting, whereby he declares it necessary that "all such philosophers give place to the Platonists" (Bk. VIII, 8). This, because Plato proves dependable insofar as he holds that "the true and highest good was God" and that the philosopher is "a lover of God, implying that philosophy is a hunt for happiness which ends only when a lover of God reaches fruition in God" (VIII, 8). But one must proceed with caution in honoring Plato. "In some places, Plato is on the side of the true religion which our faith accepts and defends. At other times he seems opposed; for example, on the respective merits of monotheism and polytheism in relation to genuine beatitude after

death" (VIII, 4). Alas, Plato is by tendency one who "believed in polytheistic worship" (VIII, 12), so that even should one understand his gods, whom Augustine argues nevertheless analogous to the Christian monotheists' *angels*, it is improper to worship gods or angels. Besides which, Plato very "foolishly" holds that a soul "inhabits a body" as a "punishment" for its prior worldly failures (XII, 27), in his theory of reincarnation. Whether such confusions are attributable to Socrates is uncertain, since "each of his followers picked what he preferred [of Socrates' teachings] and sought the supreme good of his heart's desire" (VIII, 3).

18. Etienne Gilson, "The Realist Beginner's Handbook," in his *Methodical Realism* (Front Royal: Christendom Press, 1990), 144–45. In the 1930s, Gilson wrote a number of essays against Cartesian dominance of philosophy, only recently collected under the title *Methodical Realism*.

19. Interestingly, Lionel Trilling's autobiographical *roman á clef, The Middle of the Journey,* might be taken as harbinger of this species of memoir from the Left. A very recent specimen is Alfred Kazin's *God and the American Writer* (1998). In reviewing this book for *Commentary* 105 ("Will to Believe," February 1998, 66–68) Carol Iannone remarks Kazin as now having "gone looking for involvements with divinity in the body of literature that has been his lifelong subject ever since his precocious 1942 study, *On Native Grounds.*" It is a daring turn for Kazin, one hazards, since it means engaging in some degree what he calls "a politicized, intolerant, and paranoiac religion, always crowing of its popularity." It "is too public, and aims to coerce the rest of us." Eric Voegelin, perhaps more kindly than I am disposed to be, might point out this characterization of religion in America as equally appropriate to the religion of Modernism itself, though that religion rather crows of its popularity over recent years in limited intellectual journals, ranging from *The Partisan Review* to the *New York Review of Books.* Iannone concludes with the judgment that Kazin is at last interested "only in the idea of belief...without any attendant personal obligations." She concludes: "After having been pulled in reading the book this way and that by his teasings (and his tantrums), one almost yearns for the settled clarity of Edmund Wilson's simple, adult words of refusal."

20. One of the complicating problems to any "provincial" is that of personal identity in relation to the world at hand as itself enclosed by the larger world. The themes of provincialism and regionalism, which we shall presently engage, intrude into our use of signs, willy nilly. For in our signs we would make markers of our present moment, and any present moment is in a contingent place to the consciousness seeking to find itself in a dark wood. That is why our literature deals always with what I call the scandal of the particular. Universalism as Modernist dream is always eroded by the insistent scandal of the particular. In our recent literature, the phenomenon called the Southern Renaissance is conspicuous, and it affected Weaver very fundamentally. If we

suppose we have outgrown the dilemma of the local to our intellectual journeying, however, leaving Weaver and his concerns for the use of sign in riddling the mystery of particularity, we need only look somewhat abroad—not too far—to see the old questions rising in the interest of the vitality of consciousness itself. Two instances I mention. In Canada there is a concern for "True North," a concern whose ideas are analogous to those of the Fugitive Agrarians before Weaver. And I have in hand, from *Northern Lights*, from Missoula, Montana, its Summer 1997 issue, "Enduring Values," once more a concern for a rescue of vital regional life from the rejections by intellectual universalists of those concerns as if mere provincialism.

21. T. S. Eliot, "Gerontion," in *The Complete Poems*, 21–23.

22. Weaver, 4.

23. Gilson, *Methodical Realism*, 133–34. The whole of this work engages the Cartesian distortions of reality as resisted by Gilson. See also his *Linguistics and Philosophy: An Essay on the Philosophical Constants of Language*, trans. John Lyon (Notre Dame: University of Notre Dame Press, 1988). For his engagement of science as failing when insufficiently guided in dealing with "approximations of reality," see his *From Aristotle to Darwin and Back Again: A Journey in Final Causality, Species, and Evolution*, trans. John Lyon (Notre Dame: University of Notre Dame Press, 1984).

24. C. W. Eliot's "The Religion of the Future" was published in his *Durable Satisfactions of Life* in 1910, as his distant cousin the poet was laboring to complete "The Love Song of J. Alfred Prufrock." The quotations used here are taken from Herbert Howarth's *Notes on Some Figures Behind T. S. Eliot* (Boston: Houghton Mifflin, 1964), 88. President Eliot's position suggests why such of the poet's teachers as Babbitt and Santayana were in revolt, advocating as a counter Humanism, which the poet could not at last embrace. See also President Eliot's confident program for reconstituting the nature of education in the academy, his *Educational Reform: Essays and Addresses* (New York: Century, 1901).

25. C. W. Eliot as quoted in Howarth, 88.

26. Gilson, *Methodical Realism*, 135.

27. See Maritain's "Introduction: The Major Categories of Ethical Systems," in *An Introduction to the Basic Problems of Moral Philosophy*, trans. Cornelia N. Borgerhoff (Albany: Magi Books, 1990), 1–7. Kant and post-Kantian philosophy are the principal antagonists, exacerbating problems with a clear moral philosophy in Maritain's view.

28. T. S. Eliot, *Knowledge and Experience in the Philosophy of F. H. Bradley* (New York: Farrar, Straus, 1964).

29. Maritain, "Introduction," 2.

30. In addition to Maritain's *Introduction*, see also Peter Washington's *Madame*

Blavatsky's Baboon: A History of the Mystics, Mediums, and Misfits Who Brought Spiritualism to America (New York: Schocken Books, 1993), in which Kant's contributions as philosopher are remarked in discovering a continuity from Kant into the New Age fads of our moment. The denominator is the deracination of intellect effected by separating intellect from nature, stirring sentimentality with a desire to recover that relationship.

31. Gilson, *Methodical Realism*, 138.

32. T. S. Eliot, "Preludes," in *The Complete Plays*, 12–13.

33. Richard M. Weaver, *The Ethics of Rhetoric* (Chicago: Henry Regnery, 1953), 112.

34. *Ibid.*, 25.

35. Weaver, *Ideas*, 4.

36. Ivan Karamazov's "poem," his "Grand Inquisitor" (Part II, Book Five, Chapter 5 of *The Brothers Karamazov*), is the more famous account of the diabolic pretending service in a good cause, the position taken by Nihilism. But Dostoevsky's treatment of Ivan's intellectual and spiritual crisis that leaves Ivan a destroyed intellect at novel's end is more crucial to Dostoevsky's concerns for Modernism's destructions of intellect than the highly Romantic presentation of the Grand Inquisitor, which might be taken (as it somewhat sadly is by Ivan's brother Alyosha) as Ivan's self-portrait as intellectual.

37. In his *Quaestiones disputate de veritate*, Thomas addresses our simple intellect (as quoted by Josef Pieper in *Leisure: The Basis of Culture* [New York: Pantheon, 1952], 27): "Although the knowledge which is most characteristic of the human soul occurs in the mode of *ratio*, nevertheless there is in it a sort of participation in the simple knowledge which is proper to higher beings [i.e., the angels], of whom it is therefore said that they possess the faculty of spiritual vision." Elsewhere Thomas speaks of rational intellect as an extension of intuitive intellect. The difference between the angel's intuitive intellect and man's discursive intellect is introduced by that great antihierarchic Milton, in his great hierarchical poem *Paradise Lost*.

38. Julian of Norwich, *Revelations of Divine Love: Shewed to a Devout Ankress by Dame Julian of Norwich*, edited from the manuscript by Dom Roger Hudleston (London: Burns, Oates & Washbourne, 1927), 9.

39. Flannery O'Connor, "The Grotesque in Southern Fiction," in her *Mystery and Manners: Occasional Prose*, ed. Sally and Robert Fitzgerald (New York: Farrar, Straus & Giroux, 1969), 48–49. Earlier in the same essay the writer (who had read Voegelin's *Order and History* with care) says: "All novelists are fundamentally seekers and describers of the real, but the realism of each novelist will depend on his view of the ultimate reaches of reality. Since the eighteenth century, the popular spirit of each succeeding age has tended more and more to the view that the ills and mysteries of life will eventually fall before the scientific advances

of man, a belief that is still going strong even though this is the first generation to face total extinction because of these advances. If the novelist is in tune with this spirit, if he believes that actions are predetermined by psychic makeup or the economic situation or some other determinable factor, then he will be concerned above all with an accurate reproduction of the things that most immediately concern man, with the natural forces that he feels control his destiny." She adds, recognizing that by such attention to what we are concerned with, which Weaver dismisses as the supposed "independent constitution of nature and behavior," that by his very attention to such particularities perceived with immediacy as inhering in the actual nature of the thing such a writer may witness beyond his own recognition of his witness: "Such a writer may produce a great tragic naturalism, for by his responsibility to the things he sees, he may transcend the limitations of his narrow vision" (pp. 40–41).

40. St. Augustine, *City of God,* XI, 26.

41. Gilson, *Methodical Realism,* 34.

42. *Ibid.*

43. An excellent and succinct engagement of this responsibility, out of a critical examination of the failures of Modernism, is Josef Pieper's small book, *In Tune with the World: A Theory of Festivity* (New York: Harcourt, Brace & World, 1965). For instance, he counters the Rousseauistic formula for festivity. Rousseau, in a letter to M. d'Alembert cited by Pieper (18), advises, "Plant a flower–decked pole in the middle of an open place, call the people together—and you have a fête!" To the contrary, says Pieper, "festivity, in its essential core, is nothing but the living out" of our "affirmation of the world." For "[t]o celebrate a festival means: to live out, for some special occasion and in an uncommon manner, the universal assent to the world as a whole" (23, emphasis in original). That our Puritan fathers could not recognize this distinction is dramatically narrated by Hawthorne in his "Maypole of Merrymount."

44. Donald Davidson, "The Ninth Part of Speech," in his *Poems, 1922–1961* (Minneapolis: University of Minnesota Press, 1966), 3–7. T. S. Eliot, "Ash Wednesday," in *The Complete Poems,* 60–67.

45. Richard M. Weaver, "The Pattern of a Life," in Oran P. Smith (ed.), *So Good a Cause* (Columbia: Foundation for American Education, 1993), 103–05.

46. Weaver, *Ideas,* 57.

47. *Ibid.,* 119.

48. *Ibid.*

49. Among the hymns I have in mind particularly, in the Anglican Hymnal version, "Now, my tongue, the myst'ry telling" (#199) and "Humbly I adore thee, Verity unseen" (#204), with which I am weekly familiar. See as well the collection of Thomas' prayers and hymns, *Devoutly I Adore Thee,* ed. Robert Anderson and Johann Moser (Manchester: Sophia Institute Press, 1993), and

The Ways of God, attributed to Thomas and contemporary certainly, introduced in English by the translation of Margaret Sumner and Raissa Maritain in 1942 (Manchester: Sophia Institute Press, 1995).

50. Concerning the *natural law,* Thomas says (*Summa Theologica,* I–II, q 91, a 2), "Among all others, the rational creature is subject to divine providence in the most excellent way, insofar as it partakes of a share of providence, being provident both for itself and for others. Thus it has a share of the Eternal Reason, whereby it has a natural inclination to its proper act and end. This participation of the eternal law in the rational creature is called natural law." And again, the natural law, he says (*Summa,* I–II, q 93, a 3), "is nothing other than the light of understanding infused in us by God, whereby we understand what must be done and what must be avoided." Pope John Paul II in his *The Splendor of Truth* (Boston: St. Paul Books and Media, 1993) writes in summary of Thomas's argument in the *Summa* (I–II, q 94, a 2): "Inasmuch as [natural law] is inscribed in the rational nature of the person, it makes itself felt to all beings endowed with reason and living in history. In order to perfect himself in his specific order, the person must do good and avoid evil, be concerned for the transmission and preservation of life, refine and develop the riches of the material world, cultivate social life, seek truth, practice good and contemplate beauty" (68–69). This is the complex to our intellectual responsibility as a *person* to the gift of our discrete existence which we have meant in speaking of man's responsibility as steward to the whole of creation.

51. Pieper, *In Tune.* John Winthrop, "A Modell of Christian Charity Written on Board the Arrabella on the Atlantick Ocean," in the *Winthrop Papers* (New York: Russell & Russell, 1968), II, 294–95.

52. Adams published his *Education of Henry Adams* privately in 1907, authorizing a public edition after his death (1918). He had already published privately his *Mont-Saint-Michel and Chartres* in 1904, with the first trade edition in 1913 on the eve of World War I.

53. Allen Tate, "Remarks on the Southern Religion," in Twelve Southerners, *I'll Take My Stand* (New York: Harper & Brothers, 1930), 155–75.

54. Concerning Thomas's attempt, Etienne Gilson remarks, in his *Spirit of Thomism* (New York: Harper & Row, 1964), 64: "...if we want to philosophize, being is really *the* problem of problems. In Thomas's technical language, actual existence, which he calls *esse,* is that by virtue of which a thing, which he calls *res,* is a being, an *ens.* It is the being-hood or being-ness of being, it is *be* in being. It is *to be* that makes a certain thing to be a being, *Esse* is defined by its essence, namely that which the thing is." The passage in reference, quoted by Gilson in his note, is in Thomas's *Questiones disputandum de potentia,* q. 7, a. 2, ad 9m.

55. Weaver, *Ideas,* 130.

56. John Winthrop, "Experiencia," in the *Winthrop Papers,* I, 201–02. Quoted by

David Hackett Fischer (p. 147) in his study of English exodus to the new world by the Puritans, the Cavaliers, the Quakers, and the Scotch-Irish-English border people. As a valuable background history to Weaver's own concerns, for the careful reader, see the whole of Fischer's *Albion's Seed: Four British Folkways in America* (New York: Oxford University Press, 1989).

57. Weaver, *Ideas*, 130–31.

58. *Ibid.*, 130, emphasis added.

59. See Milton's pamphlet *A Treatise of Civil Power in Ecclesiastical Causes; Showing That It Is Not Lawful for Any Power on Earth to Compel in Matters of Religion* (February 1659).

60. The mystery of conscience proved a crucial dilemma to John Henry Newman at a turning point of his journey. "Vital movements," he had said, "are not born of committees." And yet the vitality of a movement out of a single person through only the authority of his own conscience (remember John Milton) has always the difficult problem of justifying itself on any authority larger than the justifying person himself. Cardinal Ratzinger speaks to this problem, in relation to Newman: "Newman's doctrine of conscience became for us [around 1945, at the end of World War II, the "us" being Roman philosophers and theologians] the foundation of theological personalism, a subject we were fascinated with." Maritain's *The Person and the Common Good* (1946) is central to the point. Ratzinger adds, "Precisely because Newman interpreted the existence of man as originating with conscience, that is, with the relation between God and the soul, it was clear that this personalism was not individualism, and that the link with conscience did not mean there were no checks on the faculty of judgment." See Tommaso Ricci's "John Henry Newman: And Conscience Was No Longer Taboo," *30 Days* (July–August 1990), 56–59.

61. Weaver, *Ethics*, 159.

62. As quoted *ibid.*, 160.

63. C. S. Lewis, *A Preface to Paradise Lost* (London: Oxford University Press, 1942).

64. A considerable gathering of data to this point appears in "East Anglia to Massachusetts" in Fischer's *Albion's Seed.*

65. Weaver, *Ideas*, 131–33.

66. Matthew Arnold, "Dover Beach," in *Arnold: Poetical Works*, ed. C. B. Tinker and H. F. Lowry (London: Oxford University Press, 1950), 210–12.

The Ideas
of Richard Weaver

Ben C. Toledano

In late 1957, Russell Kirk invited a few of his friends to attend what we called the First Mecosta Conference at Russell's home in Mecosta, Michigan. During our few days there, two of the gentlemen, W. C. Mullendore and Louis Dehmlow, asked if I had read Richard Weaver's *Ideas Have Consequences.* I had not, but, upon returning to my home in New Orleans, I obtained and read the book. Though unprepared at the age of twenty-five to really understand *Ideas,* I was aware of the profound importance of what I was reading. Now, forty-one years later, after having reread the book many times and having personally observed and experienced the vast changes of the last four decades, I believe myself better equipped to understand the substance and consequences of *Ideas,* at least insofar as they pertain to what we inadequately refer to as "real life."

I think that a college-educated 25-year-old reading *Ideas* in 1958 would have understood more of it than would a similar young person reading it in 1998, and that is because of the accuracy of the diagnoses and prognoses in it about our human illnesses of spirit and intellect. For years, I have wondered why so few people have read Mr. Weaver's books, or have even been familiar with them. In part, it may be a case of only the believers seeking support for their beliefs, or it may be that the very nature of the subject matter necessarily limits the audience in a society which has ceased to understand or care about what he was saying.

Another problem may be the fickle nature of present day conservatives whose struggle in search of heroes is badly impaired by their own poorly formulated principles. They don't quite know what to make of Weaver. The consequences of his ideas should be alarming to many who awkwardly wear the fashionable garment of conservatism. Since he refused to be bound by a label himself, he didn't make it easy for those nourished by fast food for the mind. Thinkers who can't conveniently be pigeonholed present obstacles to frantic men scrambling to get nowhere quickly. Surely our purpose should not be to relate Weaver's work to our personal "ism," but to understand and evaluate the scholarship he has left to us.

Today we tend to view all social questions politically, and then only as they relate to government—either too much, too little, too corrupt, or too inefficient. A society's proper, public character far transcends politics and government. Public life, as defined by Jose Ortega y Gasset, should be primarily intellectual, moral, economic, religious. Contrary to what we have become, Weaver was concerned with man in the universal, transcendental sense, and can well be classified as what T. S. Eliot called a Christian sociologist, one who criticizes our social and economic systems in the light of Christian ethics.

He didn't fit into a conventional mold in another important way. Though deeply spiritual, he was not a regular churchgoer. His belief in God, in original sin, in free will, in the Soul of man and in his imperfectibility in this life were not dependent on membership in an organized religious denomination. Though the fact he was not an active churchman was of some concern to certain of his admirers, the important fact remains that he sought to teach and enlighten those of us who are ignorant, both morally and intellectually, and to provide us with "a sufficiently rational scale of values."[1] His task has been greatly complicated by the defaults of the traditional sources of instruction: organized religion, the family, and the academy.

Weaver defined the ultimate issue clearly: "whether there is a source of truth higher than, and independent of man."[2] Do universals and transcendentals have any real existence or are they only abstract terms? Though no optimist, I cannot believe that most people consciously view themselves as the ultimate reality and truth—that is, if they view themselves at all in any meaningful sense. Perhaps Weaver was giving man too much credit and was therefore expecting a level of being which we have not yet reached. It has been my experience that most people, left to their own devices and desires, are not capable of making critical moral and spiritual decisions for themselves. They need first to be taught and then to be sustained.

For us so-called post-moderns, Edmund Burke, Alexis de Tocqueville, José Ortega y Gasset, T. S. Eliot, Russell

Kirk and Richard Weaver have well described and explained our sad and sorry plight. Surely, we are not without great teachers who have clearly outlined for us what we have lost, why we have lost our way, and what we must recover in order to be loyal servants of God and worthy defenders of Western Civilization. Mr. Weaver has likened our task to "finding the relationship between faith and reason for an age that does not know the meaning of faith."[3]

He has taught us that our society has given up its form, has lost its structure and sources of genuine value, has ceased making those distinctions which are essential to a just and proper system of authority. Mass has replaced substance, and the masses have replaced cultured man. We have replaced thinking with feeling; we consume rather than build. And what we view as security turns out to be anxiety, uncertainty and amorality. Government, once properly viewed as the servant of man in community, has become what Weaver calls "a vast bureaucracy designed to promote economic activity"[4] and what Burke called "a partnership in things subservient only to gross animal existence."[5]

Weaver believed in a system of morality and ethical idealism which affirms basic principles, rules of conduct, and eternal values, and which gives priority to the spiritual and mental over the material and sensuous. Yet, how can we consider the relationship of men to God when the relationship of men to men is only that of sellers and buyers? Persons once understood to be gentlemen have been replaced "by politicians and entrepreneurs, as materialism has given its rewards to the sort of cunning incompatible with any kind of idealism."[6]

Early on, Weaver saw the absurdity of what today's liberalism demands we call multiculturalism. As he observed:

> We have been enjoined against saying things about races, religions, or national groups, for, after all, there is no categorical statement without its implication of value, and values begin divisions among men. We must not define, subsume, or judge; we must rather rest on the periphery and display 'sensibility toward the cultural expression of all lands and peoples.'[7]

He called that process "emasculation"; today we call it "political correctness."

Much more so than in 1948, thoughtful people today "wonder why the world no longer has use for a liberally educated class."[8] Since everyone cannot be a philosopher in the more general sense, then no one should be. Since the term "higher education" clearly indicates levels of attainment, then the quality of the process has to be lowered so that all can participate equally. The most valuable lesson we all learned from Don Vito Corleone, even when members of his own family were killed, was: "It's nothing personal; it's just business." We have substituted that truth in time for timeless truths, and not surprisingly we feel empty, lost and unfulfilled.

Fifty years ago, Mr. Weaver told us egotism was the order of the day. It is even more so now. We have made our separate selves "the measure of value." Self-centered and self-important, we evaluate all things in terms of our personal interests. We have rejected altruism because it involves sincere concern for the welfare of others. In our world of self-deification, one is reminded of the first two lines of Arthur Hugh Clough's poem "The Latest Decalogue."

> Thou shalt have one God only; who
> Would be at the expense of two?[9]

Prominent throughout *Ideas* is the theme that modern man has allowed himself "to be blinded by the insolence of material success."[10] Coexistent with that development is the fact that we feel a decreased rather than an increased sense of true well-being. That seeming contradiction is explored throughout the writings of the late Walker Percy. In his essay, "The Delta Factor," Percy asks:

> WHY DOES MAN feel so sad in the twentieth century? Why does man feel so bad in the very age when, more than in any other age, he has succeeded in satisfying his needs and making over the world for his own use?[11]

Walker Percy did not analyze our modern dilemma so much as he well described it. Many of his characters show the effects of what Weaver calls the "decline of belief in standards and values" and "the loss of those things which are essential to the life of civility and culture," but unlike Weaver, Percy did not specifically do battle with an age dominated by materialism.

Walker Percy and I were friends for thirty years, and I know he knew why man feels so sad in the 20th century. From time to time, I'd ask him why he didn't just lay it out for his readers. "Tell 'em what's at stake," I'd say. "Let 'em damn well find out for themselves," he'd respond; "I'm not gonna tell 'em." On the other hand, Mr. Weaver also knew full well why we feel a decreased rather than an increased happiness within our perfected material estate, and he, not being a fiction writer, chose to lay it out very clearly in *Ideas*.

THE INSOLENCE OF MATERIAL SUCCESS AND OF UNDISCIPLINED WANTS

Because of the several meanings which the term materialism can have, I must define my meaning of the term. By materialism I mean a position or state of being based primarily upon material interests, upon the acquisition, use, enjoyment, and control of goods and things. I basically subscribe to John Fiske's definition of materialists as "persons who worship nothing but worldly success, who care for nothing but wealth, or fashionable display, or personal celebrity, or sensual gratification."[12] I may not go so far as to say "nothing but," but, in terms of actual priorities, I would say "essentially."

Whether we direct our concern towards hedonism, nihilism, relativism or any of the other "isms" related to materialism, the end results are the same. We do not "feel equal to life";[13] there is no pattern or order to our lives; we are anxious, unsettled, self-indulged, undisciplined, and void of any meaningful standards and values—all in the midst of plenty—slaves to our great technology and productivity. As Eliot asked:

> Where is the Life we have lost in living?
> Where is the wisdom we have lost in knowledge?
> Where is the knowledge we have lost in information?[14]

In an earlier line from his choruses from "The Rock" written in 1934, Eliot wrote that endless invention "Brings knowledge of motion, but not of stillness." It is of interest that, one year later, Donald Davidson in his poem, "On a Replica Of The Parthenon At Nashville" used the terms "classic stillness" and "blind motion."[15] And Mr. Weaver wrote in a foreword to a later edition of *Ideas* that:

> It seems to me that the world is now more than ever dominated by gods of mass and speed, and that the worship of these can lead only to the lowering of standards, the adulteration of quality, and, in general, to the loss of those things which are essential to the life of civility and culture. The tendency to look with suspicion upon excellence, both intellectual and moral, as 'undemocratic' shows no sign of diminishing.[16]

In his *A Pattern of Politics* (1947), August Heckscher asked why "a modern generation, in the midst of a world so charged with passionate and deep-moving forces, should have continued to suppose that nothing was very real or very worth while." He answered his own question in part by stating that man had been reduced to a "creature of undisciplined wants" in a "world drained of all values and all moral significance."[17] Life was reduced to a series of demands upon the state, upon others, but not upon self, and thus lost its coherence, reasonableness, and sacred honor. That was Heckscher's view in 1947. Today, the problem is far worse. For the most part, the causes of moral and intellectual integrity have been abandoned if not actively undermined, especially in the realm of higher education.

Weaver taught us that once "antecedent truth" is denied, it is a short step to materialism in all its unstable and corrupt forms. Leave all things in man's hands subject only to man's laws and interpretations, and economic incentives and endeavors and their natural progeny become paramount. Our conduct is now governed by the presence or absence of "controlling legal authority" rather than by moral absolutes. As Weaver wrote: "Man created in the divine image, the protagonist of a great drama in which his soul was at stake, was replaced by man the wealth-seeking and consuming animal."[18]

Tocqueville wrote that "Democracy encourages a taste for physical gratification; this taste, if it become excessive, soon disposes men to believe that all is matter only."[19] At that point, "unintelligent selfishness" causes men to live apart, centered in themselves, unconcerned for the community. Men in a democratic nation, he wrote, live "in the midst of noise and excitement" and "little remains to them for thinking." "The zeal which they display in business puts out the enthusiasm they might otherwise entertain for ideas." In the absence of a "settled order of things," men become mentally and spiritually earthbound, with limited powers and unlimited desires, locked "within the narrow circle of domestic interests." Tocqueville dreaded that men, under such conditions would:

> ...at last so entirely give way to a cowardly love of present enjoyment as to lose sight of the interests of their future selves and those of their descendants and prefer to glide along the easy current of life rather than to make, when it is necessary, a strong and sudden effort to a higher purpose.[20]

Is there any wonder why we marvel over the genius of that young Frenchman, only 26 years old, who landed in

America in 1831, and later wrote Parts I and II of *Democracy in America* in 1835 and 1840? Every time I read his works, I constantly shake my head from side to side and ask, "How did he know?" How did he know that:

> Men living in democratic times have many pas-
> sions, but most of their passions either end in the
> love of riches or proceed from it. The cause of this is
> not that their souls are narrower, but that the impor-
> tance of money is really greater at such times. When
> all the members of a community are independent of
> or indifferent to each other, the co-operation of each
> of them can be obtained only by paying for it: this
> infinitely multiplies the purposes to which wealth
> may be applied and increases its value. [I believe we
> refer to it as the service industry.] When the rever-
> ence that belonged to what is old has vanished,
> birth, condition, and profession no longer distin-
> guish men, or scarcely distinguish them; hardly
> anything but money remains to create strongly
> marked differences between them and to raise some
> of them above the common level. The distinction
> originating in wealth is increased by the disappear-
> ance or diminution of all other distinctions.[21]

How did he know so early on?

Mr. Weaver's idea of private property was quite different from ours today. In expressing his meaning of the
concept, he wrote:

> At this point I would make abundantly clear that
> the last metaphysical right offers nothing in
> defense of that kind of property brought into being
> by finance capitalism. Such property is, on the con-
> trary, a violation of the very notion of *proprietas.*

This amendment of the institution to suit the uses of commerce and technology has done more to threaten property than anything else yet conceived. For the abstract property of stocks and bonds, the legal ownership of enterprises never seen, actually destroy the connection between man and his substance without which metaphysical right becomes meaningless. Property in this sense becomes a fiction useful for exploitation and makes impossible the sanctification of work. The property which we defend as an anchorage keeps its identity with the individual.

Not only is this true, but the aggregation of vast properties under anonymous ownership is a constant invitation to further state direction of our lives and fortunes. For, when properties are vast and integrated, on a scale now frequently seen, it requires but a slight step to transfer them to state control. Indeed, it is a commonplace that the trend toward monopoly is a trend toward state ownership; and, if we continued the analysis further, we should discover that business develops a bureaucracy which can be quite easily merged with that of government.... Respecters of private property are really obligated to oppose much that is done today in the name of private enterprise, for corporate organization and monopoly are the very means whereby property is casting aside its privacy.[22]

Eliot also expressed many of the same concerns. In his radio broadcast, "The Church's Message to the World," delivered in February 1937, he said:

Perhaps the dominant vice of our time, from the point of view of the Church, will be proved to be

Avarice. Surely there is something wrong in our attitude towards money. The acquisitive, rather than the creative and spiritual instincts, are encouraged. The fact that money is always forthcoming for the purpose of making more money, whilst it is so difficult to obtain for purposes of exchange, and for the needs of the most needy, is disturbing to those who are not economists. I am by no means sure that it is right for me to improve my income by investing in the shares of a company, making I know not what, operating perhaps thousands of miles away, and in the control of which I have no effective voice—but which is recommended as a sound investment. I am still less sure of the morality of my being a money-lender: that is, of investing in bonds and debentures. I know that it is wrong for me to speculate: but where the line is to be drawn between speculation and what is called legitimate investment is by no means clear. I seem to be a petty usurer in a world manipulated largely by big usurers. And I know that the Church once condemned these things.[23]

Distinctions originating in wealth have also had adverse effects upon "education centered about ideals and ideas." Professor Mark Edmundson at the University of Virginia cites among the causes the fact that "the kids come to school immersed in a consumer mentality" and "more of what's going on in the university is customer driven."[24] Even admission offices, according to a college financial officer, have become "marketing departments" directed towards obtaining tuition cash. The so-called institutions of learning have embraced the "culture of consumption" with great enthusiasm. It is unlikely the damage will be undone voluntarily. Everywhere we look, economic factors have become "ultimate determinants." A recent nationwide survey of college freshmen revealed that 75% of those interviewed chose "to be very well off financially" as their goal for higher education. Such an attitude seems to be encouraged by the likes of Governor Frank Keating who recently said, "In Oklahoma, we have a vision. It is to get rich."[25]

Weaver taught us that "Belief in nonmaterial existence" is required to prevent the laws of economics from becoming "the ordinances of all human life."[26] Yet, so confused have things become that Michael Novak, the former Catholic seminarian and now full-time apologist for finance capitalism, in a respected journal devoted to religion, described the business attributes of boldness, know-how, sound practical judgment and realism as "the moral qualities" necessary for entrepreneurship. *Moral qualities!* He concludes his article with the following thoughts:

> In the twenty-first century, economics has a great deal to teach us, and much of it complementary to the wisdom we have learned down through history. It is the vocation of economics to help us to be better women and men; to make better choices; to see more clearly what our alternatives are, and their comparative costs and advantages; to invest shrewdly in our fellows and in ourselves; and to use our freedom more advantageously and wisely. Economics is a noble vocation. It is also, I am arguing, a humanistic vocation.[27]

To use Mr. Weaver's words, the "enthronement of economic man" is now complete. If, as he wrote 50 years ago, the "place where a successful stand may be made for the *logos* against modern barbarianism"[28] is small-scale private property, then the battle has been lost. Barnes and Noble, WalMart, Home Depot, Office Depot, and the like are now firmly in control. And banks which were once local, then statewide, then regional, then nationwide, may soon become international. Some of us share Mr. Weaver's fear that once merger and consolidation have taken place in every economic sphere, it will be an easy thing for an all-powerful central government to control the relatively few consolidated industries. The trend toward monopoly is surely a trend toward state ownership. I make no real distinction between government aid for business and government aid for welfare recipients, except for the fact that the latter group has a more legitimate need. As a result of my involvement in politics, I learned some valuable lessons, firstly, that business is politics and vice versa. Secondly, I learned that, once the good guys finally get in, they want the exact same things the bad guys wanted when they were in. "Throwing the bums out" usually results in putting a new group of bums in. After working nearly 30 years to build a two-party system in the Deep South and particularly in Louisiana, we finally elected a Republican governor in Louisiana almost 20 years ago, and, within a day or two after we ardent proponents of so-called good clean government won, I was besieged by requests from our altruistic supporters for various state contracts, licenses, charters, certificates, leases and other unselfish benefits. One loyal supporter told me he'd like to have three licenses for nursing homes. Just for the heck of it, I asked him why one wouldn't be enough. Without batting an eye, he told me he'd like to help as many people as possible. I regret not having said the words on my mind: "Yourself, your wife, your partners, your kids, your grandchildren and who else?" In another of our successful, Southern gubernatorial elections, more money was raised during the two days after the victory than had previously been raised during the entire campaign.

EQUALITY

Mr. Weaver identified "undefined equalitarianism" as "the most insidious idea employed to break down society."[29] It can only exist in an undefined condition because we live in a society which scrupulously avoids definitions in favor of code words. That strategy is carefully planned to spark emotions and to avoid at all costs reasoned understanding. The only obligation required by our mindless allegiance to "equality" is lip service. Ours is an "equality" without quality and a brotherhood void of human relationships.

What Weaver observed fifty years ago has only gotten worse. Suspicion, hostility, and lack of trust and loyalty have increasingly become the hallmarks of our "equality." As he wrote: "People do not know what to expect of one another. Leaders will not lead, and servants will not serve.... No one knows where he belongs."[30] Any idea of superiority, outside of money-making, athletic ability and other entertainment skills, is resented and is called anti-democratic. I often think of Eliot's statement, "If anybody ever attacked democracy, I might discover what the word meant."[31] The same thought applies to "equality." As Weaver wrote, "equality before the law has no effect on inequalities of ability and achievement." He charged that we have sought to avoid the questions inherent in a hierarchy of values and of men by producing and encouraging "economic man, whose destiny is mere activity."[32]

Tocqueville saw early on that the unbridled cult of equality had definite and destructive implications.

> No power on earth can prevent the increasing equality of conditions from inclining the human mind to seek out what is useful or from leading every member of the community to be wrapped up in himself. It must therefore be expected that personal interest will become more than ever the principal if not the sole spring of men's actions; but it remains to be seen how each man will understand his personal interest. If the members of a community, as they become more equal, become more ignorant and coarse, it is difficult to foresee to what pitch of stupid excesses their selfishness may lead them; and no one can foretell into what disgrace and wretchedness they would plunge themselves lest they should have to sacrifice something of their own well-being to the prosperity of their fellow creatures.[33]

Though it is impossible to bring all men up to the level of those who are superior in morality and ability, it is an easy thing to bring men down to the level of the less worthy, if not all the way down to the level of the least. Weaver pointed out many of the contradictions which exist in the insidious idea of equality, except for equality before the law. For example, if equality means equal opportunity for advancement, doesn't that mean rising above and getting ahead of others? What does best or more qualified mean if all people are equal? What are we to do with ability and achievement? And freedom? And liberty? Where do they fit into undefinable equalitarian-ism? Of course, we do make a few exceptions. We recognize, applaud and even envy Bill Gates' wealth and Michael Jordan's athletic ability. But when it comes to distinctions among men regarding morality, culture and knowledge, we don't make them because we're all equal. As Ortega wrote in *Revolt of the Masses*:

> *The characteristic of the hour is that the commonplace mind, knowing itself to be commonplace, has the assurance to proclaim the rights of the commonplace and to impose them wherever it will.* As they say in the United States: 'to be different is to be indecent.' The mass crushes beneath it everything that is different, everything that is excellent, individual, qualified and select. Anybody who is not like everybody, who does not think like everybody, runs the risk of being eliminated.[34]

When Ortega wrote of "select minorities," of "select men," he did not mean persons who thought themselves superior to others; he meant those who demand more of themselves than do others. His division of society into masses and select minorities was "not a division into social classes, but into classes of men," and had nothing to do with "the hierarchic separation of 'upper' and 'lower' classes." Nearly seventy years ago, Ortega recognized the predominance "of the mass and the vulgar...even in groups traditionally selective."[35] Think how much further we've come in that same direction. It is easy to blame the various news media, the motion picture industry, the publishing and advertising businesses for the low level of culture in our society. I believe the fault lies in us. Our gross ignorance, our vulgarity, our coarseness all give rise to, in fact demand, like responses from all forms of communication and entertainment. People who have no standards for themselves are hardly positioned to elicit standards from other sources. It's not that the bottom rail's on top; it's that there is no top rail, it has fallen off, and the bottom rail is the only rail. And since cultural peasantry is dominant, it will dictate what is sold in the marketplace. If the greatest number wants the greatest filth and stupidity, that is what will be sold. If Tupac Shakur's lyrics replace those of Cole Porter, if Oliver Stone replaces Edward Gibbon, if Andres Serrano replaces Paul Cézanne, who can object in the midst of our equality and our democracy? We mindlessly say, "to each his own," but where's mine? Can it only be bought? What became of Burke's "unbought grace of life"?

Weaver wrote that the gentleman is a secularized expression of Plato's "philosopher-king" and of the philosophic doctor of the Middle Ages. The gentleman was educated in the humanities and liberal arts; he was trained to deal with all interests of society and "refused to put matters on a basis of materialism and self-aggrandizement." He was a man of his word; he was courteous; he was not egotistical. But, Weaver observed, he was "ousted by politicians and entrepreneurs" because materialism gave "its rewards to the sort of cunning incompatible with any kind of idealism." Following the South's defeat in the Civil War, "the gentleman was left to walk the stage an impecunious eccentric, protected by a certain sentimentality but no longer understood."[36] Weaver's thoughts regarding the extent to which specialization develops only part of a man, thus deforming him, are quite consistent with the thoughts of Ortega in his chapter entitled "The Barbarism of 'Specialization'" in *The Revolt of the Masses.* Ortega wrote:

> And such in fact is the behaviour of the specialist. In politics, in art, in social usages, in the other sciences, he will adopt the attitude of primitive, ignorant man; but he will adopt them forcefully and with self-sufficiency, and will not admit of—this is the paradox—specialists in those matters. By specialising him, civilisation has made him hermetic and self-satisfied within his limitations; but this very inner feeling of dominance and worth will induce him to wish to predominate outside his speciality.[37]

I wish I had a cigar for every time I've seen highly successful financiers and businessmen placed on the boards of universities, museums and symphonies, in the absence on their part of any knowledge of or even real interest in education, art or music. Perhaps they are there simply to raise funds, but I fear it is more than that. They are today's very special though specialized heroes, and for that they are given positions of honor and respectability. Of the seventeen members of the LSU Board upon which I once served, I would dare say that less than a third of the members had read a book since their graduation from either high school or college. Once I raised a question about why we were paying assistant football coaches three times more than Ph.D.s in English or history. After the laughter subsided, I was told how stupid I was. One member did explain to me that it was a market situation. "We can buy all the Ph.D.s in English we want at 18 thousand a pop," I was told, "but we have to pay a helluva lot more to compete for good coaches." Why had I not understood how simple the whole matter was? It was a market question.

Once again, we turn to our teacher and friend, Edmund Burke. To him, manners were far more than a system of etiquette; they were a way of life involving behavior and values. In his *Reflections,* Burke wrote:

> But the age of chivalry is gone. That of sophisters, economists, and calculators has succeeded; ...*The unbought grace of life,* the cheap defence of nations, the nurse of manly sentiment and heroic enterprise, is gone! ...
>
> But now all is to be changed. All the pleasing illusions which made power gentle and obedience liberal, which harmonized the different shades of life, and which by a bland assimilation incorporated into politics the sentiments which beautify and soften private society, are to be dissolved by this new conquering empire of light and reason. All the decent drapery of life is to be rudely torn off. All the superadded ideas, furnished from the wardrobe of a moral imagination, which the heart owns and the understanding ratifies, as necessary to cover the defects of our naked, shivering nature, and to raise it to dignity in our own estimation, are to be exploded, as a ridiculous, absurd, and antiquated fashion.[38]

Burke observed that from the moment ancient opinions, rules of life, and old manners are eliminated, we no longer have a "compass to govern us," much less a port to seek. To him, "all the good things which are connected with manners and with civilization" had always depended upon two principles, "the spirit of a gentleman, and the spirit of religion." He saw with great clarity that learning, and "its natural protectors and guardians," once debauched by ambition, would "be cast into the mire and trodden down under the hoofs of a swinish multitude." So did he see that commerce, trade, and manufacture, which had grown "under the same shade" as learning "would also decay in the absence of the old, fundamental, protecting principles." And the overall result would be a coarse and vulgar nation "of gross, stupid, ferocious, and at the same time poor and sordid barbarians, destitute of religion, honor, or manly pride, possessing nothing at present, and hoping for nothing hereafter."[39]

Mr. Weaver, in his chapter entitled "Distinction and Hierarchy," tells us that if we are to succeed in restoring our society and its distinctions, we must always keep in mind "that society and mass are contradictory terms."[40] Burke, in similar fashion, wrote of the distinction between a people and an accumulation of persons, and he believed that the desired social entity could only be built and maintained by what he called "a Natural Aristocracy," as contrasted to the hereditary form. Natural aristocrats, those persons most fortunate within society morally, intellectually and financially, must conduct their lives as instructors of their "fellow-citizens in their highest concerns" and are to act as reconcilers "between God and man." Burke wrote that without a natural aristocracy there could be no nation because such persons form "the leading, guiding and governing part," as does the soul to the body. When we are "abandoned to our vulgar propensities, without guide, leader or control," we follow and bow to fortune, "admire successful though wicked enterprise," and "imitate what we admire." "In a mass we can not be left to ourselves. We must have leaders. If none will undertake to lead us right, we shall find guides who will contrive to conduct us to shame and ruin."[41]

> You do not imagine that I wish to confine power, authority, and distinction to blood and names and titles. No, Sir. There is no qualification for government but virtue and wisdom, actual or presumptive. Wherever they are actually found, they have, in whatever state, condition, profession, or trade, the passport of Heaven to human place and honor. Woe to the country which would madly and impiously reject the service of the talents and virtues, civil, military, or religious, that are given to grace and to serve it; and would condemn to obscurity everything formed to diffuse lustre and glory around a state! Woe to that country, too, that, passing into the opposite extreme, considers a low education, a mean, contracted view of things, a sordid, mercenary occupation, as preferable title to command! Everything ought to be open,—but not indifferently to every man.[42]

Earlier, I mentioned Burke's idea of a natural aristocracy within a society enlightening and protecting those who are naturally and materially less fortunate. One of the saddest and most devastating features of our contemporary society is the substitution of the cruel and cynical term "equality" for the necessary, in fact indispensable, concept of leadership. The values and permanent standards of civilization cannot be preserved without the presence of a class of responsible persons whose function is to maintain the fundamental social and cultural processes.

The term "nobility" has fallen on hard times for at least two reasons. Firstly, it smacks of anti-democracy. Secondly, those who don't object to it for the foregoing reason don't know what it means. The overall cause of its demise is ignorance, of every variety and kind.

It was not always so. In his ballad *Gentilesse,* Chaucer wrote that: "What man claims to be noble must tread in the steps of Him Who was the first stock and father of nobility, and set all his wit to follow virtue and to flee vices. For unto virtue belong dignities, and not, I dare safely hold, unto iniquity, although he wear mitre, crown or diadem."

And when the knight in "The Wife of Bath's Tale" objected that his wife was of such low birth, she delivered her extraordinary sermon on the nature of true nobility.

> Whoever loves to work for virtuous ends,
> Public and private, and who most intends
> To do what deeds of gentleness he can
> Take him to be the greatest gentleman.

***

> Gentility must come from God alone.
> That we are gentle comes to us by grace
> And by no means is it bequeathed with place.

None other than Niccolò Machiavelli has told us why in times of peace and tranquillity—and we might add prosperity—men of merit are neglected: "For jealous of the reputation that such men have acquired by their virtues, there are always in such times many other citizens, who want to be, not only their equals, but their superiors."[43] Today, we take small account of men of merit outside of commerce and entertainment. However, I don't recommend Machiavelli's solutions. He proposed keeping the citizens poor so that they couldn't corrupt themselves and others, and to be ever organized and prepared for war so as to always need "men of merit and reputation."

How far have we progressed in a human sense? "Oh Fame, Fame, how many lives of worthless men you have exalted!" Was that written yesterday or today? No; by Euripides, *nearly 2500 years ago.* And, in the 6th Century A.D., Boethius wrote: "For many men have achieved a great name based on the false opinion of the masses," but it matters not for the wise man "measures his virtue by the truth of his conscience, not by popular esteem."[44]

I was of the last generation in New Orleans to grow up familiar with the term *noblesse oblige,* and many of us knew well what it meant, whether we followed it or not. What once meant "nobility obligates," now, simply stated, means the more fortunate and blessed one is, the more obligated one is towards those who are less fortunate.

At one time, I made an effort to determine where and when the term *noblesse oblige* was first used. I was unable to go any further back than 1811 when there appeared a book in French entitled *Maximes et Essais* written by Pierre Marc Gaston, Duc de Levis. In it, *maxime* 51 is *"Noblesse Oblige."* Also, in discussing those opposites, equality and nobility, he wrote:

> Equality, daughter of mediocrity and envy, you
> are trying in vain to introduce yourself, under the

guise of justice, among free men; nature rejects you and banishes you among the slaves.

In a well ordered state, the people have to derive more advantages from nobility than nobility itself does.

When nobility is not accessible to merit, the distinctions it bestows offend justice and assure the indignation of every independent and proud soul.

Despotism is the only form of government which does not include the establishment of a nobility...for the despot needs only blind agents of his superior power.[45]

For those who see comfort as a seduction and who believe that "the fetish of material prosperity will have to be pushed aside in favor of some sterner ideal,"[46] the question remains what can be done to align themselves with the values and standards of God's kingdom. Whether they can regain a sense of wholeness and harmony or whether they can recover what Professor Joseph Schumpeter called "the hidden necessities of human nature"[47] cannot be predicted with any reasonable certainty.

My admiration for Richard Weaver and for his scholarship should be quite apparent by now. At the same time, my remarks should be suspect if everything I had to say were only filled with praise. Though I don't disagree with his three "means of restoration" set forth in the final three chapters of *Ideas*, I do not find them sufficient for the task at hand. He writes of man's necessary relationship to private property, of the need to rehabilitate language, and, finally, of man's need to recover the ancient virtue of piety regarding nature, his neighbors and the past. Though piety is synonymous with religiousness, it is also more than that—and sometimes less. It is, according to Mr. Weaver, "that general respect for order, natural and institutional," and "a discipline of the will through respect."[48] Of course, that is not all he offers us on the subject. To me, piety has always meant a moral quality which causes us to love and obey God. I do not doubt for a moment that Mr. Weaver fully accepted that meaning and lived his life accordingly. Yet, he wrote that he had "tried, as far as possible, to express the thought of this essay in secular language."[49] We can't help but ask, "Why?" Even when he admitted that it had proved impossible "to dispense with appeal to religion" at certain points, his appeals were most often vague and indefinite. One familiar with Mr. Weaver and with his writings can never doubt the deep spirituality at all times apparent in him and in his work. Why he sometimes appeared more concerned with the defense and preservation of Western Civilization than with Christianity is a question beyond my knowledge. Perhaps he thought the two were so intimately related that they could not be separated.

Specifically, how and through what means does Mr. Weaver propose we be reinspired or restored with ideals? He identifies the ideals; he declares that we have lost them; he defines our predicament; but he doesn't tell us how the desired process is to come about—even if we are willing to pay the price. If, as he writes, ignorance is "virtually institutionalized," then how do we *learn* to seek what he calls "true knowledge"?[50] From whom are we to learn in a society which for generations has fostered and promoted our moral and intellectual ignorance?

Though I am more inclined than not to agree with Mr. Weaver's possibility that only some painful and sorrowful means can effect the change we seek, I still feel a need to present some proposal a bit more hopeful than simply preparing ourselves for an inevitable catastrophe.

As we enter what Professor Vigen Guroian refers to as a post-Christendom era, we desperately search for cures to the moral and spiritual diseases of our social order; but we do so without being able to rely upon our American culture "to socialize individuals into something approximating a Christian way of life."[51] T. S. Eliot wrote that a society has ceased to be Christian "when behaviour ceases to be regulated by reference to Christian principle."[52] Since we no longer have a culturally established faith, those who care must seek new ways to "enable Christians to live the gospel and show others the way to the kingdom of God." Already, we have lost the critical battle against society's distinction between public secular conduct and private religious morality. Our modern day method of proclaiming the good news is to say "You're entitled to your beliefs; I'm entitled to mine." There is no longer any recognized belief in Christian ethics being "what all Christians do together in community."[53]

At present, most of us have accepted a pagan culture whether we admit it or not. Nonetheless, the truly faithful must continue through their personal conduct to give evidence of their beliefs in order for the Christian tradition to survive and hopefully prevail. They must constantly reject both the market economy and the legal system as the ultimate sources of morality.

I believe our present spiritual condition is too grave to be significantly altered by either our families or our schools and universities. Once moral leadership has been ignored, if not opposed, by those traditional sources of authority and education, there is no catching back from within. It would be no less than the blind leading the blind.

The only sources of hope I see are those branches of organized religion which are committed to fearlessly preaching and teaching the Gospel of Jesus Christ. However, the teachers must be believers themselves in order to be worthy of belief; there can be no equivocation. There must be an absolute willingness to suffer hostility and intolerance from non-believers in a world not unlike that which the early Church had to face in the Roman Empire. My fear is that many of the people who represent organized religion are not religious believers. Consider the extent to which certain mainline liberal Protestant denominations have become almost totally preoccupied with such issues as homosexual marriage, women in the ministry, race relations and various political and social questions. Jesus Christ and His teachings often appear to be incidental considerations, if any at all. Even regarding the profound question of abortion, many of those in opposition to the procedure appear to view it as a cause rather than an effect of moral degeneration. First principles dictate that the sacred nature of human life be firmly taught and believed in order for proper, moral conduct to prevail.

Only organized religion can possibly effect some profound transformation, and that work must be done with the young, either in church schools or directly through church instruction. Then, those children, when they become parents, teachers, and hopefully, natural aristocrats, can assume the traditional moral responsibilities placed upon parenthood, education, and leadership. The harm that has been done cannot be undone by those who have done it or by those to whom it has been done. The damage is too extensive.

During what time remains in this life, members of the community of Christians can bear witness daily to their beliefs, can exhibit lives better than their enemies, can give unto others as best and in whatever ways they can.

Endnotes

1. Richard M. Weaver, *Ideas Have Consequences* (Chicago: University of Chicago Press, 1948), 1.

2. *Ibid.*, 3.

3. *Ibid.*, 34.

4. *Ibid.*, 38.

5. As quoted *ibid.*

6. *Ibid.*, 55.

7. *Ibid.*, 59.

8. *Ibid.*, 62.

9. Arthur Hugh Clough, "The Latest Decalogue," in *The Poems of Arthur Hugh Clough*, ed. H. F. Lowry, A. L. P. Norrington and F. L. Mulhauser (London: Oxford University Press, 1951), 60.

10. Weaver, *Ideas*, 17.

11. Walker Percy, "The Delta Factor," in Walker Percy, *The Message in the Bottle* (New York: Farrar, Straus and Giroux, 1975), 3, emphasis in original.

12. John Fiske, *Outlines of Cosmic Philosophy: Based on the Doctrine of Evolution, with Criticisms on the Positive Philosophy* (Boston: Houghton, Mifflin, 1874), vol. 2, 433.

13. Weaver, *Ideas*, 15.

14. T. S. Eliot, "Choruses from 'The Rock,'" in T. S. Eliot, *The Complete Poems and Plays, 1909–1950* (New York: Harcourt, Brace, 1952), 96.

15. *Ibid.*; in Donald Davidson, *Donald Davidson: Poems 1922–1961* (Minneapolis: University of Minnesota Press, 1966), 64.

16. Richard M. Weaver, "Foreword," in Richard M. Weaver, *Ideas Have Consequences* (Chicago: University of Chicago Press, 1984 [1948]), vi.

17. August Heckscher, *A Pattern of Politics* (New York: Reynal & Hitchcock, 1947), 223–24.

18. Weaver, *Ideas*, 6.

19. Alexis de Tocqueville, *Democracy in America* (New York: Alfred A. Knopf, 1945), vol. 2, 145.

20. *Ibid.*, 263.

21. *Ibid.*, 228–29.

22. Weaver, *Ideas*, 132–33.

23. In T. S. Eliot, *The Idea of a Christian Society* (New York: Harcourt, Brace, 1940), 102–03.

24. Mark Edmundson, "On the Uses of a Liberal Education," *Harper's Magazine* 295 (September 1997), 43.

25. Comments made at the Southern Republican Leadership Conference held in Biloxi, Mississippi, February 27–28, 1998, and quoted in a column by David Broder, "GOP Needs a Leader and A Message," *Biloxi Sun Herald,* March 4, 1998.

26. Weaver, *Ideas*, 143.

27. Michael Novak, "Economics as Humanism," *First Things* #76 (October 1997), 19.

28. Weaver, *Ideas*, 147.

29. *Ibid.*, 41.

30. *Ibid.*, 43.

31. Eliot, *Idea*, 12.

32. *Ibid.*, 44; 51.

33. Tocqueville, vol. 2, 123–24.

34. José Ortega y Gasset, *The Revolt of the Masses* (New York: W. W. Norton, 1957 [1932]), 18, emphasis in original.

35. *Ibid.*, 15–16.

36. Weaver, *Ideas*, 54–55.

37. Ortega y Gasset, 112.

38. Edmund Burke, *Reflections on the Revolution in France,* in Louis I. Bredvold and Ralph G. Ross, eds., *The Philosophy of Edmund Burke* (Ann Arbor: University of Michigan Press, 1960), 125–26, emphasis added.

39. *Ibid.*, 128–29.

40. Weaver, *Ideas*, 35.

41. Burke, 145–46.

42. *Ibid.*, 220–21.

43. Niccolò Machiavelli, *The Prince,* trans. Christian E. Detmold, in *The Prince and the Discourses* (New York: Modern Library, 1940), 462.

44. Boethius, *The Consolation of Philosophy,* trans. Richard Green (Indianapolis: Bobbs–Merrill, 1982), Book 3, Prose 6.

45. Pierre Marc Gaston, Duc de Levis, *Maximes et Essais* (Paris: C. Barrois, 1811), author's translation from the French.

46. Weaver, *Ideas*, 187.

47. Joseph A. Schumpeter, *Capitalism, Socialism and Democracy* (New York: Harper & Row, 1975 [1942]), 158.

48. Richard M. Weaver, *The Southern Tradition at Bay* (New Rochelle: Arlington House, 1968), 82; *Ideas*, 172.

49. Weaver, *Ideas*, 185.

50. *Ibid.*, 184.

51. Vigen Guroian, *Ethics after Christendom* (Grand Rapids: William B. Eerdmans, 1994), 12.

52. Eliot, *Idea*, 9.

53. Guroian, 25–26.

The Legacy of
Richard Weaver[1]

M. STANTON EVANS

I feel somewhat reticent about coming up to this podium and addressing an audience of distinguished academics, many of whom know much more about the topic of this symposium than I do. I am not an academic. As my vita suggests, I am a journalist, albeit a conservative journalist, which is a bit of an oxymoron. I have dabbled in these matters and have long been an admirer of Richard Weaver, and am someone who did know him slightly—not as well as Professor Ebbitt—but I did know him and learned much from him. He had a great influence on me at an early age, and that influence has remained to this day.

Allow me just a few anecdotes that relate to my first contacts with him, going back exactly forty years. This is the fiftieth anniversary of the publication of *Ideas Have Consequences*. It is the fortieth anniversary of my individual acquaintance with that book. I happened to find a copy of it in 1958, and read it and was awestruck by it, by what it had to say and by the way in which it was said. I have gone back and reread the book a number of times since, because I did not at that age fully understand what Richard Weaver was saying. But I understood enough to know that this was a powerful book, a book that would endure and have enormous impact. And I did my bit, as I told Ted Smith, out of my meager resources (I was then making eight thousand dollars a year) to promote it. I wrote to the University of Chicago Press and bought ten hardcover copies. (This was before the paperback edition of *Ideas Have Consequences* was published.) And I mailed those copies, when I got them, to ten people, saying: "You must read this book." So I became a kind of evangelist for the cause of *Ideas Have Consequences* at a very young age.

I had the opportunity about a year later to meet Professor Weaver in person when Don Lipsett wanted to have a seminar on conservative philosophy—libertarianism, traditionalism, and related matters. Don asked me to come up with the speakers, and so I did. The speakers I signed up were Milton Friedman, Frank Meyer, and Richard Weaver—which is not a bad parlay I think for a conference on these matters.

The conference was held in Brown County, Indiana, and there I met Richard Weaver, who gave a marvelous paper which is reproduced in the book *Life Without Prejudice*, an anthology of some of his essays, and was there entitled "Conservatism and Libertarianism: The Common Ground." It reads very well to this day, and contains much truth. After the formal presentations, even as the case is here, there was to be a dinner. I was in charge of keeping track of these celebrity speakers, and I looked up to find that we had lost Professor Weaver. He had just disappeared. Now this was at a state park in

Indiana, and it's a rather rustic setting, with a lodge where they have events of various kinds. Just by chance I decided to look into this lodge where they were having a square dance and fiddle playing was going on. I went in and there was Richard Weaver, with a beatific smile, just observing this square dance and enjoying the fiddlers. And I was stunned because this austere intellectual whom I had listened to and read with awe obviously was an aficionado of country music. And that endeared him to me even more, because I liked country music also.

The third anecdote that I will share with you is one on which George Nash has refreshed my recollection, as we say before committees in Washington. It relates to a conference that was held in Indianapolis under the auspices of ISI. (I had originally thought it was the Philadelphia Society, merging these matters together in my increasingly inadequate memory, but Ted Smith reminded me that Richard Weaver died in 1963 and the Philadelphia Society was not founded until 1964, so it could not have been the Philadelphia Society. Therefore, ineluctably, it was ISI.) The way I remember it is that someone asked Professor Weaver during the questions and answers what did we need to redeem the times, to turn the country around? The essence of what I remember his saying was that we needed "unshakable books," which was an interesting thing for him to say to a group of activists and people, such as myself, who were more interested in journalism. Unshakable books.

Well that's what Richard Weaver did: He wrote books that could not be shaken. And he inspired me to write some books that are perhaps a bit more shakable than were his. But that is a point of connection with the remarks that I am making. Going back in preparation for this event, in looking at Weaver's books—and I think I've read virtually everything that is available between hard covers—I realized how much influence he had had on me, influence of which I was not even conscious. How often the things that I have tried to say in my more pedestrian fashion are things that he said long ago, and so much better, and were lodged in my memory banks.

My most recent book is *The Theme Is Freedom*. The essence of my argument there is that the liberty and all other beneficial aspects of Western society that we've enjoyed in the United States are products of our Christian faith, and that if we lose our faith, we lose all the rest. That's the essence of my argument. Richard Weaver did not make the argument quite so overtly, but I think that is what he was saying in his books as well.

I've got to be careful with so many scholars and classicists in the room, and students of the Fathers, but I believe it was Augustine who said: "A man is known by what he loves." And Professor Weaver added to that: A man is known by the way he argues. That was one of his principal assertions. I would add that in the case of Professor Weaver, a man could be known by his aversions, of which he had many. He was a famous technophobe, and this was not just a pose. He lived this. He did not like automobiles. Now I've got to admit, I'm pretty much of a Luddite. I still use a manual typewriter. Not an electric typewriter, mind you, but a manual typewriter. But Professor Weaver had me beat by a mile. He did not like cars, he did not like airplanes, he did not like radio, he did not like TV, which was just starting to take hold when *Ideas Have Consequences* came out. He did not like newspapers, and I can appreciate that. He did not like big cor-porations, big unions, big government, big anything. He had a lot of such aversions, but underneath these were deeper and more profound aversions, and very justifi-able ones they were. His deepest aversions of all were to the "isms" of modernity.

Empiricism, pragmatism, positivism, naturalism, behav-iorism, however you want to phrase it, in essence every form of relativism that denied universals, that denied objective criteria of value; every form of immersion in mass and number; every form of judgment by mere externals: all of that he rejected and condemned. He did so in order to make clear what he affirmed, which were the universals, the objective criteria of right: Faith, meta-physics, creed, right reason, memory, standards, tradi-tion, place—these are words that appear repeatedly in his writings.

One of the things he said, of which again I find an unconscious echo in my own writing, is that the most important thing about any human being, man or woman, is his or her worldview. The worldview determines everything else—all the particulars are controlled by that. Going back and looking at my own efforts, and I had totally forgotten that he had written that, my version of it I call theological determinism. I said that theology deter-mines the metaphysics, which determines the philoso-phy, which determines the politics, which determines the economics, which determines the technology. The reli-gious presuppositions of a culture determine all the par-ticular aspects of that culture down this chain of causation. That is what Weaver was saying in a different way, it seems to me, when he talked about the worldview determining everything else, because our worldview is ultimately our theology.

A word that appears over and over again in his writings, and I think is indicative of what made him so powerful, is the word "center." There must be a center by which all other things are brought into scale and made coherent. If that center is not there, then all you have is random facticity. This is opposed to the moderns who work from the outside in, from the periphery. He talked about that: just taking the facts on the periphery and focusing on them, working from the outside in. Richard Weaver worked from the inside out. And his reasoning on this, it seems to me, is incontestable. Without that center, without that core of absolutes, then nothing else is possible. There is no right, there is no wrong, everything is flux, everything is random, everything is opinion. There is no intelligibility.

Facts, as Professor Weaver said in essence (and "essence" is another word you see a lot in Weaver), do not construe themselves. They don't mean anything unless there is a framework by which you can determine what the meaning will consist of. To pick an example from the realm of politics, or social advocacy, take the word "progress." Weaver annihilates the usual treatment of that word. What does "progress" mean, unless you know where you want to go? What are your goals? What are your objectives? The word is purely a word of relation and tells you nothing unless you know what the substance is that is to be achieved.

All of Weaver's writings converge, it seems to me, on these themes: on the center, the core, the body of belief that holds things together and gives meaning to existence. And if those central precepts are lost, then all the rest is chaos. That is what it seems to me he told us in many, many ways, and told us very well indeed.

In preparing for this occasion I went back and looked to see exactly what I had said about Weaver in my book, and I said some of what I'm saying now. Just in passing, I said that he had stated these matters with an "incomparable gift of language." Having looked at his writings more carefully and more recently, I would modify that a bit. He indeed had great gifts, but his use of language was not simply given to him. It was earned. He had a great craft of language. He was a great student of language. As a writer, as many in this room are, you can read Weaver not only for the substance but for the style, for the way in which he expressed himself. Many of his sentences and statements are virtually aphorisms. He was no great admirer of Bacon, but if you read Bacon, you can see a similarity. There is phrase after phrase, sentence after sentence, that is a quote. Just take it and put it in Bartlett's. And there is some of that in Weaver.

I think he was not striving for those effects, but he achieved them because of the clarity and the rigor of his thought, because he knew exactly what he wanted to say and he knew how to say it. He had the concision of the poet. You may know that he writes about poetry in *Ideas Have Consequences* in a chapter called "The Power of the Word." And like a poet he dealt sometimes in paradox, or what seemed to be paradox. I jotted some of these down on the US Airways flight from Washington today. This is just a sampler. He was a superb writer who, on occasion, would question the efficacy of writing. He was a detester of big cities, another big thing he didn't like, who lived and worked in the middle of Chicago. He was a conservative who had the temerity, as Peter Stanlis knows better than I, to chastise Edmund Burke, and a Confederate who wrote admiringly of Lincoln. These indeed are seeming paradoxes, but seeming only, in my view.

There is no real paradox in Weaver because he had the penetration to see the unity and connection of things disparate, and also to distinguish aspects of a subject that others would lump together. You have to read him carefully to see the way in which he divides and then recombines ideas and themes that are totally original with him. His writing is not historical in the sense that he would sit down to write the history of a period; it is conceptual. And yet, in his treatment of conceptual matters, one can trace the arc of Western intellectual history. You can see in his affirmations where the good things in our society came from and, conversely, see what threatens those good things. And the continuum he is describing is the Christian cultural heritage, although he was sometimes very subliminal about that. His writing is deeply religious, in my view, though with a strong Classical component. He was a student, as we all know, of Plato above all, and also other writers of the Classical era. But he also had a great appreciation of the Middle Ages, the medieval period, that is in the conventional history lesson (what I call the liberal history lesson) always disparaged. He did not develop it at great length, but he understood that this was in some ways the high synthesis of Western thought and practice. (And there has been a lot of recent scholarship, I might add, that fully affirms that view.) He understood and appreciated the British heritage of liberty under law, which was derivative from the medieval settlement. The British common law—a widely unappreciated fact—was penetrated with ideas from the canon law. All the great legal minds of, say, the thirteenth century and before, were also clerical minds. They were steeped in the canon law. The notion that, for example, Edward the First expresses in calling the Parliament of 1295, when he said, "What touches all should be approved by all," was derivative from the canon law, a treatment of Roman law, in a Christian framework.

This was more or less repeated by John Winthrop in 1632 when he issued a call for the first elections in Massachusetts. And Weaver, again uniquely for a strong Confederate, had an appreciation of Puritan New England. He understood how this heritage from the medieval period and the British common law had been transplanted to these shores by the founders of those colonies, even as he understood the somewhat different translation of those principles to the aristocratic and agrarian South. He saw the tensions between the Puritan New England view and the Southern agrarian, aristocratic outlook. He saw their distinctness, but he also saw, in a deeper way, that they were complementary.

Out of this, it seems to me, he achieved a uniquely American summation which is indeed different from the British, even though derivative from the British. I go back to pick up again, with great trepidation—Peter Stanlis staring me in the eye as I speak—Weaver's treatment of Burke, which is a chapter in *The Ethics of Rhetoric*, followed by a chapter on Lincoln. Weaver attacks Edmund Burke in this chapter for empiricism, for arguing from circumstance. Weaver writes repeatedly about two styles of argument, two forms of argument, the dialectic and the rhetorical. Burke would be in the rhetorical camp: theme; illustration; emotive, powerful, poetic argument. Weaver contrasts that with the dialectic, which is essentially an argument from propositions, which is what he attributes to Lincoln. He juxtaposes these. You have to read the chapters together to see what he is saying, but it is basically that in the British Whig tradition—if not necessarily in Burke, because I think Peter Stanlis has answered pretty well that focus isn't all of Burke—their position essentially was an argument from circumstance. Weaver tells us this is a position that is not conservative and that is ultimately doomed, both in terms of principle and in terms of effect.

To this he contrasts the Lincoln style of argument, which is the argument from axioms and definitions. (Whether he overappreciated Lincoln is another question I will avoid.) If you take the two positions, the Whig position in England, and the argument from propositions, you can see that Weaver identified rather clearly the difference between the American view of these matters and the British. The view of the British common law is essentially that precedent rules. That was never the American position. Going back to the Stamp Act and before, the American position always was that there are things that transcend precedent. There are principles that are antecedent and that must govern. The entire argument of the American Revolution between those who became identified over here as Tories and those who were identified as Whigs—although they were the opposite of Whigs in the English sense—was about this. The Tory argument over here was that Parliament was supreme by virtue of accepted precedent. Parliament had become supreme essentially with the Glorious Revolution of 1688, and whatever Parliament said, that was the law. That had been established by precedent in England, and was so argued by all of the British ministries of the era.

The American patriots, to a man, categorically denied this. They said: "We don't care what your precedents are. We don't care what is the established rule there. That is not the rule here. And if one were to accept that rule, then there would be no hindrance to the exercise of totally arbitrary power by Parliament." That was the constitutional issue on which the American Revolution was fought. That distinction was then translated in our system into our federal constitution. So there is a continuity between the arguments of the revolution and the constitutional settlement. It was the same issue every step along the way.

It seems to me this is what Weaver is getting at in this juxtaposition of the argument from circumstance and the argument from propositions. Richard Weaver was a great admirer of Edmund Burke. He was a great admirer of tradition. He was a great admirer of precedent. But he always said that this is not enough. Precedent alone is insufficient. There must be enduring, unchanging axioms and principles that govern the whole process. That is the distinctive insight of the American system of liberty that Richard Weaver presented, not in a political context perhaps, but in a philosophical context. He sought fixity in value, language, obligation, law; fixity over against the endless flux of change and randomness that he saw in modern life, and which we see so much more of now. It is from that fixity, in turn, limiting the reach of power, that we derive our freedom.

I was asked at the dinner table about events in Washington, and I really don't intend to dwell on them too much. I prefer not to, if I can avoid thinking about them. But I did jot down one Weaver quotation from the Burke chapter, which is really not about Burke, but about the Whigs, both English Whigs and the nineteenth century American Whigs, the Henry Clay Whigs. This is one of Weaver's many aphorisms. I could have written down fifty of these, but this one is so apt: "A party does not become great by feasting on the leavings of other parties." I invite your attention to what is happening in Washington, D.C., where we see the drift of what is supposed to be the opposition to the Clinton administration. I think of some of the great initiatives that have come forth from our Republican leadership—and I am a conservative Republican, as you might have guessed—and I recall to your memory, if you have forgotten it, that the principal legislative initiative that Republican leadership has been able to get through this Congress to date is Puerto Rican statehood. I went back to the "Contract with America" to see if that was in there. It was not. This was done not, it would appear, because the leadership thought Puerto Rican statehood intrinsically was a good idea. That was not argued at all. It was overtly said that, if we do this, we can get the Hispanic vote. This is the leadership that we now have in Washington, D.C. It seems to me that Weaver's annihilation of the non-Burke Whigs is totally applicable to such episodes as this.

In my view, Richard Weaver was one of the three or four authentic founding fathers of modern American conservatism. His work and his example for, lo, these fifty years have nourished countless students and shaped their thinking and their own advocacy and argument for the better. The image I think of when I think of Richard Weaver, is a quiet, unassuming man, who was never in the public spotlight and certainly did not seek it, who went about his writing and his teaching up there at Chicago and then would come back down to Weaverville. A further image that comes to my mind is that of Archimedes, who said: 'Give me a place to stand and I can move the world'—a free translation. That was what Richard Weaver was about. And he talks about that in *Ideas Have Consequences*: getting a place to do battle, ground on which to carry the fight forward, clearing a space to be able to accomplish that. It seems to me that he did that very well indeed. In so doing, he reversed an old cliche, to read as follows: Don't just do something, stand there. Richard Weaver stood there, and he moved the world.

ENDNOTES

1. The text presented here is an edited transcript of Mr. Evans' remarks at the banquet for participants in the Richard M. Weaver Symposium on the 50th Anniversary of the Publication of *Ideas Have Consequences* held at Belmont Abbey College on March 27, 1998.

About the Contributors

Wilma R. Ebbitt is an emeritus professor of English at The Pennsylvania State University. She has written extensively in the field of composition and rhetoric, including four editions of the *Writer's Guide and Index to English*, edited with her husband, David. From 1945 to 1966 she taught English in the College of the University of Chicago.

M. Stanton Evans is the former Editor of *The Indianapolis News*, columnist for the Los Angeles Times Syndicate and a commentator for CBS. He is presently the Director of the National Journalism Center and is the author of seven books, most recently *The Theme Is Freedom*.

Mark G. Malvasi teaches history at Randolph-Macon College in Ashland, Virginia. He is the author of *The Unregenerate South: The Agrarian Thought of John Crowe Ransom, Allen Tate, and Donald Davidson*, recently published by the Louisiana State University Press. He is currently at work on a study of Agrarian thought after the Agrarians and a memoir about his Italian-American family.

Marion Montgomery is a poet, novelist, and critic who lives in Crawford, Georgia. His most recent work is a

Thomistic exploration of Romanticism in three volumes, the first called *Romantic Confusions of the Good: Beauty as Truth, Truth Beauty,* the second *Intellectual Philandering: Poets and Philosophers, Priests and Politicians.* The conclusion is called *Making: The Proper Habit of Our Being,* now in press.

George H. Nash graduated *summa cum laude* from Amherst College and received his Ph.D. degree in history from Harvard University. An historian and author of five books, including *The Conservative Intellectual Movement in America Since 1945,* he writes and lectures frequently about American conservatism. Dr. Nash lives in South Hadley, Massachusetts.

Lawrence J. Prelli is an associate professor in the Department of Communication at the University of New Hampshire. His general research interests are in rhetorical theory and criticism, with special emphases on rhetorical studies of science and of environmental policy.

Robert A. Preston is President of Belmont Abbey College. He holds a doctorate in philosophy from the Catholic University of America. He continues to teach metaphysics and ethics to undergraduates.

Ted J. Smith III is an associate professor in the School of Mass Communications at Virginia Commonwealth University. The author or editor of eight books, he is currently writing a biography of Richard Weaver for the University of Missouri Press.

Ben C. Toledano, a native of New Orleans, is a lawyer and writer. His articles and reviews have appeared in such publications as *National Review, Modern Age, The Georgia Review, Texas Monthly, Arlington Quarterly, The Washington Times, Chronicles,* and *The Wall Street Journal.*